How
They
Started

In tough times

How They Started

In tough times

Edited by David Lester
and Beth Bishop

This edition first published in Great Britain 2010 by
Crimson Publishing, a division of Crimson Business Ltd
Westminster House
Kew Road
Richmond
Surrey
TW9 2ND

A catalogue record for this book is available from the British Library.

ISBN 978 1 85458 549 3

Printed and bound by TJ International, Padstow

Contents

PR AND MARKETING

SERVICES

Acknowledgements

Thanks to our lead author, Kim Benjamin for her hard work and determination to get the book finished. Thanks also to contributing authors Sara Rizk, Stephanie Welstead, Jon Card, and to all the founders and companies involved for their help and inspiration.

Introduction

Welcome to our third *How They Started* book. The companies in this collection have been selected as shining examples of what can be done when a company starts up in tough economic times. Some began and thrived despite the recession, some actually because of it. Our particular aim in publishing this book is to show the sheer quantity and variety of businesses which have been started in recessions. The idea came initially from one of our journalists on startups.co.uk while researching a speech for one of our events. To be honest we were amazed when we saw just how many truly great companies had been started in tough times. And everyone we discussed this with shared the surprise, and went away more encouraged and confident about the future.

There is a prevailing view that says that recessions are bad times for business, and that therefore it must be a bad time to start a business. Britain is still a country which is naturally more cautious about new ventures than, say, the United States, and that caution seems to go into over-drive in tough times. Yet the reality is that it can be an excellent time to start a business. And we hope that this book will help demonstrate that, promote it, and by doing so help boost the confidence of the many people wondering whether or not to take the plunge and start a business.

As with the previous two *How They Started* books, every story included here has been meticulously researched by a team of experienced, professional business writers. In every case we go way beyond a typical corporate profile to answer some of the really tricky questions, such as how they made their first sale and what their very first steps were to turn an idea into a business. Wherever possible, in fact in all but three cases, we have spoken to the companies themselves about the businesses; wherever we were unable to speak to the founder, we did additional research to find and confirm the answers to our questions.

We see the *How They Started* series of books as having three purposes. The first is simply to entertain; these are enjoyable stories for anyone who is interested in business or who enjoys programmes such as *Dragons' Den* or *The Apprentice*. The second is to inspire you, whether you are running your own business, thinking about it, or merely interested in people who do.

Our third aim is to provide you with a good sense of what it is like to start a business from scratch. We know how hard it is to do, and that many people want to set up a company but don't really know where to start. We believe that this is a fascinating collection of some of the most inspiring business stories in the world which any business student or practitioner will find both entertaining and useful. Of course every business is different, but anyone wondering whether or not they are suited to setting up their own business will get a good sense of what it is really like from reading these stories. In fact we have heard from many readers of the first two books who have gone on to start up themselves as a result of reading some of the stories in these books; we wish them ongoing success.

These stories demonstrate the variety of problems and solutions which young businesses face. You are highly unlikely to face many of the same problems yourself, but hopefully the approach you have seen 25 other businesses take to solve their problems will equip you well to address your own challenges.

The hope is that the stories in this collection will inspire you through tough times, whether that is a global recession or a decline in your specific business sector, and to prove that there can be advantages to starting a business in a difficult economic climate. The biggest advantage to starting in tough times is that you can buy what you need for the new business for substantially less money than you would need to pay in more benign economic times. The two most obvious costs which can be cheaper are staff and premises – two of the highest costs for most startups. Better still, a new business might well be able to secure people or premises on much more flexible terms when times are tough – for example part-time or on a short lease. Advertising can be cheaper in a recession as well – some media owners accept lower rates, but even where they don't, as the volume of advertising noise falls (due to other companies reducing their advertising spend) it takes less spend by a new company to break through and get noticed.

During tough times startups can find fantastic deals which would not be available to them in a better economic climate. Retail property landlords are often willing to do 'turnover rent' deals whereby a tenant pays a percentage of actual sales in rent, rather than a fixed sum per month – which considerably reduces the new retailer's risk. Some media owners, such as television stations and websites, are willing to do similar deals with advertising, seeking a percentage of any sales which result from the advertising, rather than just a fixed sum of money.

These reduced and more flexible costs also both help reduce the total sum of money it takes to start up a business. So it can cost considerably less to start a business in a recession than at other times. For some businesses, that might make the difference between the founders having enough to start up, or not. This was the case for at least one business featured in this book.

Another significant advantage is that a new business may well be able to do a deal with a customer or supplier which would not consider working with a small startup at other times. Startups are often viewed as risky, especially by suppliers who sell to them on credit. If times are really good, a supplier will often not want to take the risk of supplying a small new business with unknown potential, so they might well decline to deal with them at all. But if times are harder, the supplier will be keen to get all the sales it can.

So there are a number of strong advantages to starting up in a recession. It is important not to get carried away by this, though. For every successful startup born during a recession, there are a number which won't last. Simply starting in a recession is not a guarantee of success! All the fundamentals of starting a business still apply – providing customers with something they want at a price which they are willing to pay and at which level you can at least cover your costs.

Our book is called *How They Started In Tough Times* rather than *How They Started in a Recession*. This was a very careful decision as many of the effects of a recession will last for months and even years after a recession is formally over. At the time of writing this, most European and Western nations are thought to have emerged from actual recession, though the data is not in yet to confirm that. However the impact for many people and their businesses is yet to show through as many of the effects of recessions lag behind the recession itself.

Part of this is due to percentages. If an economy shrinks by 5% in a recession, and then grows by 5%, it will still be smaller than it was just before the recession started. It's also because much of the impact of a recession lags behind the recession itself. Many people who lose their jobs during a recession will have sufficient redundancy payment to enable them to continue to spend money for a while after their job ends; as time goes on though, unless they can find new employment at a similar income level, they reduce their expenses.

Typically a recession will last for a few quarters (five would be a very long, deep recession) however the effects of it will be felt by millions of people for probably years after the recession has technically ended.

We should also be clear that a recession might be a very bad time to start certain sorts of businesses. High end restaurants struggled in 2009 compared to previous years, for example, as people eat out less. In Britain Gordon Ramsay, Tom Aikens and Antony Worrall Thompson, all high profile chefs with high end restaurants, have seen high profile losses. Yet Dominos Pizza thrived, as some people trade down to a take-away pizza instead of eating out. Even luxury items at supermarkets are thriving for the same reason.

Given the tough economic environment which so many people presume makes it tougher to start a business during tough times, an obvious question is why did the founders of the businesses featured here start when they did? Opportunity is the clear answer for almost all the businesses we cover here. The founders spotted what they believed to be a gap in the market, and decided to set up a business to fill that gap. Entrepreneurs almost always have tremendous passion, energy and optimism, and that enthusiasm for and utter belief in their idea was a much more powerful force for the founders we feature than any concern about the risk of starting in tough times.

How They Started in Tough Times

And recessions affect different industry sectors very differently. A growing market can carry on growing despite a recession – for example, the personal computer revolution of the 1980s and 1990s continued despite those recessions, even as other sectors bore the brunt of the economic downturn. We have tried hard to find a collection of businesses which started in a wide variety of different sectors, and from different recessions dating from the late 19th century to as recently as 2009 to show that it is not just some sectors which consistently buck the trend.

At this point it is inspiring to make particular mention of four of the stories within this book, each of which stand out from the crowd of impressive businesses with something distinctive.

Microsoft's story is not simply that of another high tech startup; there have been many of those, all impressive in their own way. What makes the Microsoft story special is the extent of Bill Gates' ambition, vision and ruthlessness. Very early on he very clearly saw that the personal computer revolution would become enormous, and set out to position his company to be at its forefront. He also showed remarkable determination and guile at a very young age, for example when getting out of Microsoft's first real business contract. And while he was not the sole founder of the company, it is apparent that the business ambition which has pushed Microsoft to its enormous success is his. There cannot be many other men his age who would have continued to work the extreme hours he did when already worth literally billions.

Meetingzone is not a household name today, nor is it likely to become one. It provides conference calls to businesses. Why does it deserve a special mention then? Meetingzone stands out not for its product, but rather for its consistency in delivering on its plan. Throughout its life it has been the proverbial text-book case study of how to build a business, growing impressively year after year, with 40% growth in 2009 alone, an impressive feat in a year which saw most companies decline rapidly. Its founders are highly skilled and very impressive and have managed to retain a 40% share in the company.

Three Sixty Entertainment is one of the youngest of the businesses featured in this book. And it is the most successful business ever to have won the Startups Business of the Year Award, which it did in November 2009. The speed with which it achieved profitability in a very difficult economic climate; the fact that it raised a substantial amount of investment in the hardest climate for raising capital in several decades; and the degree to which it has innovated within its industry and impressed its customers are sufficient together for it to be worth a special mention here. Yet even more than these, its ambition is also immense, and admirable, and we expect that it will see dramatic growth over the next 10 years, and will indeed become a major household name over that time.

The story of how IBM began is rather different from any other we have featured in any of this series of books. The company we now know as IBM began as a rather motley collection of businesses, that turned into one of the world's most highly impressive, well-run corporations ever, guided by Thomas Watson Senior. The story in this book tells of how this collection of companies was put together and melded into IBM, and of how one of those pre-IBM companies got its start. Its founder, Herman Hollerith, set up a business to automate data collection in the 19th century, when there were no computers anywhere, and very nearly failed, several times. It took Herman years and years of hard, dogged persistence, and forced him to endure many hardships, before his company broke through to profitability. His story is remarkably similar in that regard to James Dyson's, featured in the original *How They Started* book.

We ought to point out that one of the businesses featured in this book, Impressions, was started by David Lester, one of the editors of this series and the founder of both www.startups.co.uk and Crimson Publishing, the publisher of this book. The story has been selected because it demonstrates some of the benefits of starting in tough economic times – and benefits from greater level of detail as a result of our better than normal contact with the founder!

We hope you enjoy reading this collection of stories as much as we have enjoyed producing it. We believe passionately in the advantages small businesses, and new startups in particular, bring to an economy, and hope that this book will help those of you in the midst of building a new business through any tough times of your own, and help you make your own success.

Recessions are dull, frightening, depressing times. They sap energy and enthusiasm from society, and shift countries' moods from positive to negative. Confidence tumbles. And confidence is what societies need to start to emerge from recession into growth. Economies need people and businesses to invest in a better, brighter tomorrow, whether that be a new division, marketing campaign, piece of equipment or merely new furniture.

It has been said that the best time to sell is when everyone else is buying, and the best time to buy is when everyone else is selling. The founders of the businesses featured in this book invested when others around them were not, and have shown courage when others around them were fearful. And they have indeed thrived, and have achieved great things. Let us salute their courage and success – and learn from them ourselves as we help drive our own businesses or employers forward.

David Lester and Beth Bishop
February 2010

MEDIA AND ENTERTAINMENT

The Walt Disney Company

Creative to the core

Founders: Walt and Roy Disney

Age of founders at start: 21, 29

Background: Cartoonist and Naval officer

Year of foundation: 1923

Business type: Entertainment

Country of foundation: USA

Countries now trading in: Global

Current turnover: $37.8bn

Disney is the largest entertainment company in the world. While we might naturally associate Mickey Mouse with the company's inauguration, the real story involves a rabbit, and several years of hard graft, creditor disagreements and mutiny. With a failed business behind him at just 21, Walt Disney and his brother Roy started their company from their uncle's garage in California in 1923. Armed with a truck load of talent, and little else, the Disney brothers' story is littered with highs and lows reminiscent of a rollercoaster found at Disneyland. The business, which today turns over nearly $40bn a year, and employs 150,000 people, is a remarkable story of survival and creativity.

Hard knocks

As you might expect, Walt Disney had always been fascinated with illustration. He took an active interest in drawing from a young age; he was even commissioned to draw his neighbour's horse. Aged 10, he continued his love of drawing, attending Saturday School at Kansas City Art Institute. But Walt soon realised he was not good enough to pursue traditional illustration, and turned his attention instead to caricatures and cartoons. When the family moved to Chicago, the teenage Walt became cartoonist for his school's newspaper and took night classes at the Chicago Institute of Art. After leaving school Walt intended to become a cartoonist, but the advent of World War One meant he joined the Red Cross as soon as he was old enough, and served in France for a year in 1918. Throughout this time he continued to hone his drawing skills, submitting numerous pieces to national magazines and upon his return home in 1919, he started a concerted effort to find a job in illustration.

Walt received numerous rejections but eventually got a job at a commercial art studio which produced marketing materials and corporate stationery. Here he met Ub Iwerks, the man who would later become his first business partner and eventually, a loyal member of the Disney empire. Both men were quickly let go from the studio once a busy period ended, and at a loose end, they decided to set up their own company in January 1920. Iwerks-Disney Commercial Artists was a short-lived venture, but gave Walt valuable business experience. The pair won a few small contracts producing similar content to the studio they had been fired from. However, it was all over within six weeks, when Walt accepted a position at the Kansas City Film Ad Company for $40 a week, and persuaded his bosses to take on Iwerks too.

The company made silent cartoon advertisements, mostly in black and white, and working at the ad company gave Walt a real taste for bringing his artwork to life – he decided to become an animator. He found he was able to improve the company's basic and somewhat lacklustre animation significantly, and started to work on his own cartoons in his spare time. His boss at the ad agency let him borrow a camera to experiment at home.

Walt began working on a series of cartoons with the aim of selling them to the nearby Newman Theatre. He called them the 'Newman Laugh-O-gram Films' and presented them to the theatre manager who was impressed enough to ask how much they cost. For all the time he'd spent on the cartoons, he hadn't actually worked out how much he'd need to charge to make a profit. Without thinking he offered up a price of 30 cents per foot, the price it had cost Walt to produce them, and the theatre manager promptly accepted. The deal was done and it was too late to renegotiate the price to try and make a profit, but Walt had his first commission and didn't intend to waste the opportunity. Walt needed to get help in to produce the cartoon strips, but with no money to pay staff, he had to come up with another way of attracting talent.

For all the time he'd spent on the cartoons, he hadn't actually worked out how much he'd need to charge to make a profit... it was too late to renegotiate the price, but Walt had his first commission and didn't intend to waste the opportunity.

A scratchy start

As a way round his staffing problems Walt placed an advert looking for boys who wanted to learn to animate. He offered applicants training and a share of any future profits. He put together a small team, including colleagues from his work, and they spent evenings after work creating a series of cartoons that could be made into films and sold to theatres. The Laugh-O-grams were a great success, and became popular in theatres throughout the Kansas area.

Walt's team began working on other projects, and created an animation of *Little Red Riding Hood*, which proved a hit at local theatres. This success gave Walt the courage to leave his job at the Kansas City Film Ad Company and concentrate on his fledgling business full time. He persuaded some of his former colleagues to invest in the business, and set up Laugh-O-gram Films in 1922, having raised $15,000. At 20 years old he owned his first company, although he later joked that it 'was probably illegal' to be president of a company at that age. Now in charge of a 'proper' company, Walt rented some studio space, brought in his former colleague Iwerks and took on another handful of budding young animators who earned very modest wages.

The team began to work on more animations, and were working nearly every hour of the day producing some excellent results. But Walt desperately needed to find someone to distribute his products. With no advertising budget, Walt struggled to get his company noticed, and eventually had to hire salesman Leslie Mace. Leslie took the films to New York and secured a deal with Pictorial Clubs of Tennessee, a company that hired out films to schools and churches. The deal was for a series of fairytale cartoons. Walt accepted a down payment of $100 on the understanding that a further $11,000 would come through once the series had been delivered. But six months later, just as Laugh-O-gram Films was about to deliver the finished series, Pictorial Clubs of Tennessee went out of business. With no income, and salaries to pay, employees gradually began to quit. Walt was booted out of his apartment, for failing to pay rent, and soon became the only member of the company.

> With no income, and salaries to pay, employees gradually began to quit. Walt was booted out of his apartment, for failing to pay rent, and soon became the only member of the company.

Walt spent the next year accepting meagre commissions, including one from a local dentist who wanted a film encouraging children to brush their teeth. The dentist offered him $500 and asked Walt to come by and finalise the deal, but Walt couldn't even afford the trip. Times were tough and his only pair of shoes were being held ransom by the cobbler until he could pay his bill. He finally admitted this to the dentist who promptly paid the cobbler's bill, and the cartoon deal was finalised. The money allowed Walt some breathing space and he soon began working on a new idea – the one that would eventually lead to the creation of the Disney Brothers Cartoon Studio.

Alice's Wonderland

Walt began to develop ideas for a new cartoon series based on Lewis Carroll's *Alice's Adventures in Wonderland*. New York distributor Margaret Winkler had expressed interest in the cartoon after Walt wrote to her describing it. However, Laugh-O-gram's debts were holding him back and he didn't have anywhere near enough cash to finish Alice. He had little choice but to declare the company bankrupt and move on. It was a tough period for Walt but he later said that he thought it was 'important to have a good hard failure when you're young.'

In 1923 Walt set off for Los Angeles, believing it to be the only place he could really bring his visions to life with any success. At the age of 21, with $40 in his pocket he arrived in Hollywood and rented a room from his uncle, Robert Disney. His brother Roy was also in LA, having been transferred to a hospital there to receive treatment for tuberculosis.

Walt first approached the big movie studios to offer his services, but was turned down categorically. He decided to once again set up his own studio, this time in his uncle's garage.

Walt first approached the big movie studios to offer his services, but was turned down categorically. Encouraged by Winkler's interest in the Alice cartoons, Walt decided to once again set up his own studio, this time in his uncle's garage. He wrote back to Winkler informing her that he was 'no longer connected with the Laugh-O-gram Films Inc' and that he was setting up a studio to produce the cartoons she was interested in. On October 16, 1923, a deal was done for the Alice series: six cartoons for $1,500 each, but with no advance.

Walt realised from his experience with Laugh-O-gram Films that his skills didn't really lie in cash flow management. The solution was to bring in Roy, who discharged himself from hospital, put up $200 of his own savings and borrowed a further $500 from their uncle. With both their sons at work on the same project, the boys' parents also chipped in, re-mortgaging their home to stump up another $2,500. Walt and Roy then hired a small staff of animators, bought a second-hand camera and hired a one-room apartment before setting to work on the cartoons. Disney Brothers Cartoon Studio was up and running. At this point, Walt declared to his father that the name Disney would eventually be famous all over the world.

Walt declared to his father that the name Disney would eventually be famous all over the world.

Although the studio had a steady income from Winkler, the distributor proved a tough client to keep happy. Demanding constant tweaks and improvements to the cartoons, Winkler was soon reducing the company's profits to virtually nothing. To stem losses,

How They Started in Tough Times

Walt decided he needed a more professional animator to join his team alongside the junior staff. His old friend Iwerks had returned to the Kansas City Film Ad Company after the collapse of Laugh-O-gram. Walt offered him a salary which was $10 a week less than what he was earning in Kansas, but Iwerks accepted it and moved out to Hollywood to join him.

By 1924, payments from Winkler were becoming increasingly late and the fee for each cartoon soon turned from $1,500 to $900. Winkler had recently married and her new husband Charles Mintz had taken over her business operations, much to the dismay of the Disney brothers. As their profit margins evaporated, the brothers had to face their client. Walt pleaded with Mintz, insisting that the quality of the Alice series could not be maintained if the right amount of cash was not stumped up. His frankness appealed to Mintz's better judgment and a new agreement was reached – a further 18 Alice cartoons were commissioned for $1,800 each as well as a share of any subsequent profits. The arrangement continued for a further three years and more than 50 Alice cartoons, although this period was fraught with fee negotiations and more late payments on Mintz's behalf. By 1927 the New York Distributor grew tired of the Alice series and requested something new, possibly involving a rabbit...

Oswald the Lucky Rabbit

Tired of the Alice series himself, Walt found a new lease of life with his creation, Oswald the rabbit. Over the past three years, Walt had realised his talents were best placed operating as the creational force of the company, and not in the animation itself. He declared: 'around here, we don't look backwards for very long. We keep moving forward, opening new doors, and doing new things, because we're curious'. The business greatly benefitted from having a leader that recognised the limitations of his own talent, and allowed others to take over where he left off.

'Around here, we don't look backwards for very long. We keep moving forward, opening new doors, and doing new things, because we're curious.'

The Oswald series soon became immensely popular, and before long Mintz was paying $2,250 per cartoon. The production schedule was tight, and Walt later recalled: 'in the early days of making these pictures, it was a fight to survive. I used to throw gags in because I was desperate. I didn't even like them but I had to get one out every two weeks'. Despite the pressure on the studio, things were running smoothly.

Fortnightly payments were being hand delivered to the Disney studio by Mintz's brother-in-law in exchange for each new cartoon. Oswald was also responsible for the first Disney merchandise. Badges, stencil sets and even a 5 cent chocolate bar were produced.

By February 1928, it really looked as though the company, recently renamed Walt Disney Productions, was starting to make an impact. Walt convinced Roy that his name alone on the cartoon credits would make for a more trusted brand. Roy agreed that a single name would convey more confidence – audiences would associate one entertainer with the enjoyment they gleaned from the cartoons, as opposed to a factory style corporation churning out commercial entertainment. But the company was heavily reliant on its Oswald contract with Mintz – a contract that was up for renewal. Walt set off for New York to negotiate a new deal. He left with high hopes, but what was to follow was one of the darkest periods in the history of the Disney organisation.

Mutiny in the ranks

Walt had been working his staff hard over the preceding few years, and the fortnightly collections of the Oswald reels meant he had to make tough leadership choices. He joked: 'every once in a while I just fire everybody, then I hire them back in a couple of weeks. That way they don't get complacent. It keeps them on their toes'. However, some of the staff did not appreciate his methods. The animators began talking in secret with Winkler, working on behalf of her husband, and she offered them better pay to come and work for Mintz directly.

When Walt arrived in New York to meet Mintz, he asked for an increased fee of $2,500 per cartoon – a fair increase as the cartoons were so popular – but Mintz had other plans. He offered a mere $1,800, which Walt immediately rejected. However, it was too late. Mintz had hired almost all of Walt's animators out from under him. Ub Iwerks was the only animator to remain loyal. But the company had not only lost its staff – it lost Oswald too. The terms of the original contract clearly stated that Walt Disney Productions did not own the rights to the cartoon – Mintz did.

Goodbye Oswald, hello Mickey

With no cartoon character, no distributor and virtually no animators to return home to, Walt set off home to Hollywood. He sent a telegram to Roy from New York insisting that it would all be ok and that he would tell him all the details when he returned. However, the reality was stark, and even he could not have predicted that the company's fortunes would be turned around.

There are several accepted versions of what came next for the company. One version goes that Walt began doodling a new character on the train back home from New York. However, the more accepted version of the story is that the studio's next creation was the result of crisis meetings back home in LA with Iwerks and Roy. Stung by the disloyalty of his staff, Walt kept the ideas quiet for some time, holding secret meetings and ideas sessions with his brother and loyal friend. Even the drawings for the new cartoon were hidden under Oswald sketches if others entered the room. This new character provided the inspiration Walt needed to get back on his feet, and put the Oswald fiasco behind him.

The character was a little mouse, dressed in white gloves and button pants. He was named Mortimer Mouse, but Walt's wife Lilly eventually persuaded her husband to rename him Mickey.

During 1928, Ub began creating two new Mickey Mouse cartoons. But 1928 was a groundbreaking year for motion pictures, and the first film with synchronized sound – *The Jazz Singer* – was released. Walt was impressed, and poured all the studio's resources into a third cartoon, which would have fully synchronized sound. They decided to scrap the first two creations, and concentrate their efforts on this film, entitled *Steamboat Willie*. While Ub produced the drawings, Walt provided the voice of Mickey. A Disney employee at the time described how 'Ub designed Mickey's physical appearance, but Walt gave him his soul'. Walt continued to be the voice of Mickey until 1946. Walt partnered with businessman Pat Powers and with his help, *Steamboat Willie* premiered at the Colony Theater in New York November 18, 1928, and was a roaring success. Mickey Mouse was an immediate hit around the world and Walt released the first two Mickey cartoons, after they had added a soundtrack.

While Ub produced the drawings, Walt provided the voice of Mickey. Ub designed Mickey's physical appearance, but Walt gave him his soul.

Booming cartoons

The success of Mickey Mouse did not, however, mean plain sailing for the business. In 1929 Walt Disney Studios released the *Silly Symphonies*, a series of comedy animations, each one containing different characters. During this time, Walt was getting increasingly annoyed by Powers, whom he thought was taking too large a cut of the distribution profits and in 1930 he struck a new deal with Columbia Pictures. Disgruntled, Powers persuaded Ub to leave Disney and open his own studio, poaching their chief animator.

Mickey's popularity rocketed throughout the 1930s, as he overtook Felix the Cat in popularity, but the *Silly Symphonies* had not been as popular as Walt had hoped.

In 1932, Walt was approached by engineer Herbert Kalmus who persuaded him to re-do one of the symphonies, using new technology that meant the previously black and white animations could be in full colour. *Flowers and Trees* proved a phenomenal success, and won the Academy Award for Best Cartoon in the same year. Disney Studios went on to win this category for the rest of the decade. From then on, all Silly Symphonies would be produced in colour, and the series grew in popularity. The most famous Symphony of all, *Three Little Pigs*, was released in 1933, and contained the classic song, *Who's Afraid of the Big Bad Wolf?*, which became the anthem of the Great Depression and ran in theatres for many months.

Faced with the popularity of a new character from a competitor studio, Popeye the Sailor, Walt turned Mickey colourful in 1935, and soon launched the familiar spin off characters of Donald Duck, Pluto and Goofy. Never one to rest on his laurels, Walt announced his plans to create a feature-length full-colour animation of *Snow White and the Seven Dwarfs*. This would take years of production, and both Roy and Walt's wife tried to persuade him against it. Meanwhile, competitors dubbed the project 'Disney's Folly' and were sure this would be the end of the Disney success. They were nearly right, as by 1937, the studio had run out of money and had to show a rough version to the Bank of America to get a loan to finish the animation. *Snow White and the Seven Dwarfs* premiered at the Carthay Circle Theater on 21 December, 1937, and received a standing ovation from the audience. It went on to become the most successful motion picture of 1938 and earned over $8m from its original release.

'*I don't make pictures just to make money. I make money to make more pictures.*'

Where are they now?

The success of Snow White marked the start of the 'golden age' of Walt Disney Studios. With the profits, Walt was able to build new studios in Burbank, and family favourites such as *Pinocchio*, *Fantasia* and *Bambi* followed in quick succession starting in the early 1940s. The onset of World War Two saw Disney create training and instructional films for the military. After the war, Disney produced a few mediocre films, until the release of *Cinderella* in 1950 and *Peter Pan* in 1953. Around this time Walt came up with the idea of a theme park full of Disney characters, after wishing he had somewhere fun to take his daughters on his day off, and, funded by a loan from the Bank of America, Disneyland was officially opened on 17 July 1955.

Walt once declared: 'I don't make pictures just to make money. I make money to make more pictures'. This telling statement emphasises the true depths of the passion the man had for his craft, but while it may be true, it masks Walt's innate gift for commercialising entertainment. When Walt Disney died in 1966, he had cemented his legacy. He had created an entertainment juggernaut which encompassed everything from animated creations, feature films, money-spinning merchandise and of course, the most famous theme parks in the world.

Penguin

Paper passions

Founder: Allen Lane

Age of founder at start: 34

Background: Book publishing

Year of foundation: 1935

Business type: Book publishing

Country of foundation: UK

Countries now trading in: Worldwide

Current turnover and profit: £903m and £93m

I t is a touch ironic that the man who founded Penguin, now one of the world's biggest publishers, didn't actually enjoy reading himself. He may not have been an avid reader, but Allen Lane was a shrewd businessman, quick to spot opportunities and not afraid of taking risks. Allen set out to radically change the way the book industry worked. He wanted to make reading affordable, bringing books to the masses without compromising on quality. His Penguin paperbacks are now classics, and with this vision, he succeeded in changing the reading habits of millions around the world.

Keeping it in the family

In 1919, at the age of 16, Allen Lane Williams left Bristol Grammar School and joined the family business, a publishing company called The Bodley Head. The business had been set up by Allen's uncle, John Lane, and by the time Allen joined had published works by several prominent authors including Oscar Wilde. John did not have any children and to ensure The Bodley Head remained very much a family business, he made it a condition of Allen's employment that he and the rest of his family – his parents and three siblings – change their surname to Lane.

In his first few months at The Bodley Head, Allen learnt about the book publishing industry from the bottom up, helping out wherever he was needed, working as an office boy and general dogsbody. At the time, the market was dominated by a number of established London publishers, who were mainly only reprinting and making very slight revisions to Victorian novels. Most books were hardback, with few contemporary topics available. Cheap paperbacks weren't widely available, and the production and design of the few that did exist was often of a poor quality.

Allen was doing well at The Bodley Head, and was rewarded with a promotion. He was given more responsibility in the royalties and accounts department and was dealing with a wide variety of suppliers, including printers and bookbinders. This helped him build a range of contacts in the publishing world. He also became friendly with younger authors published by The Bodley Head, one of whom was Agatha Christie.

Pockets of potential

In 1924, five years after joining The Bodley Head, Allen was promoted to co-director, and John died a year later. When John's widow died a year after that, Allen received a majority share in the company, but this proved a mixed blessing. The business had become insolvent at the time of John's death and remained so until it officially went into liquidation 11 years later. The publisher continued trading during this time; funded by sporadic injections of cash from some of the directors, rather than actual turnover and profits. As The Bodley Head struggled to stay in business, the world economy was in turmoil; the 1929 Wall Street Crash in the USA sparked the worst economic depression the country had ever seen and its effects stretched far and wide, triggering a recession in the UK.

During this time, Allen's resolve to remain in publishing was seriously tested. He made a series of misjudgements that could have been disastrous, but actually taught him some valuable lessons about the industry. His first mistake was his backing a book of 'diplomatic memoirs' that turned out to have been written by an unemployed actor and proved libellous. Allen took the author to court, accusing him of obtaining money under false pretences – a legal cost the failing business could have done without. On top of this Allen also gave the go-ahead for a disastrous series of children's books that failed miserably, and incurred further losses at The Bodley Head.

Yet Allen also displayed touches of the brilliance and forward thinking

Founder Allen Lane never gave up his vision, despite scepticism from the whole of the publishing industry

that were to stand him in good stead in later years. He published James Joyce's *Ulysses* in 1960, a book that other British publishers had turned down and which had even been burned by customs officials in Folkestone in the early 1920s, accused of containing 'glaring obscenity and filth'. The other directors made Allen personally liable for any legal costs incurred, for fear of being prosecuted, but there were none – instead this publication became one of Allen's earliest successes.

Mass market appeal

Despite some success, business continued to be very difficult, and the future of The Bodley Head remained uncertain. Allen was on the lookout for a way to improve the business. In 1934, after a weekend spent with the novelist Agatha Christie in Devon, Allen was travelling back by train and was looking for reading material while waiting at Exeter station. He was disappointed to find only popular magazines and hardback reprints of dry Victorian novels. He was sure there was a gap in the market for good quality, contemporary fiction, available in paperback, at an affordable price.

While the paperback was not a new concept entirely, Allen's vision was. The current paperbacks were very cheap, low-quality reprints. WH Smith, for instance had started a chain of railways stalls selling cheap paperbacks, but these were hard to read as they were printed with double columns and used a small typeface. Other paperbacks at the time had rather lurid covers and carried advertisements, making them look and feel cheap. Allen intended to keep the cheap price of current paperbacks, but increase the quality of the design and production to set them apart from existing ones.

He also wanted the books to be available in as many places as possible, and not just follow the norm of railway stalls. He saw the product as mass market: these books, he said, 'need to be bought as easily and as casually as a packet of cigarettes'. He intended to reprint popular hardback books in paperback and sell them in Woolworths, libraries and chain stores for sixpence each. By reprinting and not commissioning new books, he would save himself money, and he would be publishing books that he knew would be popular with consumers.

> Allen's vision was that these books would 'need to be bought as easily and as casually as a packet of cigarettes'.

Allen was convinced consumers would buy his high-quality paperbacks, but before he could prove this, he had the mammoth task of convincing the publishing industry – publishers, distributors and book shops – that his vision would work. This would prove his biggest challenge: the publishing industry was known for being very traditional and for lacking innovation. Throughout the 1920s and early 1930s, when the book trade could have been moving with the times, it stood still and watched as other types of media emerged to compete for consumer attention. By 1935, cinemas had become increasingly popular and there were more than 4,000 of them in the country. Although the book trade was weathering the recession better than some industries, it could not rest on its laurels much longer. What the industry needed was an injection of life and creative thinking, and Allen was just the man to do this.

With his vision still fresh, Allen attended a conference of publishers and booksellers near Oxford. The publishers were all encountering the same problems: rising production costs, which led to reduced profit margins, and slow sales. It was here that Allen outlined his vision for the business that was to eventually become Penguin. The conference delegates were less than receptive towards Allen's idea – they did not want to risk getting involved with this new proposition when their profit margins were already so delicate. Rather than be put off by negativity from industry peers though, their response only made Allen more determined than ever before.

Details make a difference

In 1934, only a few months after he came up with his radical new idea, Allen set about putting his plans in motion. The other directors at The Bodley Head agreed that he could publish as an imprint under the Bodley name initially, but he would need to find the titles and any investment needed himself. This gave Allen use of the company's resources and employees, so he did not have the burden of these costs while starting up. It was not until 1936 that Penguin was established as a separate company.

Allen used some money that had been given to him by his aunt, and his parents mortgaged their home to help fund the new venture. Since Allen intended to publish reprints only, his first task was to approach other publishers to see if they and their authors would be willing to license him the rights. He also worked out a rough business plan, to ascertain how much he could afford to pay for the licences, and how many books he could print.

Allen also had to decide on the design and format of the books – which would be key in differentiating his books from existing paperbacks. Allen did not like the traditional style of images on the covers of books as he felt this made the product look cheap, and covers were often badly designed. In all his years in publishing, Allen had never been able to understand why cheap books should not be well-designed, as he felt that you could still achieve a good design for a small price. Instead, he drew inspiration from the jacket designs of German publisher Albatross Books, who also produced mass market paperbacks. Their covers had no images and were quite simplistic in their design. Allen had long admired Albatross, and incorporated elements from their books into Penguin's design, for example, Albatross used a simple image of the bird on their cover, very similar to Penguin's iconic cover.

A mock-up of what would become Penguin's classic book covers. Allen wanted the design to be simple but appealing

Allen had never been able to understand why cheap books should not be well-designed, as he felt that you could still achieve a good design for a small price.

Allen also wanted to ensure that the books would easily fit into people's handbags - again going against the convention at the time for bulking out books to make them look better value for money. His books would be clean, modern and attractively presented.

Building a brand

For Allen, building a brand was important from the start. He did not just intend to bring good books to market - he wanted to create a line of books that could become collectors' items. With a strong series design, people would be more likely to buy new editions, and want to own the complete set of books. This translated into bold, simple covers using bright blocks of colour. The books would be colour-coded too: orange for fiction, blue for biography and green for crime, mirroring a technique used by Albatross which Allen had admired.

Allen also needed to find a name for his new imprint. He wanted a 'dignified but flippant' image for his brand and gathered the employees of The Bodley Head together one morning to come up with ideas. A host of different animal and bird names were suggested and swiftly rejected as being too close to competitors (one of the favourites was actually Albatross). The name Penguin, ironically, did not come from any of the meeting's participants, but from Allen's secretary, who was working on the other side of the room and happened to suggest the name after hearing other contributions. Allen liked it at once; the name was chosen and an employee was sent to London Zoo to draw pictures of penguins.

A frosty reception

The Penguin imprint was to launch in August 1935 with 10 titles, carefully chosen by Allen. He told the publishing trade magazine *The Bookseller* in a later interview that 'the test I applied to each book was to ask myself: is this a book, which, if I had not read it, and had seen it on sale at 6d (sixpence), would make me say, "This is a book I have always meant to read, I will get it now"?'.

However, convincing publishers to license him rights to their titles proved problematic. The first Penguin paperback book to be published was André Maurois'

Ariel, and as it was published in hardback already under The Bodley Head imprint, it was easy for Allen to secure the rights to it. But thereafter, Allen met with resistance at every turn.

'The test I applied to each book was to ask myself: is this a book, which, if I had not read it, and had seen it on sale at sixpence, would make me say, "This is a book I have always meant to read, I will get it now"?'

The problem was that other publishers thought the Penguin paperbacks would drive down the price of books in general and challenge the sale of hardbacks. Allen argued that this would not be the case as Penguin was publishing reprints of books that had long been unavailable and therefore any sales would add to existing ones, rather than take away from hardback sales. But few publishers, if any, were convinced.

One publisher, however, seemed prepared to give Allen the benefit of the doubt. Jonathan Cape had started his own publishing business in 1921, and had built it into a business with a formidable reputation. Allen met with him to see if he was willing to license some of his titles, based on an advance of £25 for each book, payable on publication, and a royalty of a farthing (a quarter of a penny) per copy. Jonathan was willing to take a punt on him, but wanted a £40 advance on each book (around £2,000 in today's money), and royalties of one and a half farthings (three-eighths of a penny) per copy. Allen intended to sell the books for sixpence, and would make a reasonable profit with this royalty, so happily accepted. Allen later found out that Jonathan, like everyone else in the industry, believed that he would go bust within months and thought he'd better take an advance off him now before the business folded.

Jonathan's publishing firm provided six of the first 10 titles, which included Ernest Hemingway's *A Farewell to Arms*, while The Bodley Head added Agatha Christie's *The Mysterious Affair at Styles* alongside *Ariel*. The remaining two titles came from two other publishers. One was *Carnival* by Compton Mackenzie, which was licensed from Chatto and Windus, who had originally been reluctant to support Allen. The 10th book was a novel by crime writer Dorothy Sayers, added to the list after Allen had persuaded Ernest Benn to release the rights. While it seemed Allen was slowly winning over the publishers, his next battle was convincing booksellers to stock the titles.

Little interest

Again Allen faced substantial opposition. To begin with he simply couldn't get booksellers to buy or stock the books. Like the publishers, they thought Allen's profit margins were too small to warrant attention. By selling the books for sixpence, Allen's gross margin was a penny a copy; whereas other publishers were struggling to make money on books being sold at the much higher price of 7 shillings and sixpence. The bookshops also believed that the smaller format would attract pickpockets and that the books would spoil easily and look tattered on the shelves. Even the minority who did agree to take them ended up putting them in a sales bin outside their shops, confining the books to 'bargain bucket' status. Allen was dealt an even bigger blow when he found out that the largest book retailer at the time, WH Smith, also refused to stock the Penguin books. Publishing was known as a conservative industry anyway, and at a time of recession, booksellers were even more risk averse, focusing on those books that were guaranteed to sell rather than taking a gamble on something new.

There was, however, a sliver of success with department store Selfridges, which had reserved a window in anticipation of displaying Penguin's first 10 titles when they were published at the end of August 1935. They ordered 100 copies of each title.

The negativity from the booksellers was a big blow to Allen. He asked a friend if he knew anyone who would be willing to take the business off his hands and was left to contemplate his huge stock of books that no one was willing to take a gamble on.

He had ordered a print run of 200,000 (20,000 for each of the 10 titles) half of which had been bound. Each copy had cost two and a half pence to produce. To break even, Allen would need to sell between 17,000 and 18,000 books, but with no one willing to stock the books it seemed an impossible task.

Pulling out all the stops

In early August 1935, three weeks before publication of the books, Allen made a final attempt to drum up book orders by getting in touch with an old industry contact at Woolworths' head office. Clifford Prescott was the buyer for the haberdashery department, which, strangely, also sold books, most of them at the cheaper end of the market. Conveniently for Allen's pricing strategy, Woolworths' slogan at the time was 'Nothing over Sixpence'. Luckily, Cliff's wife liked the titles, and persuaded him to take a gamble: he ordered 63,500 copies. It proved the breakthrough Allen needed.

The first 10 Penguin titles were published at the end of August 1935 and in only a matter of days, Selfridges had almost sold out and immediately ordered another 100 copies of each. The books also sold strongly in Woolworths and orders from other branches followed.

The press was quick to pick up on this demand and the books received good reviews. Others in the industry were also quick to spot the potential. Playwright

JB Priestley, for example, told Allen: 'these Penguin books are amazingly good value for money. If you can make the series pay for itself – with such books at such a price – you will have performed a great publishing feat'. Previously sceptical and dismissive booksellers rang Allen and asked to order the range.

Playwright JB Priestley told Allen: 'these Penguin books are amazingly good value for money. If you can make the series pay for itself – with such books at such a price – you will have performed a great publishing feat'.

As Penguin thrived, however, The Bodley Head continued to decline and the business went into liquidation in 1936, a year after the Penguin imprint launched. Allen set up a new company that same year and rented premises in the Crypt of the Holy Trinity Church on Marylebone Road, using a fairground slide to receive deliveries from the street above. The Bodley Head staff that had been working across both Penguin and Bodley joined the newly created company. Allen paid staff a modest wage, but they would be paid an extra 10% of the profits every six months.

The first year

Allen worked long hours in Penguin's first year as a separate company, often packing and invoicing books himself. Penguin books were now prominent in both railway stations and bookshops, and were selling well. Allen had proved his idea worked; and the once-sceptical publishers were suddenly all interested in leasing rights to him. Now, Allen's problem was not persuading publishers to take a chance on him, but choosing which books to publish.

In the first nine months of trading as an independent company, the business made a net profit of £4,500; and in the first year, Penguin sold a staggering three million books. The darling of the publishing world, Penguin was still regarded with suspicion by some authors and traditional publishers. At the time George Orwell commented that 'the Penguin Books are splendid value for sixpence, so splendid that if other publishers had any sense they would combine against them and suppress them'.

Sales rocketing

By 1937, Penguin had moved to warehouses near to where the future Heathrow Airport would be located, and Allen began to grow the existing business. In that same year, Penguin launched its Pelican imprint: non-fiction books based on contemporary issues. And in 1940, Penguin began publishing non-fiction picture books for children, under the Puffin imprint.

Having first struggled to get booksellers on board, Allen was keen to not rely solely on bookshops, and decided to sell his books directly to the public. He set up a slot-machine book dispenser (similar to cigarette machines), called a 'Penguincubator', in London's Charing Cross Road. He inserted business reply cards in some of the books, encouraging the public to make suggestions and leave their details, which he then added to a mailing list. Using these contacts, he set up a direct mail division so Penguin could to sell directly to consumers.

The outbreak of the Second World War in 1939 actually proved to be advantageous for Penguin. Penguin's book *What Hitler Wants* achieved record-breaking sales, and books were ordered in huge quantities to be delivered to the armed forces. To Penguin's advantage, low-priced fiction and non-fiction was particularly sought-after. One of the bestselling titles during the war was *Aircraft Recognition*, used by both civilians and the army to recognise enemy planes.

In the 1960s, the publisher courted controversy by publishing DH Lawrence's novel, *Lady Chatterley's Lover*, resulting in a charge under the Obscene Publications Act. Penguin fought this charge however and within six weeks, had sold more than two million copies as people rushed to buy the book that had caused such a storm.

Where are they now?

In 1961, Penguin became a public company on the London Stock Exchange – such was the popularity of the business that the offer was oversubscribed by more than 150 times. Allen Lane died in 1970 and the company was acquired that year by international media group Pearson. Today, Penguin has offices in 15 countries and keeps more than 5,000 different titles in print at any one time.

Impressions

Making a big impression

Founder: David Lester

Age of founders at start: 20

Background: Trainee accountant

Year of foundation: 1988

Business type: Computer games publisher

Country of foundation: UK

Countries now trading in: 20 at its peak

How They Started in Tough Times

Computer games are now a bigger industry than films worldwide, with the top individual games generating sales of over $1bn per year. In 1988, though, when David Lester set up his games business, Impressions, as a hobby with some friends, even the biggest games sold just a fraction of that. The major recession which hit the world as the company was getting properly started hurt the business initially but ultimately provided it with the opportunity to break through to significant profitable growth.

Inspiration

In 1988 the computer games industry was in its infancy, but set to grow rapidly. David Lester was a trainee accountant with a keen interest in computers, having reviewed some computer games for consumer magazines before university and during summer holidays. Through this, he had become friends with a few guys who developed games and had formed plenty of ideas for games himself. His friends were making good money from the games, and although not a programmer, he wondered if he could sell some of his ideas.

David sent several game ideas to a few game publishers; as well as some straight rejections he received a reasonable amount of interest. A number of companies liked the ideas, but wanted David to find people to develop these ideas into prototypes, which they would then consider publishing. This gave him the confidence that his ideas had some value, but he was frustrated at needing to do more work before agreeing a deal.

David got to know some developers, and they would meet in the evening after work or at weekends to try to get their games made and published. The other developers had had a few games published, but were frustrated with the publishers. New publishers came and went pretty quickly at this time, often leaving unpaid debts when they went. David and his friends felt sure they could do it themselves at least as well as some of the others they knew. So, as many groups of friends do after a few drinks, one day David said 'Why don't we set up a publisher ourselves?' After a pause, they agreed, and set out to find out what it would involve.

David began to investigate the different facets of games publishing: from manufacturing, marketing and sales, while his developer friends worked on which games they should produce first.

The outcome of this research was promising – they worked out they could break even fairly easily, with a good chance of making a profit, so they went for it. At this stage it was more about the satisfaction of doing it, with a chance to make a bit of extra money if things went well. David, the youngest of the friends with fewer commitments, was willing to put in more cash than the others (which he had saved from his student journalism jobs), and so ended up being the majority shareholder, with two developer friends, David's brother and two non-developer friends making the balance. In total they raised around £12,500.

The founder, David Lester

At this stage it was more about the satisfaction of doing it, with a chance to make a bit of extra money if things went well.

First success

For their first game they decided to publish a football management game. Several of the developers had made a game like this before, and they felt they could improve on the competition. To make their game stand out from the crowd, they decided to try and licensse the rights to a famous football manager to brand the game. The most successful manager at the time by far was Kenny Dalglish, at Liverpool FC. With no contacts in the football world, David took the bull by the horns and phoned Liverpool FC directly. Amazingly, he was put through to Kenny straight away. Kenny was keen, and David made a deal with his agent – agreeing to pay Kenny a royalty on sales.

With no structure yet in place, Impressions formed a joint venture with an existing publishing company to publish the football game. The game was launched in 1989 and was an instant hit, staying at number one in the games charts for weeks. This led to the company making a profit of £30,000 in its first year. Despite this success, David and his friends wanted to carry on with their plans to do all the publishing themselves, and so ended the joint venture after that game.

With no contacts in the football world, David took the bull by the horns and phoned Liverpool FC directly. Amazingly, he was put through to Kenny straight away. Kenny was keen, and David made a deal with his agent.

They set about finding suppliers to help publish the games. At this stage one of the other founders, Ed Grabowski, took on more responsibilities. David and Ed scoured trade magazine advertisers, and eventually found a sales agency, a disk duplicator, a warehousing business, a printer, and a box manufacturer. They learnt which questions to ask as they went along, and found that most of the people they spoke to were happy to help them.

The next game they decided to publish was *Raider*, for the Commodore Amiga, created by a programmer they knew. Their new-found suppliers worked well, the sales agent they had selected generated some orders, and Impressions launched its first game. *Raider* received more modest reviews and sales than the founders had hoped, but this game wasn't make or break. Impressions published some more Kenny Dalglish games, as well as a few others, and soon built a modest reputation in the gaming world.

After about a year, Ed went full-time, and Impressions moved to a small serviced office, and employed a full-time PR person and an office manager. David carried on with his trainee accountancy job, working on Impressions in the evenings.

Now that Ed was full-time, and they had some employees, David began to start planning the business seriously. He began to talk to developers and started forecasting sales and profits. They were a little shocked when profits they thought they'd made rapidly turned into losses, as some of the games they had sold started to be sent back, in the form of returns. They hadn't taken this into account, and as a result received less money than expected. This meant they had to delay paying a few suppliers, and learnt a keen lesson in cash flow.

Legal battle

In 1990, Impressions faced their first major challenge, when they found themselves up against one of the most powerful UK game publishers at the time, Mirrorsoft. Impressions were publishing a game called *Chariots of Wrath*, produced by some freelance developers. This was a 'science fiction shoot-'em-up' game with some similarities to a very major game, *Xenon 2*, due to be published by one of the largest games company at that time, Mirrorsoft. Impressions promoted their new game in the press, and shortly afterwards received a legal letter from Mirrorsoft alleging that *Chariots of Wrath* infringed their rights in *Xenon 2*, and had copied a level.

Impressions couldn't afford to lose a legal battle – and really needed sales of this new game to boost income. David was sure they were not guilty of plagiarism, and so fought the allegations. He got himself an excellent solicitor, and set up a meeting with Mirrorsoft. While David was sure of their innocence, he had to admit there were remarkable similarities between the games, and in the end, to avoid further prolonging any dispute, agreed to change the controversial level. The game was published on time, after a frantic rush, and ironically, the new level ended up being far better than the original.

Meanwhile, David had failed his tax exam at the last stage of his accountancy qualification, and decided he could no longer work full-time at an accountancy firm, study to retake the tax exam, and run the games publishing business. So he resigned from the firm in early December 1990, to study full-time for a week before his last exam, and would then try to make a go of Impressions. In fact he passed the exam, and qualified as an accountant, but would never go on to work as one.

Tough times, change of tack

Early in 1991, though, recession really took hold, and business started to get tougher. Their second Kenny Dalglish game hadn't done as well as the first, and they were still getting more returns than expected, leading to real financial problems. They already had a bank overdraft, which David was personally guaranteeing, and the survival of the business was in doubt. They stripped their staff right back and left their office, with David and Ed going back to running the business from their homes.

Although turnover was growing fast, cash flow remained very tight throughout 1990 and 1991. To save money, David took over sales from the agency, and started calling customers himself, which he says helped him get close to the market. He also dealt with suppliers and did the invoicing. He admits he took too much on, and ended up in a horrible administrative mess, often leaving it far too late to send out invoices to customers, which meant that they paid up even later than they should have. Money was tight, and David remembers, 'it was enormously stressful, and I stayed awake for night after night, working out who we could pay when, and trying to work out whether we would ever be able to pay all our bills off'.

By early 1991, David was personally guaranteeing well over half a million pounds of debt. 'It was scary', he remembers, 'I was also getting worse at coping with my workload, and with working from home. At this stage, the business was far more stressful than enjoyable. We knew we had to change things for it to be worth continuing'.

'It was enormously stressful, and I stayed awake for night after night, working out who we could pay when, and trying to work out whether we would ever be able to pay all our bills off'.

Impressions was now producing quite a few games, but not spending much time or money on each one. David and Ed had noticed the games industry was becoming saturated with games (many of them poor), and the better games started to far outsell the poorer games. So they decided to concentrate on fewer, better titles.

Impressions also decided it was time to specialise in one genre. They had had some success with strategy games (things like Risk or chess) – and David admits that their action games just couldn't compete with the market leaders. Focusing on strategy games would mean cutting out most of the market. Most games sold in Europe were action, not strategy games. To make a success of the business, Impressions would therefore have to sell their strategy games in either Japan or North America, both of which had huge markets for these sorts of games. Without one of these markets, the business would not survive.

America or bust

They couldn't just export their European products to customers in America: 'At that time Americans looked down on European games, and wanted American addresses on American boxes' David recalls. Most UK software publishers achieved this by licensing their games to companies in the USA, taking a small cash advance, and leaving the rest up to the Americans. But Impressions depended more on the US income than most UK publishers, and so needed a bigger share of the US sales.

David and Ed visited the States several times, attending trade shows and meeting other small publishers and distributors that Impressions might be able to work with. David was still based in London and speaking on the phone with American contacts late into the night, due to the time difference. His English accent went down a storm – and his tactic of playing dumb and asking a lot of questions (which, he says, was pretty easy, as he didn't know how things worked over there) gained him precious knowledge.

America has a reputation as a dangerous place for UK businesses to launch, and several big UK games publishers had made substantial losses by opening there. Yet when David and Ed researched the American market in detail, it offered Impressions three significant advantages over the European market. Firstly, they could sell games at a higher price and manufacture there for less than in Europe, so their gross profit was much higher. Secondly, there were just three main US games magazines compared to over 15 in Europe, which meant they could spend less money on advertising and still end up with a far more prominent campaign than in Europe. And thirdly, the strategy game market was bigger than in Europe so they could expect to sell more copies of their games.

His English accent went down a storm – and his tactic of playing dumb and asking a lot of questions (which, he says, was pretty easy, as he didn't know how things worked over there) gained him precious knowledge.

After considering several options, David decided to open an office in America, and sell to retailers and wholesalers directly rather than using a partner. Although it would cost to set up an office, they only needed two members of staff: one to 'Americanise' the products and the other to provide customer service. They found freelance sales reps to sell the games and a manufacturer in Florida to create and dispatch the games.

A selection of Impressions' games

Raising enough money

However, before they could launch in America they needed to raise enough money to fund the expansion. They needed £50,000 and the deadline was tight: without the US market, Impressions would go out of business.

Raising money was tough. David wrote a brief business plan, and talked to lots of venture capitalists – none of whom were interested in investing. David changed tack and approached his family and friends. His father, brother and some friends invested, but it still wasn't enough. Then David thought of approaching their suppliers: people who knew the business, and saw its potential. One of them was interested, and Impressions scraped together £48,500, which at the time, due to the depth of the US recession, equalled about $100,000, to fund the US venture. David, who had just turned 26, bought a one-way ticket to Boston and rented a small office in Connecticut, near an American games developer he'd met during his research.

In 1992 America, Connecticut in particular, was in the depth of recession. This enabled Impressions to get a really good deal on an office; it also made it easy and affordable to hire staff. Even so, money was very tight. Their $100,000 would not have been enough had it not been for the recession.

Playing problems

Impressions launched their first game in September 1992, called *Air Force Commander*, which David remembers did 'fine; not great, not terrible.' Their second release, *Air Bucks*, where players built an airline from scratch, had done well in Europe, and US magazines had already written glowing previews. The game generated pre-orders of about 17,000 – by far their biggest order to date.

Although this was before the internet, there were several 'online services' active in America – such as AOL, Compuserve and Genie. Using a dial-up modem, David could visit message boards where players were discussing different games. On the release of *Air Bucks*, he went online to view the feedback. The news wasn't good. 'In short, they hated it', David recalls. It meant they could expect a ton of returns, which would mean they would not get paid the cash they had expected from the game. Worse still, they'd already used most of the expected income to pay rent and wages.

David spent an enormous time discussing the game with the customers online long into the evenings every day, asking them in detail what they didn't like. The good news was that they still really liked the concept of the game – David saw that it might be possible to fix the parts the American gamers didn't like. He offered to fix the problems and told people online that he'd give them a copy for free, if they would be patient. This was met with much scepticism, but word also spread that here was a company doing things differently, where they actually talked to customers directly. Luckily, enough of these gamers were prepared to give Impressions a chance, and didn't return their games, but had to wait months for the new version. By factoring (borrowing against the amount of money trade customers owed them), Impressions managed to scrape through to early 1993.

He offered to fix the problems and told people online that he'd give them a copy for free, if they would be patient. This was met with much scepticism, but word also spread that here was a company doing things differently, where they actually talked to customers directly.

In need of a hit

The next game needed to be successful, and problem-free, or they might lose the rocky customer base they'd built so far. The now well-known game *Sim City* had become a hit over Christmas 1991, and this inspired Impressions' next game: *Caesar*, which let players build cities in an ancient Roman empire setting, adding game elements such as combat. David designed the game with one of their better developers, Simon Bradbury.

They tested *Caesar* extensively in the aftermath of the *Air Bucks* fiasco, trying to put in all the elements they now knew American gamers wanted. *Caesar* launched in America in February 1993. It was an instant hit. The press loved it, and the customers loved it. Sales rocketed – they had sold tens of thousands of copies within a few months.

Just after the successful release of *Caesar*, Impressions released the new version of *Air Bucks*. *Air Bucks 1.2* was launched in new packaging, and true to his word, David mailed it for free to several thousand customers. And it worked. The customers loved the game they ended up with. Impressions had built their reputation from the crisis, and were now established as a company that listened to its customers.

Since making a small profit in their first year of trading, Impressions had lost money in each of the following three years, despite growing turnover substantially year on year. At the end of their first year trading in the USA, they had made a profit of several hundred thousand pounds. Business boomed from here, and their assessment of the US market proved accurate: they made considerably more money than they could in Europe. They moved the office to Boston, hired more people (this office soon had 40 staff), and switched to developing games aimed mainly at the US market.

The growth in sales and profits continued, but it was far from event-free. The autumn is the biggest time for game sales, so Impressions had one major game launch planned for every autumn. In the autumn of 2003, the big game was *Global Domination*. Despite rigorous testing procedures, one of the production staff managed to approve a disk for manufacturing which was missing one file. This meant that anyone who bought it and didn't already have that file on their PC couldn't play the game. This proved disastrous, and most of the games were returned. Fortunately, though, the 'B' game for that autumn, an American Civil War game developed by Ed, took off to such an extent that overall sales were greater than expected.

To the next level

Although Impressions was doing well, they were still small fish in a big pond, and the software industry was growing rapidly. Some of their retail customers started to take advantage – charging a lot of money for promotions, and taking ages to pay their bills. One key retailer took five months to pay up. The cost of developing the games was also increasing dramatically, as customers expected bigger and better games every year. David felt it could be time to try and raise some capital.

By this time, they had already been approached by a number of American venture capital companies. While David knew they needed investment to grow, he was really enjoying running Impressions, and didn't particularly want to lose control of the business or give up many shares. He looked to alternative means of making more money.

In 1994 Impressions changed their sales agency to a company called Davidson, one of the largest educational software companies in the USA. David negotiated a great deal for Impressions, so that Davidson's commission was lower than the deal with the previous sales force and payment terms were far more favourable. This meant Impressions could grow without needing venture capital investment, leaving the existing shareholders with all the shares in the company. In fact the deal proved a mixed blessing, as Davidson weren't earning enough to bother doing a good job of selling Impressions games. Nevertheless Impressions published better games, growing turnover substantially and making more than £1m in annual profits for the first time, and by mid-1995 they had over £1m cash in the bank.

Where are they now?

In June 1995, Impressions was sold to Sierra On-Line, then the largest PC games publisher in the world. In 1997 David returned to the UK, still working for Sierra. After designing *Caesar 3*, which came out in 1998 and went on to sell more than two million copies, generating very substantial profits for Sierra, David stopped working with computer games altogether. Impressions carried on for several years but eventually its key developer talent left, and what remained was shut down. Sierra

On-Line is now part of Activision Blizzard, the leading global publisher of interactive entertainment.

Since his gaming success, David has invested in many private businesses, as well as investing in Watford FC, where he was on the board for five eventful years. In February 1999, David launched Crimson, a book, magazine and website-publishing business. David is passionate about helping small business and is dedicated to providing Britain with the same quality of advice and practical help as he found during his time building Impressions in America.

Three Sixty Entertainment

A magical business story

Founders: Matthew (Mat) Churchill, Charlie Burnell, Colin Wilkinson and Henry Meakin

Age of founders at start: 42, 48, 41, 60

Background: Theatre and events production

Year of foundation: 2008

Business type: Theatrical entertainment

Country of foundation: UK

Countries now trading in: UK

Current turnover and profit: £5.4m and £2m (operating profit)

Shows like *Les Miserables*, *Cats* and *Phantom of the Opera* have wowed audiences for generations, selling out venues worldwide. Mat Churchill and Charlie Burnell wanted to create a similar theatrical phenomenon, but their vision was to create a production with a twist – theirs would be performed in a tent and use state-of-the-art video production technology projected on its walls. The business model evolved significantly during two years of planning and along the way, the founders faced scepticism from industry experts, who questioned this new and risky concept. But Mat and Charlie resoundingly proved them wrong, with the financial help of Colin Wilkinson and Henry Meakin. Following the success of their first show, *Peter Pan*, staged in London, the company, Three Sixty Entertainment, is now setting its sights on productions in the USA and Australia.

Ideas over dinner

Mat Churchill and Charlie Burnell both had solid backgrounds in theatrical production, and Mat had worked for several years producing performances in theatre tents. They met through industry contacts, become firm friends, and always wanted to find a project to work on together. It was over dinner in London in 2006 that they developed the idea for a production that would be truly unique.

For some time, Mat had wanted to put on a tented theatre performance in London's Kensington Gardens. The iconic gardens, situated within Hyde Park, had never before

Mat Churchill and Charlie Burnell

Mat and Charlie wanted their tent to look cool and sleek, and to be the first tented theatre in Kensington Gardens

housed a show. Mat felt the situation and wonderful surroundings would make the perfect location. Meanwhile, Charlie had noticed the growing appeal of children's stories for grown-ups. A recent production of Michael Morpurgo's *War Horse* had captured the imagination of thousands of theatre-goers, and had become the most successful play the National Theatre had ever staged. Charlie wanted to uncover the story of Peter Pan, which previously had primarily only been produced by Disney Studios, or lost to the realms of 'Christmas pantos'. He intended to restore this classic to its original glory, and shared this idea with Mat.

The pair decided to try and put together their ideas: to make Mat's dream event in Kensington Gardens a landmark production of Peter Pan. The intended venue was particularly poignant: Kensington Gardens was the very place where author JM Barrie used to meet with the Llewellyn-Davis children (the inspiration for the Lost Boys) and where Pan's adventures were inspired. They realised that no major stage production of Peter Pan had been produced for decades in either the UK or the US yet Peter Pan is an internationally adored story and a major brand in its own right. The rights were available. Done right the Peter Pan story was an enormous opportunity.

The intended venue was particularly poignant: Kensington Gardens was the very place where Pan's adventures were inspired.

A spectacular vision

For the production, Mat had envisaged creating a 'tent to end all tents'. For most of us the image of spending an evening in a tent conjures up images of rather jolly but dingy circus shows. Mat's idea was altogether different: he wanted to upgrade the image of a show in a tent into a chic, urban night out.

Canadian entertainment company, *Cirque du Soleil*, had already put on major-scale shows featuring spectacle-based entertainment at more than 100 locations around the world, often, but not always, using tents. This had proved that high ticket prices could be charged for tented shows. However major Broadway scale theatre productions moving from town to town in their own tent bringing a sophisticated day out to audiences had never been done. To deliver on all levels, particularly quality and cost, a vast amount of intellectual capital and talented managers needed to be assembled. The founders felt that although similar ideas had been tried they had lacked the over arching vision and ability to deliver a premium experience at viable cost. The one exception was a major National Theatre production that Mat had toured in one of his theatre tents in 1998; it had sold out wherever it went.

The plan was to invest several thousand pounds of their own money to kick start the business and then raise funds through theatre angels (private investors backing theatrical shows), a traditional route for those seeking funding for similar shows. Additional sponsorship income would complete the finance for the project.

...then reality bites

The idea seemed perfect, but live entertainment businesses are fraught with difficulties. It is hard to make ends meet in a market where the cost of creating, then running a production and promoting a show are difficult to claw back from box-office receipts. It is also very difficult to predict whether any given script or show idea has the likely makings of a hit. Everyone knows the box office successes, such as *Cats* and *Les Miserables*, but the majority of shows don't come close to this level of success. Many fall flat on their faces.

Mat and Charlie knew they had their work cut out. Under the theatre investment model they would need this one show to cover all their costs **and** make them a profit. The equation worked well but on a restricted budget and relied on a level of sponsorship income. The restricted budget would deliver an amazing production but would not allow them to deliver the full audience experience they could see was possible. With a larger investment they could make Peter Pan a very special event which would give it a much greater ability to tour internationally. Although building a purpose-designed tent was costly, it had major advantages. Primarily they could create a stunning landmark structure that would sell tickets just by being there and they could also provide the facilities and a wow factor that audiences would love and would further drive word of mouth ticket sales. The staging could be built to the exact specifications of the space and re-used each time the show sets down, without the need to adapt it to different venues. Owning the venue also meant that none of the ancillary revenues from bar and merchandise sales needed to be shared with theatre owners. The pair had found a model that would work financially.

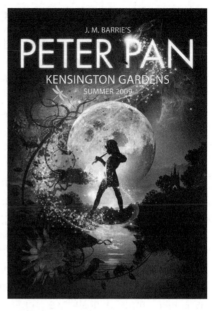

Before they could start working on the production, or even start raising finance though, they needed to overcome one major obstacle: persuading Kensington Gardens to allow them to stage a production there in the first place. If they weren't able to use this location, their plan was redundant, so everything rested on their application being accepted. The plan was to launch the show in May 2008, but despite a long lead time

The poster advertising Three Sixty's ground-breaking production

of over two years, this was hardly a walk in the park. In its entire 280-year history, Kensington Gardens had never allowed a tented theatre production to perform in the grounds. But Mat was determined to succeed. As a veteran of tented entertainment, one of his skills was completing planning applications. Gaining permission involved completing a 95,000-word document and running a minor political campaign. It took the best part of a year. The application was so extensive that it equalled the application you'd need to build a skyscraper in London. At this point there was no money to employ expensive planning consultants. Against the odds, their application was approved. The process took a year to complete, and they were granted permission at the end of 2007.

Gaining permission involved completing a 95,000-word document and took the best part of a year. The application was so extensive that it equalled the application you'd need to build a skyscraper in London.

The Three Sixty model

During the application process, Mat and Charlie concentrated on getting the production off the ground. They needed to hire a director, designer, writer and members of the cast; design and create the home for the production, a bespoke tented structure; and, crucially, fund the production.

To design the tent, Mat looked close to home, and engaged the services of his wife, Teresa Hoskyns, a Royal College of Art trained architect and expert in theatre and public space. The original idea was to design the tent with an external supporting structure so that the fabric of the tent would be hung from four exterior poles, which would mean no one in the audience had a pole obstructing their view. It would be particularly appropriate for Peter Pan as the cast would be able to fly – a key element of the show – without the hindrance (or danger!) of unsightly poles.

In mid-2007, Mat and Charlie met Bill Dudley, a multiple award winning designer of sets for Broadway and the West End. They met for the first time in Kensington Gardens on the site that had been earmarked for the show. When they told him about the design of the tent, Bill's face lit up. He saw the interior walls of the tent as a giant projection surface, three times the area of an Imax screen. But more importantly for Bill, it created the ideal structure to create a 360-degree immersive world all around the audience. He had always wanted to create a 360-degree set and he pointed out that "when the children fly to Neverland the entire audience will fly with them."

Not only were they recreating Peter Pan in Kensington Gardens, they were using groundbreaking technology that was sure to propel this production into the history books.

The idea thus evolved to create the world's first wrap-around virtual set – made up from Computer Generated Images (CGI). 'It's not film, it's CGI, so you can do anything you like with it' said Bill. 'It's where the virtual world steps out from a flat screen. Imagine looking at a great painting and having that moment where you think: "I wish I could walk right into that right now." Well, now you can.'

Although this would be an added cost, Mat and Charlie were convinced that using CGI was a must. It fitted well with their artistic vision for the adaptation and would provide them with another strong USP. Audiences worldwide would love this and it would be an incredible way to fly to Neverland. and Bill was highly experienced in using the technology. A powerful integrated concept of Peter Pan, CGI and an amazing tented environment was emerging.

Colin Wilkinson and Henry Meakin provided some much-needed business expertise

Funding plans and problems

Over the course of 2007, while they waited for the venue permission to be granted, they sought funding for the show. With not only a bespoke tent to pay for, but CGI technology and the production costs, Mat and Charlie figured they would need £1.8m. They had begun tapping into their industry contacts to raise money from theatre investors and it was also clear that this was a unique summer event worthy of significant sponsorship. The founders put as much of their own money as they could raise into the production in order to cover initial costs, including a deposit on the tent, which would cost about £750,000 in total.

But by the end of 2007, the business was dealt a severe blow. The two main backers at that point (both on the Sunday Times Rich list) pulled out citing concerns with the dark clouds gathering over the world economy. Now increasingly confident with the overall concept they had created and aware that there was a strong history of high quality family friendly productions doing well in a downturn, Mat and Charlie felt it was better to postpone and fully fund the show for May 2009, than take unacceptable risks with what they now felt was a very large opportunity.

But worse was to come. In January 2008, the economic climate really had turned sour. It was only a matter of time before the bottom fell out of the sponsorship market, as it is heavily reliant on banks and other financial institutions. A report that year predicted that the global financial crisis could have a devastating effect on sponsorship of the arts. Spending in that area had increased gradually between 2004 and 2007 to reach £170m, but was estimated to have fallen to £160m in 2008 and predictions for 2009 were even more pessimistic. New properties such as Peter Pan, however hot, were no longer getting offers.

Crisis of cash

By October 2008, they had received under 20% of the required investment.and were concerned about word in the industry of many big shows failing to find capital. They had just recruited other members of the production team, sourced from their contacts, to begin putting the show together. Writer Tanya Ronder had adapted many classic works of literature for the West End, while director Ben Harrison was a world-renowned expert of site-specific theatre. But despite getting such a skilled team on board, Mat and Charlie now felt that they should not rely on the theatrical model to deliver the funding. Mat had been following the CEO of Slingshot films Arvind Ethan David's blog. He had been blogging about funding structures in film, in particular the Enterprise Investment Scheme (EIS), which aims to help smaller, higher-risk trading companies to raise finance by offering a range of tax reliefs to investors who purchase shares in those companies. The EIS scheme seemed to fit well with their conviction that their integrated concept could have a very long life. They made initial contact with the Creative Investment Fund but were starting very late in the day with a funding model they knew little about. Mat decided to call Colin Wilkinson, a seasoned entrepreneur and fundraiser who had previously been involved

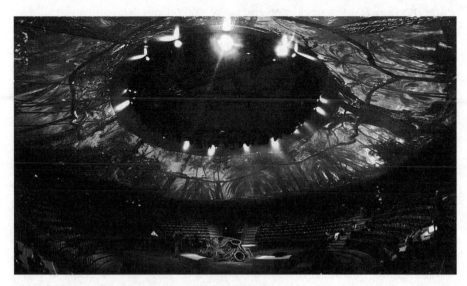

Inside the theatre tent, with 360 degrees of CGI

in managing other theatrical productions. Mat had heard had used a similar model on a theatrical company.

Colin was impressed by both the founders' vision and their perception of the market – so much so that he joined Mat and Charlie in November 2008 to help them raise the money they needed to put on the show. But even with experience on both the production and financial side, industry experts were not at all convinced the business would take off. When Mat and Charlie presented their plans to experienced operators in the market, they could not see how such grand ambitions could be realised on such slim budgets or in such tight timescales. Most shows would typically run in one location for as long as they can make a success of it, and their profit margin would increase along the way, with fixed costs such as set and design lasting the duration. Peter Pan's ambitions were different: it was to run for only 16 weeks (the length of time it had secured from Kensington Gardens) in one location and needed to make this short time profitable.

Adapting to market conditions

The business plan was changed to incorporate the international touring of Peter Pan and Charlie and Mat's ideas for new productions. From offering an investment in a single show in Kensington Gardens, it would now be possible to invest in a global entertainment business. This would open the business up to a wider pool of potential investors – not just theatre angels - who would have the opportunity to buy shares in a business, rather than just one production.

Colin persuaded Mat and Charlie to change the business plan from offering an investment in a single show in Kensington Gardens, to offering an investment in a global entertainment business.

Charlie, Mat and Colin spent the next six weeks re-examining the numbers. Colin took the lead on rewriting the business plan, and in the revised plan, they spread their costs over more than one season. 'This meant we did not need to make an instant profit from the show' explains Colin. 'We could increase our budgets from £1.8m to £2.75m, so we could now deliver our full vision for the concept, which would enable us to raise enough money to cover us for the whole of the *Peter Pan* run.' With a more long-term plan in place, they did not have the tight constraints of making one production profitable, and could consider it in a wider business perspective. The resulting company, Three Sixty Entertainment, was born out of PPKG in November 2008.

Getting off the ground

Confident with this renewed plan, marketing efforts started in earnest. They placed an ad in *The Sunday Times* in November 2008, and pulled in £20,000 of ticket sales in only one week. They forecast cash flow on a weekly basis, creating the tightest of forecasts. This gave the founders a clear idea of how much money they needed to raise each week between then and 26 May 2009 in order to keep the production on schedule. Mat, Charlie and Colin worked out ways to cut costs wherever possible to preserve cash flow, and looked at staggering suppliers' costs. For example, they reasoned that they didn't need to pay for the tent poles at the same time as paying for the tent fabric as they came from different suppliers.

In January 2009, Mat, Charlie and Colin contacted every theatre angel and investor they knew with their revised business plan. Timing was exceptionally tight. Although the production was scheduled for May 2009, they needed to raise enough finance to fund pre-production costs such as rehearsals, which were due to start at the beginning of March. Fortunately, in January, they were able to test out the flying elements of the show against a CGI backdrop, thanks to a grant from the Arts Council.

Against the odds

Raising funds was a task of 'sheer bloody-minded determination'. For three months there was a literal 24 hour operation running. Colin would be up until 4.00am calling internationally and finessing figures with Mat and Charlie taking over at 5.00am getting more pitches out and writing letters before getting on the phone at 8.30am. As each day passed, there was nothing but bad news about the current state and future of the UK economy. Companies were going into administration on an almost daily basis. While those in the industry seemed fairly positive about the new structure of the business, they endured lecture after lecture from the investment community regarding the ongoing economic freeze.

Raising funds was a task of 'sheer bloody-minded determination'.

'When we raised funds we had to present an aspirational view of how the business was going to grow' says Colin. 'We assessed the size of the market and when we were likely to make revenue.' Their painstaking attention to detail and foresight worked in their favour. Before joining the team, Colin had done some in-depth financial analysis into the theatre industry which they used as the basis for their calculations. Despite the economic downturn, it seemed that people were still willing to go out and spend money on family entertainment. Box office records for ticket sales for 2008, for example, were predicted to be better than 2007 and to rise further in 2009.

The search for funding was helped tremendously by some unplanned publicity. In February 2009, the *Observer* newspaper published a guide the Hot 10 for 2009 and Peter Pan was the only show amongst the top 10 things to do worldwide that year This gave them invaluable additional publicity in the run-up to the show, further boosting their ticket sales. It also showed investors the level of interest the show was generating.

Mat and Charlie had also looked at other ways of raising their profile for free and also to position the show in the event space as well as a theatre production. They aproached Visit London, the London tourism agency. Visit London felt that *Peter Pan* was a great fit for London so much so that it made *Peter Pan* its only featured show and event permanently displayed on the tourist's board's website in 2009. This had a huge impact on levels of awareness and ticket bookings and also boosted the business's credibility amongst potential investors.

Experience counts

Three Sixty found its investors one by one: it took 58 of them in total. However despite an enormous ground swell in interest including venture capitalists (people who invest in money in companies) operating in the event space their investment pipieline still showed a major shortfall in deposited funds.

Colin had suggested the business would benefit from a suitable chairman, someone with gravitas would also help with a final push to raise cash. After spending some time looking for the right person, they found Henry Meakin, who Colin had known from a previous business relationship. He was the founding chair of two FTSE 250 listed companies, GWR group which became the largest radio group in the UK and he was also one of the key fundraisers for Classic FM where he became chairman. Henry's arrival brought wider investment networks and was instrumental in the final rush to invest in Three Sixty; he also personally invested.

The combination of publicity, experience and faith in their vision finally paid off. By March, they had raised £1.4m, which was enough to cover their pre-show production costs. Finally after three years working to capitalise the company, two one-million pound offers arrived almost at once. So, by opening night, on 26 May, the rest of their £2.75m target had also been raised. This additional money was used to fund the show during its run and was put towards new business development. By this stage Three Sixty even had a waiting list of investors willing to back the business with up to a further £100,000. They could even afford to turn down the offer of £1m from a venture capitalist, as the terms and conditions from an alternative source proved the better option. Even more impressive is that the founders achieved all this investment, and still retained around 40% of the business, which is a huge percentage for a start-up like this.

Where are they now?

Peter Pan opened on schedule on 26 May 2009 in Kensington Gardens, and received spectacular critical acclaim. The *Daily Express* called it 'breathtaking' and Time Out said it was 'awesome'. The business grossed just under £7.5m during its 22 weeks in the UK and just under 200,000 people attended. As of writing Peter Pan has generated a multi million advance for the USA premiere which opens in San Francisco in April, less than 11 months after it opened in Kensington Gardens.

Three Sixty have been planning tours of both the US and the UK, 18 months ahead of forecasts in the business plan. The founders have also been approached by production companies around the world interested in partnering on a number of international versions of Peter Pan. As if that wasn't enough to keep Mat and Charlie busy, they have begun work on their second production. To top it off, the business was named the Startups Awards Business of the Year in November 2009. Not bad for a high-risk venture in a recession.

INTERNET

Mumsnet

A very maternal market

Founders: Justine Roberts and Carrie Longton

Age of founders at start: 33 and 35

Background: City economist and later sports journalist, and television producer

Year of foundation: 2000

Business type: Online community

Country of foundation: UK

Countries now trading in: UK

How They Started in Tough Times

For many mums, Justine Roberts and Carrie Longton are the saviours of their sanity. When the pair launched Mumsnet in 2000, they saved many a mum from the isolation of motherhood, by creating a site that combined unique parenting information, with a supportive social network and online community. From the outset, Mumsnet was unlike any other parenting site: it featured real-life parent-to-parent advice, instead of blanket advice written by 'experts'. Mumsnet launched just before the dotcom bubble burst, which caused thousands of fledgling sites to go under. Justine and Carrie, however, had bypassed the in vogue, ridiculous venture capital investments, and opted to grow organically. It was a wise move, and the site has gone from strength to strength, registering more than one million users a month and hosting thousands of forum postings every day.

Inspired by a 'holiday from hell'

Justine Roberts had worked in the City for 10 years as an economist and market strategist before switching to a career in sports journalism. During her first pregnancy in 1999, she met television producer Carrie Longton at ante-natal classes, and the two became friends. Throughout their pregnancies and with their newborns, they both agreed that the best source of parenting information was other mothers.

The inspiration for Mumsnet came to Justine during a disastrous 'holiday from hell' in Florida with her one-year-old twins. They were supposedly staying at a 'family

Justine Roberts and Carrie Longton created a unique parenting site, mixing social networking and information sharing

friendly' resort but she found the level of childcare at the resort appalling. Other mothers she talked to at the resort agreed that it would be a great if there was a website enabling parents to swap information on everything and anything – from recommendations on trusted family-friendly resorts to the best pushchairs to use. They wanted a resource where parents could pool all their information together in one place that all parents could have access to.

Home from holiday, the idea came together. Justine did some research to find out what else was out there. She found plenty of sites with parenting advice, but none that gave parents the opportunity to provide their own views, share ideas and give feedback. She wanted to create a site that offered both, and was sure this would be completely unique. 'Having done our research carefully, there wasn't really anything like our idea in the market at the time', says Justine. 'There was a site called Babyworld but it was more of an e-commerce offering rather than a resource for pooling information.'

'Having done our research carefully, there wasn't really anything like our idea in the market at the time.'

The idea for the business was an early version of the social networking sites that abound today, a place where user-generated content could be created and shared. Justine would recruit parents and mum and dads-to-be to generate the content and would finance the site through advertising.

The idea was that the members of the site would fill in a brief questionnaire, and receive a range of benefits and incentives in return, such as regular emails highlighting the developmental milestones their children were approaching. They would also be encouraged to give advice and interact with each other. Once the site was up and running, the aim was also to negotiate special offers with relevant retailers for the site's members.

Spurred on by the novelty of the idea, Justine finalised her plans for the site in November 1999 and persuaded Carrie to get involved soon afterwards. Justine recalls another motivating factor for her: she really didn't want to go back to her job as a sports writer after maternity leave, as it involved too many weekends away from family life.

Booming possibilities

Justine and Carrie spent a month writing a business plan with the aim of having a test site ready by early 2000. At this time, the business climate couldn't have been better. In 1999, dozens upon dozens of internet businesses had emerged, buoyed by large

How They Started in Tough Times

Mumsnet provides parents with advice from fellow parents, and has lively discussion boards

sums of venture capital finance and a predicted growth in broadband technologies. Many entrepreneurs boasted about securing money on the back of plans scrawled on business cards, so convinced were they that their idea was destined to be the next big thing. And it was clear that dotcoms were the next big thing, as even high street retailers made sure they also had an online presence and got in on the act. Buoyed by the economic climate, Justine and Carrie hoped to attract £500,000 worth of funding from private investors.

Late in 1999, work began on the site with the help of Justine's friend from university – a technical whizz who was willing to work on the site in his spare time. He managed all the technical aspects of building the site such as coding it and choosing a web host, while Justine and Carrie built the content pages, tested the site's navigation and came up with the design.

Both Justine and Carrie were working round the clock, juggling work and family life with evenings and weekends spent on the new business. Justine was reluctantly working most weekends as a sports journalist, and both had limited childcare available. Fortunately, they had the support of their husbands, whose jobs paid the mortgage and kept each family afloat. Writing all the original content themselves, Justine and Carrie spent many a day roving around London in search of reviews for the perfect pushchair. To get parents on board, they visited as many playgroups as possible.

Justine and Carrie spent a considerable amount of time discussing potential names for the business. The word 'Parentsnet', for example, did not seem snappy enough to them and while happy with the choice of Mumsnet, they were worried about alienating fathers and dads-to-be from the site. In the end, they decided to go with their gut instinct – the name was simple, clear and catchy and the strapline, 'by parents for parents' would include fathers.

By January 2000 the pair had already spent around £4,000 on content and technical expenses. They raised £25,000 from a friend, in return for a small percentage of the company, and began negotiations with other private investors to raise more.

From boom to bust

After months of work, the test site for Mumsnet was launched in March 2000. By this time, Justine and Carrie had recruited more than 500 parent reviewers through their contacts and research, and were actively seeking more.

Justine and Carrie were in the midst of negotiations to raise the funds they needed, when the economic environment changed considerably. Several high-profile dotcoms went bust, and people began predicting the end of the dotcom boom. One of the most infamous victims was e-retailer Boo.com, an online fashion retailer which collapsed in May 2000 through lack of funds, but not before it had burned through $120m in venture capital. Once the darling of the dotcom world, Boo.com, which had launched in a fanfare of publicity at the beginning of 2000, had fallen victim to technology glitches and poor navigation, driving customers away in their droves. It was a wakeup call for Mumsnet. 'Boo failed in spectacular fashion and put everyone off the idea of dotcoms' recalls Justine. 'This meant our chances of funding disappeared too, almost overnight.'

'Boo failed in spectacular fashion and put everyone off the idea of dotcoms... this meant our chances of funding disappeared too, almost overnight.'

That same month, IT consultancy Forrester published a report predicting that one in four UK internet companies would burn through their cash reserves in the next six months. The reasons for this were simple: many dotcoms had yet to make profits, most had low revenues and almost all of them had high burn rates (the speed at which they used up their venture capital funding). Consequently, venture capitalists pulled out of the dotcom market, leaving many companies without funds and on a downward spiral.

Failing to raise their initial funding target might have seemed a significant setback at the time, but Justine believes that ultimately, starting small helped to both save the business and shape its future. She feels the worsening economic climate made her and Carrie even more determined to succeed – they had already come so far that giving up was now not an option. As Justine explains, had the business secured additional funds from investors, the site would in all likelihood, like many a dotcom before it, have overspent on overheads and advertising, before running out of cash.

With precious little money in the business, and none on the horizon, both Justine and Carrie had to work out ways to cut costs down. This meant taking no salary apart from some money for expenses, and examining alternative ways of paying staff. By March 2000, as well as their technical expert, they had just taken on another friend from ante-natal class to work part-time. To overcome their lack of cash, they paid their technical expert by giving him some shares in the company.

Shrinking revenues

A lack of investment wasn't the founders' only worry. Soon after the site's launch in March 2000, it became clear that the revenue streams Mumsnet had originally planned for were not going to materialise. The site planned to make its money from the CPM (cost per thousand) model, where advertising costs are based on the number of page impressions it gets, that is the number of times an ad is viewed on the site. 'When we started, we had factored on getting £25 per 1,000 page impressions, a realistic figure at the time we had written the business plan' recalls Justine. 'But within a year or so, this had dropped to just £2.50 because of the dotcom crash and the subsequent economic climate. The original figures we worked out were just pie in the sky – the industry never recovered those levels again.'

Despite this setback, Justine and Carrie were actually able to use the tough economic environment to their advantage. With little financial reward available, there were no competitors entering the market. This gave Mumsnet the time to grow organically and build up its presence in the marketplace. With so many examples of other businesses that had needlessly burned through cash, Mumsnet was determined to learn from its mistakes. Thus far, it had managed on the initial investment of £25,000, and it was determined to succeed using only this.

Whatever the market conditions, and however hard it was to encourage advertisers to spend with them, there were some companies and products that Mumsnet would not accept advertising from. It believed the likes of Nestle, McDonalds, and products such as cosmetic surgery did not fit in with the site's philosophy.

Gordon Brown took part in a live web chat at Mumsnet Towers

On a shoestring

Mumsnet spent most of 2001 focusing on building up its user base and content, while keeping its outgoing costs as low as possible. According to Justine, the company spent hardly any money on marketing, bar printing leaflets to advertise the business in the first six months. Instead, Justine used her existing journalistic skills to raise their profile in the media.

This enabled them to place stories in relevant media, encouraging consumers to visit the site. As Justine explains, the site's users became the company's biggest marketers, creating original content and encouraging friends to join. Heated discussions in the forums often ended up being featured in newspapers, creating additional publicity. They learnt the power of word of mouth, and were able to grow their customer base with relative ease.

The site's users became the company's biggest marketers, creating original content and encouraging friends to join.

'An economic downturn can be a good time to start a business as long as you can afford to be austere about it' believes Justine. 'In a recession, it is best to adopt a lean approach. You have to be prepared to do everything yourself – we never had a secretary and I did our VAT returns on a Sunday morning at our kitchen table.'

Change in direction

By 2002, with online advertising sales continuing to slump, Justine and Carrie were forced to look at other ways of monetising the business. This prompted them to think about the value of their content and their member base, which amounted to around 10,000 registered users, and they made the decision to branch out into offline publishing. This had never been part of the original business plan, which had focused exclusively on the website, but was only made possible by the reputation the website had developed.

In March 2002, they launched the first Mumsnet book, *Mums on Babies*, a guide to the first year of parenting gathered from comments posted by users on the site. This was followed two years later in January 2004 by *Mums on Pregnancy*. Two handbag-sized magazine guides have also been produced; *Mumsnet Best* is a compilation of the product reviews on the website. In autumn 2004 Justine and Carrie presented a television series for Discovery Health called *Mum's the Word*, again drawing from the shared knowledge on the site and helping to troubleshoot parental questions. These activities helped to boost the number of registered users, and any profit made was ploughed back into the business.

'In a recession, it is best to adopt a lean approach. You have to be prepared to do everything yourself.'

Legal battle

In 2007, the site came under threat after it became embroiled in a legal dispute with renowned parenting author Gina Ford, after allegedly insulting comments about her appeared on the site's discussion boards, posted by users. Mumsnet clarified that it did not support the comments, removed the statements and issued an apology. Despite this, the site, and its hosting services DCS, were threatened with a libel action. Justine wanted to fight part of the action but it was unclear whether the law would be on her side or not, as no precedent had yet been set regarding how quickly content that is deemed defamatory should be taken down.

The situation raised an important new issue for websites with user content: who is liable for comments made by users of online communities? After consulting with lawyers, it became clear that Mumsnet would be a test case, which would cost time and money to fight, and there was no guaranteeing a positive outcome. The site also had no insurance at the time, which would have covered the cost of fighting or defending the case. As Justine explains, the truth of the matter was that it cost the business less to settle than it would have even if it had won in court, because the full costs of the legal battle would not have been recovered.

For Justine and Carrie, however, the legal experience was, on balance, a positive one. For one thing, it brought the site additional publicity. It also meant Mumsnet clarified its legal position, and adjusted some of the site's policies, making its terms and conditions clearer.

Where are they now?

Mumsnet has continued to explore offline publishing opportunities, signing a six-figure deal with a book publisher in 2008. In March 2009, it partnered with the National Childbirth Trust (NCT) charity to provide access to its forum, Mumsnet Talk, direct from the NCT site and has been involved in various national campaigns.

In February 2008, the site underwent its first major redesign since it was launched, to include new content across areas such as conception, pregnancy, and babies, with the aim of making navigation easier. The business also opened its first offices in Kentish Town, North London (known as Mumsnet Towers). Prior to this, its staff of 20 full-time and part-time employees worked from their own homes.

The business recorded a profit for the first time in 2007, and the bulk of its online revenues come from advertising (as initially planned), and more recently, from market research, with Mumsnet's user base completing surveys and product tests. Justine admits that the website is still only marginally profitable, although still growing rapidly with more than one million visitors each month, clocking up 16 million monthly hits. Mumsnet Talk discussion boards attract around 20,000 posts every day.

Mumsnet's early lesson in cost-minimisation has stood the business in good stead in the recent global financial crisis. Being sensible about costs, says Justine, has meant the business has weathered the latest economic downturn, with only one person in sales being made redundant. They have not used any additional investment, other than the initial £25,000 they raised back in 2000. Mumsnet's organic business story proves how careful nurturing and care can help a business grow, through even the most dire circumstances.

Wikipedia

A fountain of knowledge

Founder: Jimmy Wales

Age of founder at start: 34

Background: Day trader

Year of foundation: 2001

Business type: Online encyclopedia

Country of foundation: USA

Countries now trading in: Worldwide

Wikipedia, the online encyclopedia, has opened up a whole world of information to us – and has changed the format of encyclopedias forever. Instead of turning to a large, out-of-date book for answers, we can now search an online database of more than three million articles, and edit that information ourselves. Founder Jimmy Wales was inspired by his love of encyclopedias, and thirst for knowledge. He envisioned a world where everyone could have access to information in their own language. By using new technology in innovative ways, Jimmy was able to create a unique information source. Not your typical business story, Wikipedia is run as a not-for-profit company, a result of the vision of its founder and loyalty of its users.

A thirst for knowledge

Jimmy Wales was interested in encyclopedias from an early age. He attended a one-room elementary school in Alabama and supplemented much of his early education by browsing through sets of encyclopedias made famous by companies such as Britannica. He had early entrepreneurial aspirations, harbouring a secret ambition to earn his first million by the time he was 40. After graduating with a master's degree in finance from the University of Alabama in 1994, his ambition led him to accept a job as a day trader at Chicago Options Associates, where he rose to the position of research director. After six years at the firm, he had earned a small fortune speculating on foreign currencies and internet valuations.

As he rose up the trader ranks, Jimmy became increasingly interested in the world wide web, and this passion led him to set up his first website in 1996, while he continued with his day job. He constructed a basic search portal called Bomis.com, focusing on pop culture and funded the venture with money he'd made from trading, intending to generate money from advertising when the site was up and running. But Jimmy saw this as just the beginning. What he really wanted to do was put his passion for encyclopedias into some kind of online format.

Print encyclopedias were well established, and during the 1990s, CD-ROM technology drastically cut the cost of manufacturing and distributing encyclopedias. Publishers like Britannica and Microsoft sold their encyclopedias to millions of people. CD-ROM encyclopedias had brought sound and vision to what was traditionally print format, as well as making searches and cross-referencing easier and faster. Jimmy knew that he'd have to produce something innovative and different to stand out from the popular and well-entrenched market leaders, and putting an encyclopedia onto the web seemed the obvious route.

Jimmy's idea took shape when he observed the growth of the 'open software' movement in the mid to late- 1990s. Users were able to download software from the internet free of charge, and improve it themselves. Jimmy explains, 'the open source software movement was growing steadily and becoming more important – although at first people had tended to dismiss it. Throughout the industry, we were seeing programmers coming together in a volunteer capacity to create open software.' Collaborating was shown to be not only possible, but popular, and it could lead to some excellent results. There were many different types of software available, and Jimmy experimented with two popular open source website development languages: Apache and Perl.

Freedom of information

Jimmy had the idea to apply the open source approach to create a free online encyclopedia. He realised that by using this software he could create a site where every user – not just programmers – could write and edit web information, thereby making

Founder Jimmy Wales' main motivation was to provide free information to users

the encyclopedia open to everyone. At the time, if people wanted to work together on a document with lots of other people, the only real option was to email it round, which was both impractical and time-consuming. He saw a unique opportunity to use software to create a viable way for people to collaborate online. If this worked in reality, it would give him the means and method to get his vision for an online encyclopedia off the ground.

'The idea seemed completely obvious to me and I went into a mad panic as I feared someone else would do it' recalls Jimmy. 'Encyclopedias are low hanging fruit when it comes to collaboration, it's pretty easy to do. For example, if you have an encyclopedia article about the Golden Gate Bridge, everyone knows pretty much what the Golden Gate Bridge is and has a good idea of what an encyclopedia entry should tell you. In a collaborative environment, it's really important to have a clear vision about what you are trying to accomplish.'

'The idea seemed completely obvious to me and I went into a mad panic as I feared someone else would do it.'

Unlike print encyclopedias and CD-ROMs, his online version would never go out of date; users would not need to buy upgrades or new editions to ensure they had the most current information. While CD-ROMs were seen as the height of new technology in the early 1990s, technological developments meant they were soon viewed as a slow and costly information source, when compared to the free world wide web. And while traditional print encyclopedias were still popular, a whole set of books could be very expensive – anywhere from £500 to £2,500!

An early disaster

Jimmy did not put together a business plan for his idea. He believed that the best businesses are not cooked up by those with MBAs and extensive business plans – rather, they are those businesses that fulfil the needs of potential customers in an innovative way. By 1999, he felt the time was right to set up his vision, which he called Nupedia. At the time, the market for internet businesses was booming and had reached peaks not seen before. The NASDAQ (the US stock exchange favoured by hi-tech growth companies) had risen by more than 85% in 1999.

> Jimmy believed that the best businesses are not cooked up by those with MBAs and extensive business plans – rather, they are those businesses that fulfil the needs of potential customers in an innovative way.

Jimmy's encyclopedia, based on open source software, would be free to users, while the site would make money through advertising. He kick-started the business with several thousand dollars from his other business, Bomis. This supplied the internet access, a server and paid for staff salaries. Jimmy hired philosopher Larry Sangster as editor-in-chief (whom he knew through an online discussion forum and had met twice in person) and two programmers to build the site, with the idea that they would all work from home. The plan was to recruit other people on a voluntary basis, to update information and help develop the site.

But Nupedia wasn't the success Jimmy had hoped for. The problems lay in the set up of the business – looking back, Jimmy believes that the site was far too academic in nature and too rigidly structured, and was also difficult to manage. The open source software that Nupedia was using proved to be too clunky. After a year of operating, there were only 24 articles on the site. Having spent all that time to have so few submissions was disheartening to say the least.

Problems also lay in how the contributors were sourced. Volunteers were recruited through online discussion forums and most of them had academic backgrounds. Anyone who wanted to contribute to the site had to submit credentials outlining why they would be suitable, most often by fax. These were then checked out online, and if they matched up, they were deemed suitable to contribute. It therefore took an incredibly long time to recruit volunteers, and even longer for them to edit and post articles. The process was lengthy and Jimmy realised that the site was limiting its user base; missing all those people who wanted to contribute in whatever way possible, regardless of their background or credentials, academic or otherwise.

Towards the end of 2000, 18 months after the launch of Nupedia, it became obvious that the site could not continue in its present state and Jimmy needed to find a way of improving how it was run. Jimmy and his volunteer contributors sent emails back and forth to each other, debating ways that could make the site work better and assessing other types of software and tools. There were moments when he thought about shutting the site down, but ultimately, Jimmy says he was too passionate about the concept of creating a free encyclopedia to close the site. 'That's when the idea really seized hold of me and I wanted to make it my life's work' he says. 'There was a bit of doubt about whether I could make it work but there was never any serious question of quitting.'

Jimmy was too passionate about the concept of creating a free encyclopedia to close Nupedia. 'That's when the idea really seized hold of me and I wanted to make it my life's work.'

By this point, the market for internet businesses had turned sour. By 2001 the economy was beginning to lose speed. Many dotcoms subsequently ran out of money and it was proving harder and harder for the remaining ones to prove their business models would work.

Turning point

Despite Jimmy's devotion, it was clear that getting Nupedia to succeed would take substantially more change than merely tweaking the site. He realised that it would require a complete software overhaul. It was one of his volunteers who first alerted him to the potential of using a new type of open source software instead – a Wiki (Hawaiian for quick). Wiki had been developed in 1995 by Howard Cunningham, an American computer programmer. The volunteer had been using a Wiki for some time and thought it would be a good way to encourage people to collaborate better on the web. It allowed people to link to different web pages, and users could easily create pages with new content. Its speed and abilities were significant improvements over the software Nupedia was using at the time.

So while Jimmy did not invent the Wiki, he came up with a novel and inventive way of using it: to power his online encyclopedia. It was easy to use and implement and was relatively low-maintenance. The new online encyclopedia using Wiki-Wikipedia, was born in January 2001, and quickly took over from the Nupedia venture, as work gradually petered out in favour of focusing on this new technology and the launch of Wikipedia. As a result of the dotcom crash, Jimmy (and the other Bomis investors) took the decision not to continue funding the role of editor-in-chief and Larry officially left Nupedia, and quit Wikipedia too a month later. Following Larry's departure, activity on Nupedia ground to a halt, and the site officially closed in September 2003.

Initial funds for Wikipedia were again provided by Bomis. This would pay for editorial staff, programmers and the required servers, and advertising would be sought when more funds were needed. Jimmy also intended to establish the business with the help of Nupedia's volunteer team. He never considered asking users to pay to access the information: above all, he wanted to provide free content, where information sharing was the main focus of the business.

Early challenges

The same volunteers who worked on the editorial and technical side of Nupedia were invited to help develop Wikipedia. Excited by the groundbreaking use of new technology, many of them continued working with Jimmy, and the site was able to flourish quickly. When the first Wikipedia website was first launched in January 2001, it used a type of programming software called Perl, which was very easy to implement – Jimmy recalls that he got it up and running in 10 minutes. It was, however, quite basic and stored all articles as text files.

As a result, the search facility looked for files in a pretty basic way and the site was slow to load pages. This made Jimmy realise Wikipedia would need a proper database, and one of the voluntary programmers created a database of articles.

There was no money to spend on marketing, but because of the novelty of the idea, it soon received attention from the media, and its loyal community of volunteers ensured they mentioned it online. Word of mouth spreads fast through academic and technological circles, and Wikipedia became a talked-about web phenomenon long before social media came to the fore. By the end of the first month, there were around 600 articles on the site; two months later, this had grown to 1,300 and by the end of May 2001, there were close to 4,000 articles on the site.

Jimmy also noted the effect that Google had on the site's profile. Each time the search engine browsed Wikipedia for information, more pages would be picked up on

Google; the greater the number of pages indexed, the more people became members of the site. This had a knock on effect as the more contributors got involved, the more pages there were to index, spurring the growth of the site. In January 2002, a year after launch, there were 20,000 articles on the encyclopedia.

Not for profit

While Wikipedia had been launched successfully, the site was greatly affected by the dotcom fallout of 2002. Bomis, the company that had funded the initial start-up of Nupedia and Wikipedia, was not faring well: it had more than halved its staff numbers from around 12 in 2000 to five people in 2002.

Bomis had intended to start selling ads on Wikipedia in 2002 to pay for staffing and operational costs. Even in the midst of the deepening dotcom fall out, the number of page views on the site appeared to support the argument for ads. But Jimmy knew this would be a controversial move – supporters of open source software passionately disliked the use of online advertising and were likely to be up in arms at such a suggestion. The decision was made for Jimmy, however, when Bomis failed to attract any advertising.

Jimmy had to consider other alternatives, including the potential of setting the business up as a not-for-profit organisation. Jimmy's biggest motivation with his online encyclopedia venture had always been to share information freely, and not to make money. He was also keen to keep his loyal network of contributors onside, some of whom had been working with him voluntarily since the beginning of Nupedia. So in 2002, Jimmy decided to make Wikipedia a not-for-profit organisation, and changed its web address from Wikipedia.com to .org, to signify that it would not commercialise the site.

Raising funds

By the end of 2002, Wikipedia had grown so much that the site was being run off three servers. But at Christmas, two out of the three servers crashed, compromising the service and making Jimmy aware that a radical overhaul of the technology was due.

At the same time, there were other technology bottlenecks to manage. As the site became more populated with articles, the developers realised that the existing database server had about six weeks left of disk space and they were unsure how to resolve the problem as it was too expensive to buy new hardware. The developers asked Wikipedia's vast contributor community for advice, and through this, found a way of compressing the existing files to free up disk space.

These problems made Jimmy aware that they needed some new equipment to make the site's technology more robust. In the summer of 2003, he set up the Wikimedia Foundation, a non-profit-making charitable organisation and donated all the business's assets (such as its domain names and computers) to the Foundation.

His first round of fundraising raised $20,000, which enabled them to buy and install the much-needed new servers. These were eventually moved to a data centre in Florida, not far from where Jimmy was based at the time.

This money was raised through charitable donations directly from the site's users, as well as from major grants through grant-making foundations. Over the following years, income was also derived from business relationships, and corporate donations from businesses that support Wikipedia's purpose.

Information creation

As well as technological problems, Wikipedia also encountered challenges with the content of the site. Many contributors started to confuse dictionary definitions with encyclopedia entries, and Wikipedia had to make its users aware of the differences. A dictionary definition, for example, would simply explain what a word meant, while an encyclopedic entry gives background information and a history of the subject.

The site also realised it needed to ensure that its users knew that it was not a place where original research could be published: all information on the site must be verifiable, and not still under development. To ensure the information was as accurate as possible, Wikipedia established some strict rules and guidelines. For example, unless the members of Wikipedia could verify the information on the site, and cite sources to back it up, the site would not publish it. A community of contributors had built up during the Nupedia project, and very quickly grew to include users from all over the world who were attracted to the open participation model – not just academics.

The site also realised there would be constraints around certain articles, in particular biographies. 'If somebody is not very famous or if they are only very famous for doing something bad, it is really hard to maintain the article; it is really hard to write a balanced one,' says Jimmy. 'Those are the kinds of things where we realised that there were constraints in the social model on how detailed we could be and still maintain quality and accuracy.' The guidelines have worked well, and new information is checked for providence and any bias removed. There is also an interactive element to the editing process, where contributors can argue a point, and agree on the right wording of a fact.

An invaluable source of information

The site continued to flourish, so much so that by the end of 2004, there were more than one million articles worldwide. In 2005, the business raised $100,000 to help upgrade the servers to cope with rising demand. Through the success of the site, Jimmy had not only rivalled other encyclopedic media, but had managed to virtually wipe out the existence of CD-ROM versions. Compared to Wikipedia's constantly

Jimmy Wales, Achim Raschka and Daniel Arnold at technology coference 21C3 in 2004

updated entries, the CD-ROM just could not compete. Microsoft's Encarta eventually moved online, but in March 2009, they announced the closure of both the online and disk versions.

In early 2008, Jimmy took on search engine giant Google, with the launch of WikiaSearch, a community-based search engine that aimed to rely on user ratings and input to determine the results, rather than using algorithms like Google and other search engines. But in April 2009, Jimmy took the decision to close down WikiaSearch, even though it has established itself as the fifth-fastest growing member community in February 2008, with around just under four million users.

While Jimmy says he believes in the opportunity for free software to make serious inroads into the search space, he admits that the launch of WikiaSearch did not go as he had hoped. 'In a different economy, we would continue to fund WikiaSearch indefinitely. It's something I care about deeply' he says. 'I will return to again and again in my career to search, either as an investor, a contributor, a donor... or a cheerleader' he said.

'*I will return again and again in my career to search, either as an investor, a contributor, a donor... or a cheerleader.*'

Where are they now?

In 2008, Wikipedia also completed its fifth round of fundraising, and raised in the region of $6m compared to the $2m it raised in the previous year.

Wikipedia is now one of the world's largest reference websites, hosting more than three million articles across 18 million pages and is written in more than 250 languages. It has over 10 million registered users worldwide, from teenagers to software engineers, and attracts nearly 320 million unique visitors per month. The business now has just under 10 members of staff on its payroll, covering roles such as administration, fundraising and publicity. Wikipedia has revolutionised how to look up information, and has become a verb in its own right while staying true to its open source, not-for-profit roots.

Linkedin

Connections are key

Founder: Reid Hoffman

Age of founder at start: 35

Background: Technology and product development

Year of foundation: 2003

Business type: Professional networking site

Country of foundation: USA

Countries now trading in: Worldwide

There's an old saying in business: it's not **what** you know but **who** you know. LinkedIn set out to make this a reality in the online world, creating a site aimed at helping professionals connect with each other. Set up in 2003 in the wake of the dotcom crash, the business survived a harsh economic climate and became profitable four years after launch. Today, the company has more than 51 million members in over 200 countries and says that someone joins LinkedIn every second.

Technology guru

Reid Hoffman grew up in Berkeley, California and, ironically, during his childhood, his father had never let him have a computer, thinking it was irrelevant. It wasn't until Reid was at college, where he studied Artificial Intelligence and Cognitive Science, that he got one. In the early 1990s, he gained a scholarship to Oxford University to study Philosophy, but after a year, he realised that the world of academia was not for him. Instead, he had a few ideas for technology-based companies, one of which was a personal information manager for a hand-held device. Convinced his idea had potential, he networked his way to meeting two venture capitalists, asking friends of friends to introduce him. While they didn't turn him down flat, the venture capitalists advised him to get some experience in producing and selling products, and then come back.

Following their advice, Reid decided to try and get a job at a high-profile technology company. He landed his first job at Apple in 1994, again using his networking skills – he heard about an opening in software development through the room-mate of a good friend of his from Stanford and applied to the company directly. Nearly two years later, he left Apple for a job at Fujitsu, this time in product management and business development.

During this time, Reid always planned to work for himself one day. His aim was to build up experience, skills and confidence, and prove to the venture capitalists he was taking them at their word. At both companies, he set himself a strict timeline and mapped out the areas he needed to master before he could strike out on his own, including experience in design and product management, building a team and both producing and selling products successfully.

> Reid always planned to work for himself one day. His aim was to build up experience, skills and confidence, and prove to the venture capitalists he was taking them at their word.

Reid Hoffman had the idea for a social networking website long before most people had grasped the internet basics

In July 1997, Reid quit his job at Fujitsu to set up Socialnet, one of the earliest versions of a social networking site. He'd thought up the concept of social networking long before most people had started using the internet at all. The aim of Socialnet was to build on the kinds of relationships that people have, from potential dates to room-mates or even meeting potential tennis partners. The idea was to put users 'near' the people they'd be interested in, but online. The right person for you could be in the next building, but you'd never know it – everyone would be connected online so physical locations did not matter.

Reid realised that the only way he would get the business off the ground was to just bite the bullet and go for it. He looked at financing opportunities and went back to the original venture capitalists he had contacted years before. This time, they were impressed by his background and his ambitions for Socialnet and he raised $5m at the end of 1997.

PayPal and beyond

Just over two years later, however, Reid resigned from Socialnet as he wasn't convinced that the direction in which the company was going was the right one.

How They Started in Tough Times

A LinkedIn profile helps you improve your business connections

The business's strategy had been to partner with newspapers and magazines to encourage subscriptions to the site but it soon became clear that this was not viable and would not give them the user numbers they needed. Reid had a difference of opinion with the board and left soon after. He had learnt some valuable lessons – you can have a brilliant product but unless you know how to reach tens of millions of people, then the product will count for nothing.

'There are three words people use for retail: location, location, location. For the internet, it's distribution, distribution, distribution' Reid said. 'If you don't get this, the value of your site is zero. I hadn't realised this when working at Apple and Fujitsu as they worked with big channels of established customers.'

'There are three words people use for retail: location, location, location. For the internet, it's distribution, distribution, distribution.'

He told a friend, Peter Thiel, who had studied with him at Stanford, of his intentions to start another company. Peter was one of the founders of internet payment system PayPal, and at the time was the chief executive. Reid had been one of its board members since its launch in 1998, and Peter persuaded him to join the company as executive vice-president in charge of business development instead of starting another business.

At PayPal, Reid was responsible for external relations including corporate development, banking and international development. All the while, he continued to be fascinated by how the internet (then at the early stages of its commercialisation) accelerated the rate at which people did business. He was particularly interested in how individuals could use the internet to promote their business profile and skills and what influence this had on their careers.

It wasn't until a few years later that Reid capitalised on his online networking ideas – he believed that it wasn't possible to perfect his business plan while he was still in another job. In 2002, PayPal was acquired by internet auction site eBay for $1.5bn and Reid received $10m for his share in the business. He planned to take a year's sabbatical but just three months later, was back on the business trail, too tempted by his desire to start another online business. Even after the dotcom bubble burst, Reid was adamant that there was still potential for online success.

Thriving in a harsh climate

Reid saw nothing but advantages in the harsh economic climate of the early Noughties. He wanted to create a business that would only be possible via the internet and that would change people's lives. He reasoned that with the current climate, there would be less competition and therefore more of a chance that his venture would be able to achieve its goals. Reid had several ideas, including a worldwide online computer game, but rejected them in favour of revisiting his passion for how people could be brought together online. He wanted to start a business where professional people could establish their profiles online so that other people could find them; effectively creating a network to enhance and further their careers.

Even after the dotcom bubble burst, Reid was adamant that there was still potential for online success.

Since the dotcom bubble burst, it was harder than ever before to raise money for an internet venture. Not wishing to waste any time before launching his idea – after all, this idea had effectively been brewing for several years – he decided to use the money from the sale of PayPal to start the business.

For Reid, having enough capital wasn't the big issue at the start – his main concern was ensuring he assembled the right team. He gathered a team of people he had previously worked with and known from his college days, and whose experience and opinion he valued. The group included Allen Blue, Jean-Luc Vaillant, Eric Ly, and Konstantin Guericke. Konstantin had been a fellow graduate at Stanford; Jean-Luc had worked for Matchnet, an online dating business which had acquired Socialnet; while Allen and Eric had worked at PayPal. Over several months, they met in Reid's living room and hatched the plan that was to become LinkedIn.

Preparing for launch

As the USA officially entered a recession, the founders worked on the business plan for LinkedIn for several months before launch – having witnessed the collapse of the dotcom bubble, they needed to prove that the business could grow at a low cost, could make money and be sustainable.

In the face of a gloomy economy, Reid continued to believe that starting in a time of recession gave LinkedIn a competitive advantage – while consumer internet ventures were no longer the next best thing, LinkedIn now had the opportunity to stand out with a fantastic idea. Investors were now only interested in start-ups that could offer a solid, long-term business case, something that LinkedIn was determined to prove. It wanted to show that it had a sustainable business model based on a number of revenue streams, such as subscriptions, and at its core, a valuable proposition for prospective members.

Reid continued to believe that starting in a time of recession gave LinkedIn a competitive advantage – while consumer internet ventures were no longer the next best thing, LinkedIn now had the opportunity to stand out with a fantastic idea.

The business continued to be funded by the proceeds of Reid's PayPal shares, as the founders held off seeking additional funding until they were sure they could prove the value of LinkedIn's business model. By early May 2003, the founders felt confident enough to launch the site. But it was to take several months of hard work for the idea to catch on.

Word of mouth

Reid set himself the challenge of getting a million people to register for the site. The point of LinkedIn, where people could search for other members and share information meant the site had to have enough people signed up in order for it to be valuable. Right from the start, Reid planned to grow LinkedIn organically by word of mouth – it seemed the most cost-effective and efficient way to get members. The speed of uptake would also help to demonstrate the site's value to potential investors.

The founders planned to look for a first round of funding to support the business's growth plans once they had recruited a sizeable amount of members. The LinkedIn founders began by inviting 350 of their most important, well-connected and trusted contacts to join, encouraging them to get their friends and contacts to join, too.

This worked well. At the end of its first month in operation, LinkedIn had a total of 4,500 members in the network and the business set up offices in Mountain View, Silicon Valley (using more of Reid's money), not far from Google's company headquarters. Reid had also recruited new staff members to work on the technical side, bringing the total number of employees to 13.

The site wanted to emphasise the strength of the connections between members, so it dissuaded members from adding people to their network randomly. Instead, LinkedIn encouraged members to connect with colleagues, clients and people they had worked with in the past. Connections were therefore based on the trust and experience of those individuals. Reid believed that this increased the value of people's network by focusing on existing connections in the real world, as opposed to the random connections that are common on some social networks.

On the up

Member numbers were increasing, and timing now seemed to be on LinkedIn's side. When it launched, there were no other similar businesses in operation, enabling LinkedIn to develop its concept of online professional networking without worrying about competitors. It didn't take long, however, for other professional networks to spring up, including Tribe and Friendster. With a growing interest in the sector, it was not surprising that investor appetite was waking up to the potential of social networking sites, particularly since the US economy was showing signs of a recovery. In December 2003, the stock markets were up for the first time since the internet bubble had burst back in early 2000.

LinkedIn was now ready to seek venture capital funds. Reid recalls how he was besieged by at least a dozen unsolicited visits from venture capitalists. At the end of October 2003, he signed a deal for $4.7m from Sequoia Capital, a leading venture capital firm whose support he'd targeted in the first place. By this time, the site was doubling in size every six weeks and had gained users in more than 80 countries and 120 industries. Several months later Reid says he was still hearing from venture capitalists he'd never met, begging to be allowed to buy a piece of his company even though they'd heard about it second or third hand.

While it was common for online businesses to use advertising as their main revenue stream, LinkedIn was determined to be different, having learnt lessons from the dotcom fallout. In 2005, two years after launch, LinkedIn introduced two income streams: paid job listings and a subscription-based service, which offered users an enhanced search service, so they could connect to people they didn't already know.

While advertising was not part of the original business plan, Reid decided this would become the site's third revenue stream, as it had built up a demographic base that appealed strongly to advertisers. The self-selecting nature of LinkedIn's membership (it was targeting successful and ambitious professionals) would provide an opportunity for certain brands to reach their target audience in an efficient way. Just a year later LinkedIn turned a profit, the majority of the income coming from its premium services, such as job listings.

Where are they now?

In the last few years, a plethora of social networking sites have launched, including Facebook, MySpace and Bebo. LinkedIn, however, sets itself apart from these. The company says it is not in direct competition with these sites as they are targeted towards general social networking and games rather than conversations between professional people.

LinkedIn may be one of the few businesses that has benefited and thrived in the recent recession. Rising levels of unemployment worldwide and a sagging global economy arising from the credit crunch, have resulted in more and more people on the hunt for jobs, and for LinkedIn, this can only be good news. In March 2008, the site saw its traffic double to just under 7 million users, up from 3.3 million a year earlier. The site has capitalised on the fact that, in times of economic downturn, professionals become more aware of the importance of their network of trusted contacts.

The site continued to develop features to increase the value of its services for its users. In September 2008, LinkedIn struck a partnership with financial news channel CNBC, enabling users to share and discuss news with their professional contacts. Community-generated content such as surveys and polls from LinkedIn are broadcast on CNBC, and in return the broadcaster provides the site with its programming, articles and blogs. The networking site has since sealed similar partnerships with other media owners, including *The New York Times*. Also in 2008, original investor Sequoia Capital, together with Greylock Partners and other venture capital firms, acquired a 5% stake in the company for $53m, giving the company a valuation of nearly $1bn, a remarkable achievement for a business that was just five years old.

The number of members continues to grow aggressively, representing more than 200 countries across 170 industries, with more than 50 million members worldwide and a new member joining every second. The site is also available in a number of additional languages including English, German, Spanish and French, with more to follow in 2010. But for founder Reid Hofmann, who is often dubbed 'the most connected man in Silicon Valley,' this is just the tip of the iceberg.

TECHNOLOGY

IBM

Computing Success

Founder: Thomas Watson, Charles Flint, Herman Hollerith

Year of foundation: 1911

Business type: IT

Country of foundation: USA

Countries now trading in: Worldwide

Revenue and net income: $103.6bn and $12.3bn

U nlike most business stories, the founding of IBM is not simply a tale of one man with an idea. Rather, it is a story of several men, three in particular, who history brought together and who laid the building blocks that created a vast, technological business. It is the story of Herman Hollerith, a brilliant inventor and flawed genius, who would envisage and develop the tabulating machines which IBM would later sell across the world. And it is the story of Charles Flint, a maverick investor and an adventurous businessman, who would buy several companies, including Hollerith's, which would be forged together and made into International Business Machines. Thirdly, and most crucially, it is the story of Thomas Watson Sr, a brilliant leader and salesman, who would bring order to Flint's messy acquisitions and create a strong and vibrant culture which resonates in IBM to this day.

For many, Thomas Watson was IBM. He was its leading figure from 1914–1956, setting its course, and he was the man who gave the company its name. But Watson was no engineer or inventor – he barely understood how his company's machines worked, beyond the information he needed to tell his customers. His path to the helm of IBM is an intriguing one, but to truly appreciate this journey you have to go back to the beginning and look at how the company came into being; formed from the sparks of genius decades before.

463-465 PENNA. AVENUE.
WASHINGTON, D. C.

Founder of the Tabulating Machine Company, Herman Hollerith

HERMAN HOLLERITH

In 1879, 19-year-old university graduate Herman Hollerith took a job at the US Census Bureau, compiling statistics. The census was taken every 10 years and it was a tiresome and cumbersome affair for all involved. The data, which was recorded by hand, took years to process and Hollerith became determined to find a more efficient method. He conceived of a machine which processed data automatically, and spent the next few years of his life inventing one.

Inspired by the way in which ticket conductors punched holes in train tickets to record information such as destination and age, Hollerith predicted that the same process could be used to collect the census data. He saw that the position of a hole on a line of paper could represent answers to census questions, such as male or female, or whether a person lived in the US or was from abroad. He imagined a machine that automatically fed the paper through its processors, and a board with buttons that would electrically punch the holes in the paper. As the paper was fed through the machine, it would pass over a drum, completing an electrical circuit for each hole. The data would then come rolling out automatically, without the need for human intervention. The 'tabulating machine' would, in time, revolutionise data processing and, on September 23, 1884, Hollerith submitted his first patent application.

Herman developed his invention to include a motorised card feeder

But an invention alone does not a business make, no matter how great it is. Hollerith still needed to prove his machine worked in an office environment, he needed to manufacture it and to sell it to the world, and this required investment. Hollerith worked out that he would need around $2,500 ($60,000 in today's money) to develop his invention, and a family friend agreed to put up the cash. He then visited the Census offices and asked if they would consider using his machine to work on some past Census data, in effect, asking the government to fund the invention by providing the manpower, in the form of government clerks, to test it, to which they agreed.

Things were going well, but the machine itself was not perfect, not by any means. For one thing, the paper Hollerith was using would tear easily, and it was difficult to read the information recorded. To solve this, Hollerith switched to using punch cards the size of one-dollar bills. The advantages over paper were clear: the size of the cards meant they were easier to sort and collate, and they would not tear so easily. The process of trial and error to iron out the problems took years of dedicated work and, during this time, investors were not easy to find or keep. However, government departments were intrigued by the potential of Hollerith's machine, and they continued to test his machines. Meanwhile, Hollerith kept himself going financially by consulting on patents and working on other inventions.

In 1888, the Office of the War Department decided to rent one of Hollerith's tabulating machines for $1,000 for the year. If successful, Hollerith was told there was the chance the Navy would also be interested, as the Department of Records and Pensions wanted to compile data on the health of its soldiers. The machine performed well, Hollerith signed a contract with the Navy that same year, and he began to rent out his machines to other clients. Then, in 1889, Hollerith's patent application was finally approved and he took his machine global, exhibiting it at the Paris Universal Exhibition of that year.

By this time, the 1890 Census was fast approaching and, as the US population had grown considerably in the 1880s, it was estimated that it would take it would take 13 years to complete. The Census Bureau trialled Hollerith's creation against two other competitors – Hollerith's won. The Bureau placed an order for six machines at a yearly rate of $1,000 each. A year later, in 1890, an order for 50 more machines was placed by the Bureau.

The data collection for the 1890 Census was completed in a staggeringly short six weeks and the whole Census itself was finished in just two and a half years. Hollerith's invention had saved the taxpayers five million dollars, and earned him a PhD from Columbia University.

By 1891, demand for the machines had soared and Hollerith won contracts from other countries such as Austria, Canada, France and Russia, following his appearance at the Paris show. Every country was keen to use his invention to gather and process Census data, and the machines now had a great track record. There was also demand from private companies as Hollerith expanded the commercial uses of the machine to encompass freight and agricultural data.

At the end of 1896, Hollerith founded the Tabulating Machine Company to continue making and licensing out his machines. However, he was a far better inventor than he was a businessman, and he struggled to manage a business. Hollerith also possessed a difficult temperament, often antagonising both his staff and his customers. By 1911, he was finding it increasingly difficult to manage a growing business, was suffering from poor health, and had competitors biting at his heels. Eventually, Hollerith decided to sell the business to an investor called Charles Flint, who was putting together a collection of businesses that would become IBM.

THOMAS WATSON

The man who many regard as IBM, Thomas Watson, couldn't have been a more different character to Hollerith. While Herman was awkward in social situations, Thomas was to prove himself a savvy man-manager and motivator. Also, unlike the well-read and educated Hollerith, Watson was a man of humble beginnings, who never went to university and who started full-time work as soon as he could. After a few jobs, his working career began in earnest in 1896, where he joined the National Cash Register Company (NCR) as a sales apprentice. Watson was taken under the wing of a John Range, who taught him all about sales, and his career began to flourish.

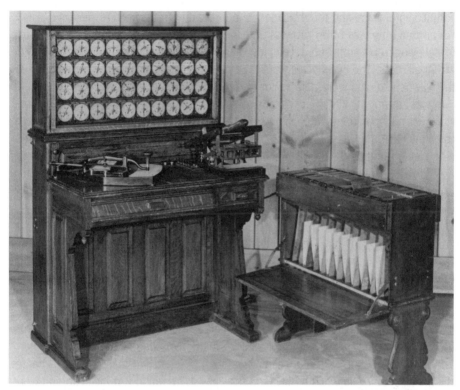

Herman's first version of the tabulator, in 1890

FAIR MEANS OR FOUL

By 1903, Watson had made a real impression with senior management and they called on him to work on a special project. With NCR backing, Watson set up the American Second Cash Register Company, which was little more than an NCR front, designed to crush the competition by fair means or foul. NCR's business was selling new cash registers, and the company was therefore threatened by companies which bought and sold second-hand ones. Watson's goal was to drive out the competition by paying over the odds for used registers and even acquiring the rival businesses on the understanding that they would not re-enter the market. The operation was highly successful, although later NCR would gain the unwanted attention of the Federal Government on charges relating to monopolistic activities. Indeed, thanks to Watson's work, NCR had gained 90% of the market by 1910.

Nevertheless, Watson's work gained him a promotion at NCR to sales manager, where he worked directly beneath the company's founder, John H. Patterson. From him, Watson learned much about running a business and leadership, and NCR's founder was to have a profound influence on Watson's own leadership of IBM. Patterson was an uncompromising and tough leader, who instilled both fear and respect in his staff. Yet although he was often ruthless and controlling, he also extolled the importance of believing in his staff and developing teams. Patterson also taught Watson how to win at all costs. The two became close. So close, in fact, that Watson became one of the few people who were able to contradict Patterson and get away with it.

It was through NCR that Watson heard about Herman Hollerith's tabulating machines. He was remarkably impressed with how they could be used to transform company data, and he hired some machines for his offices. At this stage, it is clear that Watson understood the importance of being able to measure performance, as well as the benefits of having a scientific approach to business.

FEDERAL CHARGES

In 1912, NCR's management was indicted by the Federal Government for its corrupt and monopolistic practices, and John H. Patterson and Thomas Watson were among those indicted. The charges were made criminal and Watson faced up to a year in jail. The indictment began a dark period in Watson's life, and would go on to haunt him throughout his career. At the first trial, the company was found guilty, although the defendants appealed. Eventually, a deal was made between NCR and the defendants, though Watson never admitted he had done anything wrong.

By the end of 1913, Watson was finished with NCR. However, with Federal charges still hanging over him while he awaited the appeal, he found it difficult to find work. He would have liked to set up his own business, but no-one was likely to back someone who could soon end up in jail. However, after many trips between Dayton and New York looking for a job, Watson would eventually enter the offices of Charles Flint.

CHARLES FLINT

Charles Flint is a colourful character in the history of IBM. He had been an adventurer, an explorer, an investor, an arms trader and a friend to high society, from US Presidents to dictators. Prior to meeting Watson, Flint had acquired several businesses: The Tabulating Machine Company; International Time Recording; Bundy Manufacturing; and Computing Scale of America. The new company became known as the Computing Tabulating Recording Company (CTR). However, the acquisitions were not working out, and Flint needed a strong manager to turn his sinking ship around. It was a brave decision to make, bearing in mind the charges still standing against Watson, but Flint saw in him a true leader in the making. The two struck a deal where Watson was to be manager until charges against him were dropped, when he would become president.

Thomas began work at CTR but found the experience a miserable one. Unlike the well-oiled machine of NCR, his new company was structurally flawed. Its founder's messy acquisitions did not sit well together and the company had no discernable culture.

It had 1200 employees but these were based at several locations, making managing the business virtually impossible. Financially, the business was haemorrhaging money; it was valued at $3m but had over $6m of debt – technically it was bankrupt. Instinctively, Watson wanted to impose on it the rational management techniques that he had learned at NCR, but he had two big obstacles in his way: Herman Hollerith, who had remained at the company, and CTR's chairman George Fairchild.

Hollerith had sold his business but had retained a role at the company which gave him the right to approve or veto any new technological advance or product. The effect was to stifle the company's innovation and prevent gifted engineers from bringing forward the next phase of products. This was needed, as Hollerith's patents were running out and competitors were cutting into the company's markets. However, Watson needed Hollerith as his name was synonymous with the tabulating machines and the business traded off it. George Fairchild also irritated Watson with his interference, demanding to be consulted and informed while also being unavailable. However, as a member of the House of Representatives, he offered some respectability to the company, which offset Watson's questionable past at NCR. Watson had little choice but to play the long-game and placate them both.

THE MAN PROPOSITION

Nevertheless, Watson got to work on his sales team and soon proved himself a powerful motivator. He wanted to transform the approach his managers had toward their staff, encouraging a more nurturing approach. "Every supervisor must look upon himself as an assistant to the men below him, instead of looking at himself as the boss," he told his managers.

He also introduced what became known as *The Man Proposition*. On a blackboard, he wrote out the words 'manufacturing', 'general manager', 'sales manager', 'sales man', 'factory manager', 'factory man', and so on, covering all the positions within the business. He then crossed out all the words apart from 'man', suggesting that all were equal in the company. "We are just men," he said. "Men standing together, shoulder to shoulder, all working for one common good."

The Man Proposition would be repeated regularly at IBM for the next forty years or more – and is one of Thomas' biggest contributions to the company's culture.

PRESIDENT WATSON

By 1915, the charges against the management of NCR had concluded and while most of those involved accepted a minor penalty for what they had done, Watson never admitted to any wrongdoing. However, the Federal Government declined to pursue him any further. He therefore became President of CTR on March 15, 1915, and was determined to turn the company around and to run it in as moral a way as possible.

However, it was a gruelling challenge as the US economy was in decline as The First World War raged in Europe.

Imbued by the Man Proposition, Watson looked to find the talent within his existing staff, rather than recruit from outside. "The directors told me, 'You'll have to hire outside brains before you can build up this company', said Watson. "I told them, 'that's not my policy. I like to develop men from the ranks and promote them.'"

Watson's own personal style and morality affected those around him. He never drank alcohol, and soon it became the norm for the executives to refrain from drink as well. Thomas also had a love of fine clothes, and pretty soon those below him adopted his style of suits. However, while he espoused democracy and equality, he could also behave like a tyrant, subjecting staff to brutal tongue-lashings and tirades. But he engendered a love in his staff, which meant that most forgave or tolerated him, and he developed many loyal employees.

In many ways, Watson was becoming more and more like John H. Patterson, his old boss at NCR, aping some of his ideas as well as his management style. NCR had a Hundred Point Club where salesman who hit targets would be treated to a weekend at a country club. Similarly, Watson created the Hundred Percent Club, which served the same purpose. He strove for unity and cohesion, which was easy as he was managing what were effectively separate companies. "We want all of our subsidiary companies to feel that they are all one thing, one big family," he said.

ENGINEERING SUCCESS

Against the odds, by the end of the decade, CTR was growing and beginning to really show its potential. Hollerith's influence was declining and later Watson would establish a robust engineering department that would work on and improve the tabulating machine. Although he was not an engineer himself he managed to get the best out of his men. Sometimes he would secretly set them the same task and then choose the best product, believing that rivalry brought better work. He tried many different techniques to bring out the best from his team and repeated whatever seemed to work the most effectively. He also liked to have the slogan THINK written at various places across the company, another hangover from his NCR days.

IBM

In 1917 the company moved into Canada and Watson decided to call that company International Business Machines (IBM). He later used that name as the company moved into South America and in 1924 the CTR name was dropped completely and IBM floated on the New York stock exchange. Also that year George Fairchild died and the last remaining barrier to Watson's dominance was removed. IBM was now truly Thomas Watson and it would remain that way for the best part of thirty years.

WHERE ARE THEY NOW?

During the Great Depression of the 1930s, IBM managed to grow and even launch new products, such as the Electric Writing Machine (a typewriter), while other businesses struggled. In the 1940s, the business made its first foray into computing and a decade later, had introduced its first computer. By the 1960s, IBM had recognised the potential computers would bring to business and accordingly, the business was transformed from a medium-sized manufacturer of tabulating equipment to the computer industry leader more familiar to us today.

IBM has recently shifted its focus onto software, which now makes up 24% of its total revenue. IT services, including internet security, and storage and data, for example, have continued to perform well and are a growing part of the company's offerings.

Today, nearly 100 years after the business was founded and many recessions later, IBM operates in more than 170 countries and is recognised as a world leader in computing systems.

Hewlett-Packard Company

Inspiring innovation

Founders: William Hewlett and David Packard

Age of founders at start: 25 and 26

Background: Student and engineer

Year of foundation: 1939

Business type: Technology manufacturer and services

Country of foundation: USA

Countries now trading in: Worldwide

Current turnover and profit: $114,552m (2009) and $7,660m (2009)

Willliam Hewlett and David Packard started their high tech company in a garage in California. The talented pair went on to set a number of trends as they built Hewlett-Packard into one of the world's top technology businesses. The company was founded by William Hewlett and David Packard at the tail end of the Great Depression, in a tiny garage in the heart of what is now Silicon Valley, now the home to many of the world's most vibrant hi-tech companies but back then just an ordinary middle-class American town.

A lasting friendship

William Hewlett and David Packard met in the early 1930s, while they were undergraduates at Stanford University in California. In their senior year, they became firm friends, sharing a love of and fascination for electronics and the outdoors. They spent time together hiking and fishing in the Sierra Nevada and the Colorado mountains where they discussed the dream of someday starting a company together.

Following graduation in 1934, however, plans to start a business of their own were put on hold as William decided to continue studying at Massachusetts Institute of Technology (MIT) and Stanford, undertaking postgraduate study in radio engineering. The Stanford course reunited him with Fred Terman, a professor who had taught both him and David and who was impressed with the pair.

David meanwhile had accepted a job after graduation with General Electric as an engineer. Jobs were scarce at this time – the US was slowly starting to emerge from the shadow of the Great Depression, a period of economic decline that started with the Wall Street stock market crash of 1929 and rapidly spread worldwide. Furthermore, Terman pointed out that the experience of working at GE would prove very useful in starting their own company.

In 1936, William completed a master's degree at MIT. He received one job offer, from Chicago-based Jensen Speakers. However, Fred Terman found him a California-based contract job for a doctor, building a device to measure brain waves. Now that William was back in California, Fred was keen to get William and David working together again.

Luckily for Fred, David's engineering career at General Electric was not working out as he had hoped – he felt frustrated by the lack of understanding of the future of electronics and a corporate culture that stifled innovation and good management.

Fred was able to arrange a Stanford research fellowship for Dave, and in 1938, David negotiated a one-year leave of absence from his job at General Electric (as good jobs were hard to find during the Depression) and came back to Palo Alto to work on a project involving vacuum tubes for a scientist called Russ Varian.

Bill and David were still determined to start the company they had talked about.

Starting from scratch

Once it was determined that David was returning to Palo Alto, William started looking for suitable premises to start their business. He found a house with a small garage and shed in downtown Palo Alto. David, who had recently got married, would live in the house with his wife, while William would move into the shed and the garage would become the workshop.

Having made the leap to start a business, they realized they didn't actually have any idea of what product to develop. They decided to contract out their engineering skills – and could get some excellent leads through Fred and his extensive network of contacts.

Initial contract work ranged from creating a self-flushing urinal and a foul-line indicator for bowling lanes to a shock machine to help people lose weight. While this work wasn't groundbreaking, it taught the partnership a valuable lesson. 'The miscellaneous jobs made us more sure of ourselves and our skills' says David. 'It also revealed that our abilities tended to be complementary. Bill was better trained in circuit technology and I was better trained and more experienced in manufacturing processes.' The work generated a small income to help keep the business afloat throughout 1938.

The miscellaneous jobs made us more sure of ourselves and our skills...It also revealed that our abilities tended to be complementary.

Inventive ideas

William also continued to work on a project that was the topic of his graduate thesis at Stanford – an electronic instrument used to test sound equipment, known as a resistance-tuned audio oscillator.

One of the problems with audio oscillators at the time was that they struggled to keep consistently accurate signals across a wide range of amplitude settings. The problem was getting the resistance to vary with the signal – no one had yet solved this, meaning that the audio oscillators available were either cheap and inaccurate or expensive and somewhat accurate.

William came up with the brilliant idea of using a small light bulb as a temperature-dependent resistor in one part of the circuit. It provided the resistor needed to vary resistance with the oscillator itself.

One of Fred's former students, Harold Buttner, was the vice-president of research and development for telecommunications company International Telephone and Telegraph (ITT), and Fred persuaded him to have a look at the oscillator design in mid-1938. He was so impressed with it that he offered William and Dave $500 for the foreign patent rights. This was a wake-up call for William and David – they realised the oscillator was more than a bright idea, it was a product they could make money from.

A prototype was finished in late 1938, and named the HP Model 200A. 'We thought the name would make us look as if we had been around for a while' David admitted later. William exhibited the prototype at a show in Portland in November 1938 and impressed, among other people, Bud Hawkins, a sound engineer for film maker Walt Disney Studios.

Chasing leads

Buoyed by the feedback from the exhibition, the two set about building a more professional-looking version of the oscillator and, with the help of David's wife, they produced a two-page sales brochure. They sent this to a list of Fred's contacts and a few weeks later received their first orders. 'We really didn't know if this oscillator was any good' said William. 'We simply put one together that worked pretty well, sent a letter out to universities and others, got three or four orders, and tried it again.'

According to David, one of the orders contained a cheque, and this tangible object convinced the two that their fledgling business had a future.

William and David were selling the product at $54.40 (a figure that meant something to them, based, oddly enough on a political slogan, which refers to 54 degrees latitude by 40 degrees north longitude). This was much less expensive than the competition – existing oscillators started at around the $400 mark. This seemed a wise move at the time as the economy was still recovering from the Depression, but William and David soon realised that the price was too low. It cost them more than $55 to make the product and so they couldn't break even, let alone make any profit.

We really didn't know if this oscillator was any good. We simply put one together that worked pretty well, sent a letter out to universities and others, got three or four orders, and tried it again.

They kept production costs to an absolute minimum – buying only the cabinets needed for the oscillator, but making its panels from sheets of aluminum, and baking on the enamel in David's home oven. They would assemble all the necessary pieces in the garage before taking them to Litton's labs to engrave the products.

Disney magic

Following the exhibition, Bud Hawkins from Walt Disney had been attracted by both the design and the price of the audio oscillator. He wanted to order eight oscillators for a film Walt Disney was making at the time, called *Fantasia*. William and David took a train to Los Angeles with a prototype, and successfully presented the invention to Disney.

Disney required some changes to be made to meet its specifications. William and David launched the revised model as the HP Model 200B, which they sold to Disney for $71.50 each. William recalled that they quickly learnt that they could raise the price of their product if it was good value.

In January 1939, the two men officially started their partnership and named it Hewlett-Packard (after flipping a coin to decide on the order of names). They advertised their 'resistance-tuned audio oscillators' in *Electronics* magazine and orders started to come in thick and fast. A manufacturers' representative for radio and sound recording equipment called Norm Neely had heard about the oscillator and contacted Hewlett-Packard, asking to represent them. He invited William to speak about the product at the Radio Engineers Club, where Norm had found many of his customers in the past.

David remembered that they didn't encounter too many financial problems in the first year, as steady sales kept them afloat and they didn't they take much, if any, out of the business. It helped that David had done courses in management accounting and business law as they were better able to balance figures and rarely required the services of lawyers. They made $5,369 in sales by the end of the first year of trading and had made $1,563 in profits.

Smashing growth

By the end of 1939, with two successful products under their belt, William and David were confident that they could take on the audio frequency measurement market. The company had grown to the point where they needed additional space, and they also had hired their first employee to help them make the oscillators.

They moved the business from the garage to a small, rented building not far away which was to become home to Hewlett-Packard for the next three years. Moving into new offices presented them with a series of challenges. To keep costs down, they decided to build their own oven, using a second-hand refrigerator as a means of cheap insulation. But they hadn't realised that this insulation was made out of flammable material. Flushed with the success of building what they perceived to be a working oven, William and David left it on to run overnight. Luckily, a passing truck driver noticed the flames coming from their office and the fire was extinguished before much damage was done to the building and the business!

They also noticed that the windows to their office did not offer much privacy, and their work was on display to passers-by and any snoopy competitors. To solve this problem, William and David decided to paint the windows black. This worked well, until one hot day when the black glass absorbed sunlight and cracked, shattering all the office windows. Luckily, continued sales helped pay for any damage.

William and David agreed that all employees should share in the company's success and they paid their first bonus to employees – $5 – in December 1940 (generous, as the minimum wage at the time was 30 cents per hour).

Cash flow issues

In 1940, Harold Buttner's company, ITT, put two contracts out to tender: one for a variable frequency oscillator, the other for a fixed-frequency oscillator. General Radio took the first contract, and Hewlett-Packard won the second – but fulfilling it proved an uphill struggle. William and David couldn't fulfill the contract on time without employing more people. Fortunately, they were able to recruit three talented engineers to become members of the team and finished the project to the required specifications.

Worse was to come: payment for the ITT contract was delayed and the founders soon realised they would not have enough money to pay staff. A phone call to Harold Buttner soon sorted out the payment, but a vital lesson had been learnt: even with a full order book, a business' cash flow is paramount. This episode prompted David to set up a line of credit for the company and he applied for a loan of $500. By the end of 1940, turnover was just under $35,000, impressive in the tail end of the Great Depression.

William and David continued to advertise in engineering magazines, and produced a catalogue of products. They also marketed the business through exhibitions, showing their product line at the Institute of Radio Engineering show in 1941, gaining more customers.

While business was actually going well, the US now faced a new threat that cut much deeper than any Depression: World War Two. War had been declared across most European countries in 1939, and the US was drawn into the conflict two years later. As a reserve officer, William was called up to the army in 1941, leaving David to run the company, which by then had six employees and reached a turnover of just over $106,500.

War effort

The War increased demand for Hewlett-Packard electronic equipment, much of it coming from the US Naval Research Laboratory. The business also began to develop new products that could be used by the Armed Forces, including moving into the field of microwaves.

During the war, Hewlett-Packard built signal generators and a radar-jamming device developed by the Naval Research Laboratory. In 1945, at the end of the war, Hewlett-Packard made the critical decision to continue in the microwave field, and this area quickly became an important part of the company's business.

Hewlett returned full-time to Hewlett-Packard in 1947 after completing his military service. Like many successful business partnerships, William and David brought increasingly different skills to the business. William worked alongside the engineers, while David was the face of the company, often acting as spokesman.

Diversifying the business

It wasn't until 1966 that Hewlett-Packard entered the market for computers with its first computer, the HP2116A. This was originally created to control the business' growing test and measurement products, but the company soon saw its potential as a stand-alone product. This was followed two years later by the introduction of the world's first desktop scientific calculator, the HP 9100A. Always at the cutting-edge of technology, the calculator was 10 times faster than most other machines when it came to solving scientific and engineering problems. In 1972, HP released the world's first scientific handheld calculator, the HP-35, and made the engineer's slide rule (a tool used for multiplication and division) obsolete.

Like many successful business partnerships, William and David brought increasingly different skills to the business. William worked alongside the engineers, while David was the face of the company, often acting as spokesman.

Over the following years, Hewlett-Packard continued to innovate. During the1980s it produced a range of computers, from desktop machines to portable equipment, that helped the business become a major player in the computer industry. Always on the lookout for industries that complemented its existing product range, it seemed only natural to expand into the printer market with the launch of ground-breaking inkjet and laser printers that connected to personal computers.

While the 1990s were memorable for the business' continued advances in computing and printing, it was also marked by the death of David in 1996. William passed away five years later in 2001.

Where are they now?

Spanning six decades of innovation, in 2007, Hewlett-Packard became the first IT company in history to post revenues in excess of $100bn. Today, it is the world's largest technology company, and it brings together a portfolio that spans printing, personal computing, software, services and IT infrastructure to solve customer problems. As a testament to the impact of HP's business story, in 2005 work was completed to preserve the humble garage where David and William brought their dreams of a business to life. The simple garage is now regarded by historians as one of the most significant artifacts of the electronics industry in Silicon Valley today.

Microsoft®

A technology empire begins

Founders: Bill Gates and Paul Allen

Age of founders at start: 20 and 22

Background: Students of computing

Year of foundation: 1975

Business type: Computer software

Country of foundation: USA

Countries now trading in: Worldwide

How They Started in Tough Times

One of the world's richest people, Bill Gates hardly needs an introduction. Software made by the company he co-founded runs almost all personal computers in the world today. Microsoft® is one of the world's largest corporations, making around £10bn in profit on revenues of around £40bn. Yet this company began in the same way as many others in this book, with two ambitious young people who had a dream. Back then, in 1975, there were no PCs on desks or in homes, and those few people who knew what a 'computer' was, knew them as substantial machines which took up a large room and needed specialists to operate them. Even so, the young student Bill and his co-founder, recent graduate Paul Allen, truly believed that software and computers were going to grow dramatically, and they were determined to be a part of it. Despite their foresight, even they could not have dreamt back then of quite how far their vision would go.

Computer skills

Bill Gates was born in Seattle into an affluent family and went to a private school. He was gifted at maths, but was otherwise unremarkable. In 1968, his first year at this private school, the school got its first computer – in fact it was just a terminal which linked into a PDP-10 computer made by Digital Equipment Corporation. The computer was owned by General Electric Corporation which leased it by the hour to Bill's school. It was a very long way from today's computers, though, which meant it was popular with just a handful of boys who wrote programs on it using a language called BASIC. Bill's first programs were games – first tick tack toe, then Lunar Lander, a game about landing a space shuttle safely on the moon before it ran out of fuel.

Bill would spend hours in his school's computer lab using this machine and it was here that he met Paul Allen, a fellow school pupil two years older than Bill. They continued to develop their interest in computers at school, running up enormous bills way beyond anything the school had originally imagined. The school understandably set limits on the amount of time they could spend on the computer.

Bill and Paul literally breathed computers day and night and when Bill was only 13 years old, they were tasked with their first 'IT project', for the Computer Center Corporation ('C-Cubed'). The company, recently established in Seattle, owned a mainframe computer which Bill's school hooked up to using its terminal. The company director was impressed with Bill and the other students' skills and tasked them with finding bugs in their software, in return for unlimited time on the computer after normal working hours; the boys were often there until midnight! 'It was when we got free time at C-Cubed that we really got into computers, Bill remembers. 'I mean, then I became hard core. It was day and night.' Through this the boys were able to ask the C-Cubed staff all sorts of questions, vastly expanding their computing knowledge. Bill and Paul stood out from their school friends because of their enthusiasm for computers.

'It was when we got free time at C-Cubed that we really got into computers...then I became hard core. It was day and night.'

Over the next few years, word spread about Bill and Paul's abilities and they were asked to develop a payroll system for a local company in return for receiving more computer time and some royalties on any sales of the system. After that they came up with a program that could count city traffic which they sold to the city of Seattle, but reports say they never made much profit from it.

Software adopter

In 1973, Bill enrolled at Harvard University, where he proved himself one of the most gifted students at maths. It was also there that he met fellow student Steve Ballmer, who was studying maths and science and who would later play a significant role in Microsoft®'s history. Much like his days at school, however, Bill found himself missing classes on a regular basis to indulge his passion for computers. He even considered quitting college to look for a job and had several interviews. While Bill was undecided about what the future would hold, the US economy too was looking unstable. By 1973, the US had officially entered a period of recession.

Over the next two years, while the recession deepened in the US, Bill continued to study at Harvard but he also kept in close touch with Paul, who was now working for computing company Honeywell, based in Boston. The young men were convinced that there would be an enormous computing boom, and were determined to be a part of that. After their earlier forays into the business world they knew they wanted to set up their own business, and were on the look out for the right time and opportunity to do so.

Chance sighting

In January 1975, on his way to visit Bill at university, Paul came across a trade magazine for the computer industry, *Popular Electronics*, featuring a new computer called the Altair 8080 on the cover. This machine was manufactured by Model Instrumentation and Telemetry System (MITS), a company based in Albuquerque, New Mexico, who claimed it would be the world's first affordable computer for the general public. Thousands of people had already placed orders for one, eager to get their hands on what was then a revolutionary piece of technology. The Altair bore little resemblance to the computers we use today, lacking both a keyboard and mouse. These computers had to be assembled from a kit, then programmed in binary code using switches on the front panel. Unsurprisingly, this appealed only to electronics enthusiasts.

Bill and Paul felt sure that this was the opportunity that they had been waiting for. They thought that they could write a version of BASIC for the Altair (which would be so much easier to use than the binary code). MITS would be sure to sell lots of copies of it, earning good money for Bill and Paul.

Just a few days after the magazine had come out announcing the Altair, they phoned Ed Roberts, the head of MITS to offer him a BASIC program for the Altair. This move demonstrates the pair's ambition and drive – in reality, they had talked about writing a version of BASIC but had not actually developed anything yet; they wanted to gauge the company's reaction first. Roberts explained that he had had many such calls, and that the first people to deliver a program which worked would get the deal. 'We realised that the revolution might happen without us' Bill said. 'After we saw that article, there was no question of where our life would focus.'

Risky business

The pair faced two serious challenges: neither of them had access to an Altair computer (or had even seen one with their own eyes – in fact the only one in the world was still at MITS at this stage) and they hadn't even begun to write the software. MITS asked Paul and Bill to fly out the following month to demonstrate their program, unknowingly giving them the time they needed to write it. Sensing their first real opportunity to start a computer business, Bill and Paul set about writing the software. Using Harvard University's computers, Paul worked on a program to imitate the Altair's system as closely as possible, working at nights after his day job, while Bill worked both day and night writing reams upon reams of code for the BASIC language itself. Although BASIC had already been invented, nobody had ever made a version for a minicomputer, let alone something as small as the new Altair – and many experts declared that it could not be done.

As their deadline drew closer, Paul and Bill roped in fellow Harvard students to help complete the code. Eight weeks after the phone call to Ed Roberts, Paul flew out to Albuquerque to meet MITS. None of the MITS executives believed that the program would work, and indeed just one bug could have stopped it. But, against all the odds, Paul used BASIC to get the Altair to add 2 + 2, and the machine gave the crowd watching the answer: 4. The program worked!

Paul and Bill negotiated a deal whereby MITS agreed to buy the rights to the program, even though there were still quite a few bugs that needed to be fixed. The two young men celebrated what would turn out to be their new company's first deal by going out for ice cream and soft drinks.

Things moved quickly from there. In June 1975, both Paul and Bill moved to Albuquerque, with Paul working officially as director of software at Altair (having left

Honeywell) while Bill took a leave of absence from Harvard and worked on perfecting the software code. They both signed a 10-year contract giving MITS exclusive rights to the BASIC language and the right to license it out to third parties. For their part, Bill and Paul received a royalty of between $30 and $60 for every copy sold and MITS agreed to promote and market their software. When BASIC was sold together with an Altair it would typically cost around $50, whereas when sold separately, the price could be as much as 10 times more.

The two young men celebrated what would turn out to be their new company's first deal by going out for ice cream and soft drinks.

Paul and Bill also formalised their partnership at this point, with Bill initially owning 60% to Paul's 40%, as Bill argued that he had done more of the initial programming. They later changed this split so Bill ended up with 64% to Paul's 36%. Despite being independently wealthy from a trust-fund he had inherited, Bill was determined not to use that money for his business, so he and Paul kept their costs to a bare minimum, sharing a room in a dingy Albuquerque hotel to start with.

They quickly hired two of their friends from the computer club at their school in Seattle to help them work on debugging BASIC and the other programs for the Altair. The four shared an apartment, and worked in a fanatical way, all of them utterly committed to developing software as fast as they could, and building up enormous team spirit between them. They worked at a small office next to MITS, and would often fall asleep at work. One time a MITS executive was giving someone a tour of the office and came across Bill asleep on the floor.

Orders for Altairs flooded in and MITS could barely keep up with the demand. Strangely enough though, sales of the software remained in the low hundreds, and Bill soon figured out why – his version of BASIC had been pirated and was being distributed freely among Altair users. While these users were happy to pay for the hardware and associated computer accessories, it became clear that where software was concerned, they thought it should be shared freely.

It was not a view, however, that Bill subscribed to. He already believed that software, more than anything else, would be the single most important force for the future of personal computing, and for this to happen, it had to be paid for. He was so passionate about this that he wrote a letter to a trade magazine, bemoaning the fact that people expected software to be free. If this were the case, how would developers be paid? Such was Bill's passion that his letter gained considerable support from business partners and was to lead to paid-for, copyrighted software becoming the industry standard.

It was not only the letter that was significant, but the way in which Bill signed it – 'Bill Gates, general partner, Micro-Soft.' They had come up with this name during the summer by combining microcomputer with software. Bill and Paul soon dropped the hyphen.

Microsoft® takes shape

While Paul worked at MITS, both he and Bill also developed their software company. They were enormously excited by the potential of the burgeoning personal computer market and were desperate to take advantage of this. MITS launched a floppy disk drive for the Altair and asked Paul and Bill to adapt their BASIC program to work on that.

The following year, in 1976, Paul decided to quit MITS to concentrate on Microsoft® full-time and the business decided to hire new programmers and move into its first offices, on the eighth floor of a bank building in Albuquerque. In November that year, they registered the name Microsoft® as a trade mark. Bill formally dropped out of Harvard at the end of 1976 to concentrate full-time on the business. His parents were not happy with his decision and tried to talk him out of it, but he was absolutely convinced that computers would eventually enable people and businesses to save time and money, creating an enormous business opportunity, and he was determined to be part of this impending growth.

MITS may have been the company that launched Bill and Paul towards fame, but less than two years later, it was holding back Microsoft®'s growth potential. MITS was still struggling to keep up with the demand for Altairs, and was facing some serious reliability issues with some key components – and dozens of new competitors, many of whom wanted to license a version of Microsoft®'s BASIC. Bill negotiated deal after deal with these companies, but under the terms of their deal with MITS, MITS had to approve these deals, which it felt were too competitive, so MITS withheld their approval, enraging Bill, who felt deprived of enormous income.

Bill was absolutely convinced that computers would eventually enable people and businesses to save time and money, creating an enormous business opportunity, and he was determined to be part of this impending growth.

Before long, MITS was in decline and struggling, and in 1977 was sold to Pertec Computer Corporation. Pertec knew that the Altair was in decline, and wanted MITS for its rights to BASIC. Bill and Paul knew that they had to wrestle control of their program back somehow, as their original contract with MITS had set a limit as to how much they could get paid under that deal, and they now knew that the market potential for it was substantially larger.

They consulted Bill's father, a lawyer back in Seattle. A clause in their original contract stated that MITS had to use its 'best efforts' to sub-license the BASIC program, and Microsoft® was able to prove that by refusing to sign deals with other manufacturers, MITS was in breach of the contract. Microsoft® used this to get the rights to its program back, after a three-week long hearing. Microsoft® then set about selling versions of its BASIC program to other manufacturers of computers, such as Commodore's PET, Tandy's TRS80, and Apple's Apple II, which were all taking off. Bill, who was a voracious reader of business books, negotiated the deals, while Paul concentrated on programming.

Astounding in many ways, Bill took the company to Japan as early as 1977, when it was just two years old. He found a computer whiz kid there his own age, Kuzuhiko Nishi, and used him as an agent to build business with Japan's growing computer companies.

The bigger picture

By now Bill and Paul had what at the time seemed like extraordinarily ambitious targets for their company: they wanted a computer on every desk and envisioned a future with Microsoft® on every computer. As these computers became more powerful, so the demand for more powerful software grew. It was now possible for example, to move words around documents in word-processing programs and to manipulate crude images. All this could now be achieved at much faster speeds than previously possible.

Over the next three years the founders added new programs, mainly other programming languages. They continued to work long hours, with Bill getting involved with the programming as well as driving the sales efforts. He called several big corporations to persuade them to use his software and programming languages on their mainframe computers. This approach worked wonders – as more and more companies became interested in the company's software, the business grew and hired programmers to help with this expansion, many of whom Bill knew from his high school and college days.

By 1978, Microsoft® had around a dozen employees, but Bill was finding it harder and harder to persuade programmers to move to Albuquerque, and, as Microsoft® had no more links with MITS, it didn't seem to make sense to keep the business there. Subsequently, they decided to relocate the business and although most technology companies at the time were located in California, the business moved to Seattle, close to where Bill was brought up and where his family still lived.

The move coincided with a rethink of the business. In keeping with the original vision, Bill knew that for Microsoft® to thrive, he would need to come up with something bigger and more ambitious than BASIC software systems. He wanted to tap into the burgeoning market for operating system and word processing software. Bill also needed to get more sales expertise on board and he turned to his college friend Steve Ballmer, who joined Microsoft® as business manager and who soon became an expert at promoting and marketing the business.

Golden opportunity

What would turn out to be one of the century's greatest business opportunities presented itself towards the end of 1979. Bill had found out that hardware manufacturer IBM, the world's leading manufacturer of mainframe computers, was looking for an operating system for a new personal computer (PC) that it was to launch shortly. This was IBM's first attempt to make a substantial impact in the personal computer market, which it could see was growing rapidly. As IBM wanted the product made in a short space of time, it decided not to build its own computer from scratch, but to buy in different elements from other companies.

Bill decided that Microsoft® should be the company to create the operating system IBM needed. They bought an existing software system from a company called Seattle Computer for a hotly negotiated one-off fee of $50,000 (and a few minor other rights – spare a thought for the people who sold it for relative peanuts) and used this as the basis for a new operating system they called MS-DOS® (Microsoft Disk Operating System). Microsoft® put nearly half of their programmers (there were around 60 by this time) to work on this system over the period of a year.

Microsoft® then attempted to license this software to IBM. This was a very competitive battle, with other software companies also very keen to work with IBM on what they all thought would be an enormously successful new product launch. In the end Microsoft® won, and negotiated to license their operating system to IBM on a royalty basis (having learnt from its experience with MITS, Microsoft® was insistent that it retained the rights to the program) so that every time a copy of MS-DOS® was sold, IBM would pay a fee to Microsoft®. IBM agreed, and signed the deal which became the making of Microsoft® as we now know it.

Just one year later, in 1981, MS-DOS® became the industry standard and more than doubled sales at Microsoft® – from $7m in 1980 to $16m a year later. Part of the reason for this rapid growth was that as IBM had used off-the-shelf parts to build its PCs, it was easy for other computer manufacturers to follow suit and build similar machines, all of which could run MS-DOS®. Bill was quick to capitalise on this, supplying MS-DOS® software to IBM competitors. By 1982, Microsoft®'s revenues had grown to $32m and the company had grown to around 200 employees.

Just one year later, in 1981, MS-DOS® became the industry standard and more than doubled sales at Microsoft® - from $7m in 1980 to $16m a year later.

Just a year later, however, Paul Allen took the decision to leave. Having been diagnosed with Hodgkin's disease, an illness that could be treated, he decided he wanted to focus on other interests.

Where are they now?

Throughout the 1980s, Bill concentrated on growing an international sales force for Microsoft® and developing further products, including Office® and Windows®, so named because of the separate frames that users could create on their computer screens. Microsoft® launched the first version of Windows® in 1985, though it would take several upgrades before it really began to take off.

Microsoft® went public in 1986, listing its shares on the NASDAQ, the USA's stock market for young, fast-growing companies. Investors who bought shares at the time and held onto them have seen spectacular growth since, as the company has been one of the best ever performers on the stock market.

Bill stepped down as chief executive in 2000, with Steve Ballmer taking over. In 2008 Bill announced that he was focusing on a career in philanthropy; he remains Chairman of the business.

Microsoft®, MS-DOS®, Windows® and Office® are trademarks of the Microsoft® group of companies.

MeetingZone

A new wave of communication

Founder: Tim Duffy and Steve Gandy

Age at start: 47 and 41

Background: Telecommunications

Year of foundation: 2002

Business type: Audio and web conferencing service

Country of foundation: UK

Countries now trading in: UK, Germany, Canada, USA

Current sales: 2008–2009 £8.2m

Following the horrors of the terrorist attacks in New York on September 11 2001 there was an immediate decline in executives willing to travel to business meetings. Around the same time joint partners Tim Duffy and Steve Gandy had an idea for a business which has proved to be very good for them, their customers and shareholders. They identified a gap in the market for a provider of collaboration services which took full advantage of new, web-based, technology. Focusing their attentions on creating a service that was fast and flexible, Tim and Steve launched MeetingZone in 2002, and it has grown rapidly, and with remarkable consistency, ever since; today it is one of the leading providers of such services in Europe.

Looking for a challenge

Before starting the company, both Steve and Tim were well-experienced in the field of telecommunications, having chalked up more than 25 years between them at companies such as BT and GEC in Britain and America. In his time at BT, Steve had created BT Conferencing, set up a joint venture called Quip! and had later moved on to join the Caudwell group where he also led the creation of a fixed-line business called Reach Telecoms. Tim, meanwhile, helped to run a number of small GEC Telecom companies and had moved, in the early 90s to PictureTel Corporation, then a small company, and one of the pioneers in video conferencing - it was here, in fact, that that he had met Steve when the two men had been involved in a business deal.

Late in 2001, Tim and Steve were both 'looking for new challenges' at a time when nobody was investing anything in start-up companies, following the collapse of the dotcom bubble. A few weeks after the tragedy of September 11, during a conversation in a coffee shop in London, they decided to channel their existing skills into creating a new service that allowed people to collaborate without being in the same location. At a time when most people were expecting the growth in collaboration services to come from video conferencing, Tim and Steve had come up with what they thought was a lucrative opportunity, mainly in

Founders Tim Duffy and Steve Gandy

simple voice conferences coupled with web collaboration tools. They spotted that new technology was enabling much better services, and that there was a problem with the existing providers which a new company could solve.

They decided to channel their existing skills into creating a new service that allowed people to collaborate without being in the same location. The established companies offering these services were hampered by expensive and old technology.

Although BT had just about cornered the UK market at the time, Steve and Tim felt there was room for improvement. They felt the existing companies in the market were offering a service that was 'outdated and slow'. As Steve recalls, in order to set up a conference account the customer would have to call up the company and request it – the company would then set up an account, take your bank account

View of the Oxford offices

details and, some considerable time later, get back to you with an access code that would enable you and your colleagues to join the call. It was a lengthy process every time you wanted to make a conference call, requiring call booking in advance with their provider.

The established companies offering these services were hampered by expensive and old technology which required large numbers of people to operate. Steve and Tim could see a very clear business opportunity: using the internet, they could set up a service that offered a considerably better service for customers, and at considerably lower cost to their company, than the older systems used by the established competitors. The shocking terrorist attacks on the Twin Towers translated immediately into an increased demand for alternatives to business travel, boosting demand for conference call and collaboration services.

Improving a service

Armed with this idea, Tim and Steve realised that one of the key things that their business could provide was a real time, 'transparent' kind of bill. They spoke to some of the big customers and industry analysts that they had known from previous ventures, and found that there was widespread dissatisfaction with the existing billing systems – which conference call customers felt all too often amounted to a 'messy pile of paper' with little traceability. Tim and Steve decided, therefore, to improve the billing system so that details such as who called, how long the call lasted and how much it cost were available through the customer's online account immediately after the call.

They also wanted to market their service as a lower cost alternative to their competitors, whilst providing superior service levels. As a result, they decided on a price point below the average – which was at that time dominated by giants such as BT, who had a list price of 22p per minute. Tim and Steve decided 12p a minute was a suitable price distinction without falling too low.

The two founders then focused on providing a better service. According to Steve and Tim, good service was the main advantage of MeetingZone – overall, conference call customers were not only unhappy paying the current prices; they were unhappy with the service they were getting for their money. The founders' solution was to offer customers a unique self-service model via the web where anyone could set up an account 'within a couple of clicks'. Their system didn't need customers to book a specific call time at all, but instead let them make conference calls whenever they wanted, simply by dialing in with the appropriate account code. As conference calls often took place in business environments where time was of the essence, this idea made absolute sense to them; all they needed now was enough money to build the system and start selling it.

£2 million was a lot of money for a raw start-up.

Tim and Steve spent several weeks building forecasts and drafting their business plan, which they needed to help them raise the £2m they would need to get started. Given the risk averse investment climate in 2002 they designed the plan to appeal primarily to investors interested in a low-risk, short-term venture run by individuals who were experienced and knew the market. It included carefully planned milestones and both founders made certain that 'everyone knew there were lots of checks and balances' to ensure the growth of the business was going according to plan. As well as this, when presenting the business plan to investors they made sure that they referenced the good management team they had assembled and recruited, for example, the ex-CEO of PictureTel Corporation was serving as a Board Member. This reduced the apparent risk factor a little further and encouraged investors to part with their money.

£2m was a lot of money for a raw start-up in the climate of 2002. In order to offer an 'impressive corporate service' from day one, Tim and Steve needed enough money to build really good software, as well as to fund a corporate class customer service team and professional marketing. It was their intention from the outset to get it right first time and go through only one funding round, from which they hoped to get to profitability right away, which is almost unheard of for a start-up business like this.

However, after approaching various venture capitalists in early 2002, the founders learned that most of them considered it an 'excessive' figure to attempt to raise – so they lowered their sights to raise the slightly smaller sum of £1.6m which they calculated was the absolute minimum required. Tim and Steve spent months meeting various venture capitalists and other investors such as high net worth individuals, also known as business angels. This ultimately proved worth their while – they ended up raising £2.1m. As soon as one venture capitalist (Springboard plc) had agreed to invest, they found it much easier to get others on board.

Once they had the funds, Tim and Steve began designing and building the service delivery platform and investing in hardware and software. The first investment was the billing system – which cost several hundred thousand pounds of license fees, plus extra costs. Although this was expensive, Tim reveals that most of the deals they struck were on fantastic terms given the collapse of the telecoms markets in 2002, one of the advantages of starting a business in a major downturn. The rest of the money, Tim says, went on funding the design team of software programmers that were working in offices he and Steve had borrowed in Milton Keynes over the summer of 2002. This was another key benefit of starting the business in a recession, it was very easy to secure highly skilled software development talent at a fraction of the cost.

Team photos, Christmas 2002

Do as much networking as possible so that you get to know a lot of people.

Getting out there

The founders then turned to the issue of branding and marketing. One memorable incident in MeetingZone's early days came when they tried to secure the domain name www.meetingzone.com. Having agreed the name and determined it was clear to use Tim and Steve discovered that they could only register the .co.uk domain. With global ambitions they set out to locate the owner of meetingzone.com, which turned out to be a Thai dating and 'exotic' services website. After a few fax exchanges the .com domain name was secured for a small sum, although Tim is sure the original customers of meetingzone.com were surprised at the change of what was on offer!

With the website name secured and the branding designed by a top London agency (Tim notes they got a very good deal for this due to the recession) the founders set about promoting the company. From their experience in larger businesses, they knew that their best route was simply to spread the word of their new business to existing contacts and previous clients. It is a path that both men recommend to anyone starting up their own business: firstly, do as much networking as possible so that you get to 'know a lot of people'; and then work hard to make the most of this network – it's amazing, they say, 'how important your network is'. They also spent a fair proportion of the initial funds hiring a PR agency in the hope of 'punching above our weight'. This proved very sensible, freeing up Steve and Tim to cultivate new clients, while their PR agency could work on spreading the story to potential prospects. Tim explains that they decided to use Six Degrees, a PR agency that Tim's previous company, PictureTel, had used very successfully to launch their European market entry 10 years earlier. As they specialised in providing business-to-business media relations, they were ideal for getting the word out into the wider market.

Envisaged success

The company was launched in September 2002 after the company moved into rented offices on the Oxford Business Park, and secured the business of a major FTSE company within the first few weeks. Business started to grow very rapidly as clients appreciated the new approach MeetingZone offered and word spread about its unique service. Shortly after this Tim and Steve began to experiment with online marketing, using Google, which was to become a significant new marketing approach for most businesses. As well as this, PR activities during the first six months paid off with 'considerable' press coverage in the business media, and as a result business grew at a strong rate.

The company also started to see a second benefit from its investors: contacts. Their investors had an obvious incentive to see MeetingZone succeed, and some of them provided a number of contacts which led to new sales accounts. By delivering a substantially better product for customers than its competitors, MeetingZone also grew by word of mouth, as delighted customers talked to colleagues about the new company.

Their business had high initial overheads, but the nature of their technology-based approach meant that they could scale the business without a corresponding increase in overheads. Their revenues started rising between 5% and 10% every month, with a static cost base and after about two years they broke through into profitability, without needing to raise any more money from investors, in line with their original business plan.

'MeetingZone would have run out of cash very quickly had the sales not appeared as predicted.'

Despite what may appear to be an easy success, Tim says that trying to minimise cash drain whilst retaining a high level of service was their 'biggest challenge' at this time. He adds that it was in fact always something of a 'balancing act' to ensure that money invested in sales and customer support achieved a rapid payback. 'MeetingZone would have run out of cash very quickly had the sales not appeared as predicted' Tim revealed.

Traning the newly recruited team in Oxford, August 2002

Finances are always a problem for young companies, and the founders also recall running into another cash-related problem when one of their key US suppliers was acquired by another company and attempted to renege on the original supply contract due to the advantageous terms MeetingZone had initially negotiated. As Tim reflects, although they were ultimately successful in enforcing the contract with the supplier, it took a lot of stress, time and money. Anyone starting a new business should always be aware of the possibility of such issues.

Despite this, Tim and Steve are justifiably proud that, two years after the launch, when they had reached profitability and seen through a legal dispute, they had £300,000 left in the bank from the £2.1m that had been invested.

Where are they now?

Since such early figures, turnover increased at an astounding rate; the first year's £75,000 grew to £4m by the end of 2006. MeetingZone also continued to innovate in all areas of its service offering, keeping well ahead of the competition and today has thousands of major corporations as clients and a complete suite of collaboration applications.

Such success, Tim and Steve say, is largely put down to service innovation, quality of their employees and the strength of the corporate class service provided. 'If we can't automate it we don't do it' claims Steve, 'the strength of the MeetingZone model is in the relentless application of new technology to keep overheads down and service levels high'.

From their previous jobs, Steve and Tim were both familiar with the process of early start-ups in the business world and also with the telecoms market they entered. Both men stress that this is key to the success of your business and they warn that if you are planning to start up a business you should always 'know your industry backwards'.

Retaining a 40% share of the company, both Tim and Steve are still heavily involved with MeetingZone, and are now driving an international expansion strategy. With the UK business a great success and enjoying a strong reputation with its clients,

MeetingZone is in the process of growing the business in other countries. With new ventures in Germany, Canada and the USA, MeetingZone is still growing rapidly.

2009 was another strong year for the company, and with a growing awareness of global warming, the conferencing and collaboration market is a good place to be. The company grew 40% during 2009 – impressive in yet another recessionary market. MeetingZone has featured three times in the annual Microsoft Sunday Times Tech Track 100. Their initial investors are also pleased – Tim comments that 'we now have cash in the bank and have even been paying dividends in the last couple of years, which is a real surprise for our shareholders in this environment.'

Tim and Steve attribute their success to having a consistent business model and executing on it every day with enthusiasm and a relentless focus on quality and automation. 'Customers appreciate what we do!' says Tim.

RETAIL

Whole Foods Market

A food awakening

Founder: John Mackey

Age of founder at start: 26

Year of foundation: 1980

Business type: Natural and organic food supermarkets

Country of foundation: USA

Countries now trading in: 284 stores (273 in the USA, six in Canada, five in the UK)

Texas in the late 1970s and early 1980s would hardly seem like the best place to start a business dedicated to natural and organic foods. The country is of course renowned for its fast foods – hamburgers, french fries, hotdogs and milkshakes. America is also a country which loves its meat. But it was in this meat-loving nation and the state of Texas (famous for its BBQ Ribs) no less, where Whole Foods Market was established. Its founder, John Mackey, is a tough and combative figure who has championed a brand and direction that few others would ever countenance. He and his then girlfriend Renee Lawson Hardy went through a rollercoaster ride before attaining success. Not only did they survive a tough recession and sceptical consumer base, but also a flood, an eviction, battles with conscience, not to mention many of the other challenges which can hit any business, before making a success of their natural food vision.

An organic awakening

John Mackey had no training in business; indeed, there's very little on his CV prior to Whole Foods which would commend him as a likely success. By the time he set up in business in 1978 he had dropped out of no fewer than three Texan colleges. John was a hippy and just before establishing his first company he was living in a vegetarian co-op (basically a hippy commune). He wasn't really interested in business and spent a lot of his time reading philosophy, cooking natural foods and being outdoors. 'I got interested in food when I was in my early 20s. I moved into this vegetarian co-op. I wasn't a vegetarian, but I figured the co-op would have a lot of interesting women living there' he says.

One of the interesting women he met was Renee Lawson Hardy who became his girlfriend, and later co-founder of Whole Foods. John remembers that his time at the co-op was very important to him: 'I learned how to cook and I became the food buyer. I got very interested in food; I sort of had a food awakening about what's happened to our food over the years.'

John became increasingly dissatisfied by what modern culture had to offer in terms of food and the way it was produced. He found himself at odds with the high-yield, low-cost approach that most US food producers adopt. He became concerned about health and how food impacts on a person's well-being. Also, he was troubled by the way animals were treated and became a vegetarian as a result. Later in life he would go even further and restrict himself to a vegan diet.

Garage business

In 1978 John and Renee were just 25 and 21 respectively. John's 'food awakening' had a profound effect on him. He went to work for a small natural foods store, which was his first taste of working in a retail environment, and he loved it so much he decided to open a similar shop himself. John remembers, 'I pitched the idea to my girlfriend..."hey, why don't we go do our own small store" and she loved it and we went out and hustled everybody we knew and raised $45,000 and opened the first store'. John and Renee approached family, friends and acquaintances at the co-op to raise the money – many were hippies, and were lured by John's energy and passion for natural foods, and expected a modest return for their cash.

Their first store, named Saferway (a pun on the then ubiquitous supermarket chain Safeway) was opened in Austin, Texas, and was little more than a small shop in a garage.

> 'I pitched the idea to my girlfriend..."hey, why don't we go do our own small store" and she loved it and we went out and hustled everybody we knew and raised $45,000 and opened the first store'.

Nevertheless, it was a big gamble; at the time there were just a handful of supermarkets in the USA selling solely 'organic' foodstuffs. At the time, the term 'organic' hadn't even been properly defined or regulated by the US Department of Agriculture (and wasn't until 2002, with the help of Whole Foods). John and Renee were pioneering a new concept of food, focused on using production methods that emphasise the use of renewable resources, treat animals humanely, and don't use genetically engineered pesticides or genetically modified ingredients or synthetic preservatives.

It was a fun affair, local farmers would drop off produce in old pickup trucks and John would buy nut loaves and muffins from hippy bakers. The shop was strictly vegetarian, just like its founders and achieved about $300,000 of sales in its first year. However, this didn't equate to making a profit: 'We didn't know what we were doing, we managed to lose $23,000. We lost half of the money which was invested in the first year. But I'm a quick learner, so we made a small profit in the second year. The first thing I realised was that the store was too small and we needed to get to a larger location if we were really going to be successful and compete.'

The small store didn't always have enough storage space, so Renee and John kept some of their vegetables at their rented home. However, their landlord objected to this and the couple were subsequently evicted. With cash tight and with few other options available to them they opted to live at the store. Life was far from glamorous. The store didn't have standard bathroom facilities so they had to be inventive when it came to personal hygiene: in order to bathe they used a Hobart dishwasher which they attached a water hose to.

'We didn't know what we were doing, we managed to lose #23,000. We lost half of the money which was invested in the first year. But I'm a quick learner, so we made a small profit in the second year.'

Organic growth

After two years John had learned a lot from running a business and decided that he needed to think bigger if he was to be successful. However, some of his initial investors were not so sure: they were more interested in growing the Saferway shop slowly, and making some of their investment back. But John was determined to move locations, as he explains, 'I didn't think we'd be competitive there over the long-term'. The investors were adamant though, and refused to put any more money in, unless John could find other investors. 'Their basic strategy was that they didn't think anybody would be stupid enough to invest in this business...but I was very persuasive.'

John was friends with the owners of another natural foods store and suggested that they merge to form a larger business. In some ways it was an offer that the other business couldn't afford to refuse. 'They were a competitor but they were friends of mine. So I didn't go up there and threaten them and say, "join with us or we're going to drive you out of business",' he explains. 'I went up there and said, "we're going to open a 10,000-square-foot store about a mile from here. Wouldn't it be a lot more fun to join forces together rather than compete when our store's going to be four times bigger than yours?" And they saw the logic of that argument.'

Ethical roots

John's first store, Saferway had been a wholly vegetarian focused business, but he realised that he couldn't just sell vegetables if he was going to run a supermarket. He opted to stock other products too such as meat, seafood and dairy products. As a vegetarian this wasn't an easy decision and some criticised him for this. John explains, 'when we made the decision to open a bigger store, we made a decision to sell products that I didn't think were healthy for people such as meat, seafood, beer, wine, and coffee. We didn't think they were particularly healthy products, but we were a whole food store, not a "holy food" store. We're in business not to fulfil some type of ideology, but to service our customers.'

However, John did steer clear of the many brands and suppliers that other supermarkets buy from and always focused on buying from more ethically defensible sources. Typically this meant smaller farms where animal welfare practices are higher. In other cases it meant buying food which had been grown in sustainable or fair-trade environments. Often these sources were more expensive but proponents believe that they are both more ethical and are usually higher quality products. 'To me, you make a trade off' John says. 'It might be a little bit more expensive. But you're getting a better tasting, higher quality food that's going to be better for your health and better for the environment.'

'We were a whole food store, not a "holy food" store. We're in business not to fulfil some type of ideology, but to service our customers.'

Floods of interest

The business opened in 1980 in Austin, Texas, as Whole Foods Market. It was the first supermarket-style natural foods store in the country and had 10,500 square feet of space and a staff of 19. The store was a hit with customers, sales started pouring in and the store was profitable almost straightaway. Word of mouth quickly spread about this new, sizeable health store, and people took notice – there were less than half a dozen natural food supermarkets throughout the whole of the USA at the time. Consumers, who had grown tired of processed foods and unhealthy pre-packed dinners flocked to buy Whole Foods' healthy, high-quality natural vegetables and groceries. In some cases the goods were more expensive but customers still bought them and became very emotionally attached to the company. Pleased by his customers' loyalty, John didn't yet know how important it would become.

Within a year of opening a spring flood almost wiped the whole business out. The shop was filled with water and mud and $400,000 of stock was lost. The company, which didn't have insurance to cover the damage, was brought to the brink of extinction. But that same day, loyal customers began to arrive with brushes and buckets and began work clearing the floor of the store that they loved. Even the bank lent a hand, rapidly arranging finance to keep the business afloat. Within 30 days Whole Foods Market was back up and running.

A growing business

John and his colleagues knew that they were on to a winner and looked to expand the business as quickly as possible. Its second store opened in 1982 and the business soon crossed state lines and has since moved into 38 separate US states. It did this through a mixture of organic growth but also acquisitions. Since its formation the business has made 16 major acquisitions buying companies such as Whole Food Company, Wellspring Grocery, Bread & Circus, Mrs. Gooch's, Fresh Fields, Bread of Life, Amrion, Merchant of Vino, Allegro Coffee, WholePeople.com, Nature's Heartland, Food for Thought, Harry's Farmers Market, Select Fish, Fresh & Wild and Wild Oats Markets.

Primarily these have been businesses which already closely match the outlook and ethics of Whole Foods. However, some have criticised Whole Foods, suggesting that as it grows it is likely to lose its ethical spirits. John denies that this has been the case and believes that big businesses can be a force for good. 'America has a romance with small businesses. And it has mistrust of the large businesses' he says. 'Whole Foods is out to prove that wrong. I don't see any inherent reason why corporations cannot be just as caring and responsible as small business.'

But as its business has expanded so has its range. It now offers a wide range of alcoholic drinks, meats, seafood, and even novel items such as yoga mats, as well as its traditional fare of organic fruit and vegetables. The business has grown and expanded while its founders have learned and adapted to the world around it. But John says that he never had any clearly defined plan for growing the business. 'Twenty-five years ago? No. I mean, we didn't have this in mind until a year or two before we opened the store up. There's a misconception somehow or another that there was some master plan and I've been fulfilling the master plan that we made up 25 years ago, but, I mean we've been... it's a discovery process. We've been making it up as we go along.'

'Whole Foods is out to prove that wrong. I don't see any inherent reason why corporations cannot be just as caring and responsible as small business.'

'We didn't have a plan. My girlfriend and I started it because we thought it would be fun. It was an adventure. Imagine a couple of young people that are taking backpacks and going to Europe and they know they've got three months over there but they don't necessarily have a complete itinerary worked out, exactly where they're going to go because they don't know who they're going to meet and they don't know what kind of adventures they're going to have. The plan will unfold as they go along.'

Where are they now?

In 1992, with 12 stores and $92m in sales, Whole Foods floated on the NASDAQ stock exchange to raise money for growth and acquisitions. Today Whole Foods Market is the world's largest retailer of natural and organic foods and has over 270 stores in North America and the United Kingdom. It also employs about 54,000 staff, or 'team members' as they are called. In 2009, the company had a market value of over £3.6bn. Importantly, Whole Foods has maintained its ethical stance with regards to farming and sustainable practices. It also engages and supports projects and charities that promote sustainable and equitable food production. Impressively while doing all this it has also remained a great place to work and was voted the fifth best company to work for by *Fortune* magazine.

John Mackey is still at the helm of the company, having made the transition from start-up entrepreneur to fully-fledged CEO. However, he now draws little money from the company and in 2006 announced that he was reducing his salary to $1 a year, was selling his stock portfolio to charity and was establishing a $100,000 emergency fund for staff facing personal problems. He wrote: 'I am now 53 years old and I have reached a place in my life where I no longer want to work for money, but simply for the joy of the work itself and to better answer the call to service that I feel so clearly in my own heart'.

John's lack of experience led him to try to do things which others might be afraid to do: inexperience can actually be an advantage not a drawback: 'I didn't have any biases. I didn't know how it was "supposed" to be done. I didn't have any preconceptions about how business had to be. This meant I made mistakes. We reinvented the wheel a few times but I didn't know what I couldn't do. And so I was free. We were free to be creative and inventive and to try new ways of doing things'.

Specsavers Optical Group

A better vision

Founders: **Mary and Doug Perkins**

Age of founders at start: **21**

Background: **Optometrists**

Year of foundation: **1984**

Business type: **Optical and hearing centres**

Country of foundation: **UK**

Countries now trading in: **UK, Republic of Ireland, Netherlands, Sweden, Norway, Denmark, Spain, Finland, Australia and New Zealand**

Current turnover: **£1.2bn (2008/2009)**

How They Started in Tough Times

Every once in a while an entrepreneur turns an industry on its head. Dame Mary Perkins is a perfect example. In 1984, she launched a business that changed the face of optometry for good. We might be used to visiting showrooms to purchase glasses these days, trying on frames at our leisure until we find the perfect fit, with every item clearly priced, but back in the early 1980s this was not the case. Before Mary launched Specsavers, consumers had very little choice or control when purchasing eyewear. The once state-owned optics business was going through deregulation in the early 1980s. Under its previous ownership, opticians could not even advertise their products or services. Indeed, before Specsavers came along, when you visited an optician they'd disappear out back to find a few pairs for you to try on. But Mary had a clear vision of how opticians could operate in order to deliver better value, choice and transparency to consumers. Driven by a mission of providing affordable eye care to all, she built the company around the idea of treating others respectfully. Twenty-five years later, she still describes her billion-pound international company, which she founded with her husband, Doug Perkins, as 'a family-owned business, with family values'. These days, Specsavers is a major success story, operating in 10 countries, with more than 1,300 stores worldwide, and turning over £1.2bn a year. Mary believes that much of her success has been driven by the preservation of the founding culture and ideals, and a focus on giving consumers real value and choice.

A visionary entrepreneur

Mary started her first business straight after leaving Cardiff University, where she completed her optics degree course and met her husband and fellow optometrist, Doug Perkins. Looking back, she says the idea of working for someone else didn't even cross her mind. Inspired by her father, who ran his own optical practice, Mary set up her first practice with Doug in a room above a baker's shop in 1965, sharing a waiting room with a doctor.

At the time, opticians didn't have products on display for customers to try on themselves; you could only try them on with the help of a member of staff. However, despite these hurdles, Mary was proactive in finding customers. Rather than sitting and waiting for business to come to

Visionary Dame Mary Perkins

her, she sought out new opportunities by visiting families and old people's homes in the neighbourhood and steadily growing her customer base.

With regulations restricting her from advertising, growth of the business relied solely on word of mouth recommendations. She built up a high standing in the community by delivering great service and by 'being nice to people'. It sounds simple, but this actually provided a key point of difference to the competition, says Mary, explaining that opticians had a reputation for being standoffish at the time.

> Mary built up a high standing in the community by delivering great service and by 'being nice to people'.

However, growing the business was hard work. Mary and Doug worked long hours, and balanced building a customer database and opening more practices with looking after three young children. But their hard work paid off. When they sold the business for a reported £2m in 1980 to a public pharmaceutical company, it comprised 23 practices in the west of England.

Mary recalls reaching a point where she did not want to grow the business any longer. There was growing uncertainty regarding the future of the industry at the time following Margaret Thatcher's appointment as prime minister in 1979, and increased talk of the deregulation of state-owned businesses. What's more, Mary felt that the managerial responsibilities involved with running a larger chain of shops would distract her from focusing on what the customers wanted and needed.

Starting again

Under the terms of the deal to sell their business, Mary was prohibited from working in the optics industry for three years, to prevent her from setting up a rival firm. So along with Doug and their children, she moved from Bristol to Guernsey, where her parents then lived. She spent three years working in a number of different roles, but keeping one eye on the optics industry, as it became clear that it was high on Mrs Thatcher's list for deregulation. The then prime minister wanted more openness and transparency in the industry, so that opticians could advertise and tell people exactly what they were offering.

With the deregulation of the industry paving the way for much greater flexibility, Mary and Doug felt sure that a service which gave consumers much more freedom and choice would be a big hit. Driven by the vision of giving customers a better deal, Specsavers launched from a table tennis table in a spare bedroom in Guernsey, where the head office is still based today. The first store was opened on Bond Street in Bristol on February 14, 1984.

They invested around £500,000 from the sale of their first business to get the fledgling Specsavers off the ground, buying equipment and sourcing products, establishing contacts and hiring staff. This investment also provided working capital to bring the business to profitability, which was achieved after just 12 months, despite the addition of four more stores in Guernsey, Swansea, Bath and Plymouth.

After being away from the industry for three years Mary admits to being a bit rusty to begin with. But although they had to start again from scratch, the key elements needed to get a start-up off the ground soon came back to them.

Blazing a trail

One of the key lessons Mary had learned was the importance of setting yourself apart from the competition by establishing unique selling points (USPs). As a new business, there was no point in merely copying a major player – you had to offer customers something different.

She identified a number of major problems with the way opticians were doing business at the time, and came up with a proposition that she felt was far more attractive to consumers. First of all, glasses were expensive. Mary believed that she would be able to bring prices down without compromising on quality by negotiating better buying terms and selling larger volumes. For example, instead of buying from wholesalers who added a significant mark-up on their prices, she went to factories directly.

'That first Specsavers Opticians in Bristol signalled the dawn of a new age in optics. The price displayed on the frames included the lenses – we called it Complete Price. Additional options were also prominently displayed, ensuring the customer knew exactly what they were going to pay before they got to the till.'

Another major problem she wanted to solve was the lack of transparency on pricing. She wanted to set up an optical business that focused on value-for-money, quality eye care, with clearly marked prices. People needed to know what they were going to pay before they got to the till. Mary says that after helping you choose your frame and lenses, you could get all the way to the till before finding out what your glasses would set you back. 'That first Specsavers Opticians in Bristol signalled the dawn of a new age in optics. The price displayed on the frames included the lenses – we called it Complete Price. Additional options were also prominently displayed, ensuring the customer knew exactly what they were going to pay before they got to the till.'

Until then, it had been harder for people to pick out frames that really suited them. She saw that people were quite capable of picking up a pair of glasses and trying them on themselves, and although different types of lenses carried different prices, this could be easily resolved by displaying a list of the different charges. At the time opticians were also charging higher prices for stronger prescriptions. This didn't seem fair to Mary, who strongly believed that everybody should pay the same for their lenses, no matter how bad their eyesight was. Critics said it couldn't be done, but this was the system that Specsavers introduced, and made a success.

Mary also spotted a growing trend of customers seeing eyewear as fashion accessories, and wanting glasses that looked great as well as performing their function as a visual aid. Like any disruptive business model, word soon spread, and once again Mary found that word of mouth referrals were a key growth driver in the early days. Specsavers was the first to introduce a showroom where people could walk in and try on frames, and Mary remembers customers travelling for miles to visit it. 'This was all part of our vision to provide fashionable and affordable eye care for everyone' she recalls.

A new model

Mary also devised a groundbreaking business model in the industry, which laid the foundations for a company with real scalability. 'Back in 1984 we realised that for opticians to really feel a part of their business, they had to have a stake in its ownership and profits' Mary says. As a result, they developed a joint venture partnership model that is still in place and driving growth today. 'Partnership is at the heart of our success and no matter what market we are in, it is the partnership with the professionals that allows the business to continue to grow' she adds.

Essentially, Mary believed that trained optometrists would work much harder, be far more motivated and deliver top-notch customer service as an entrepreneur running their own business rather than as an employee. She did not want to run another chain operation with a head office employing different opticians all over the country. Instead, she wanted opticians to share ownership of their stores on a 50:50 basis with her company. They had to put in half the money to get their shop off the ground – the model that still exists today. Meanwhile, Specsavers provides support services in areas such as marketing, accounting, IT, sourcing products, manufacturing and training. This removes a lot of the stress of getting a start-up off the ground for the optician owners at each store. This then enables them to focus on the day to day running of the business and delivering great customer service – something that Mary and Doug had found more difficult as the sole owners of a chain.

Rose-tinted glasses: Mary always wanted to support young, independent optometrists

'Partnership is at the heart of our success and no matter what market we are in, it is the partnership with the professionals that allows the business to continue to grow.'

Through this model, each store is run by someone entrepreneurial (rather than an employed manager) who is invested in the success of the business. They have put their own money in, depend on its success to make a living and are incentivised to grow it, look after the customers and motivate staff.

Selling the vision

This is not the type of model that an entrepreneur can launch and roll out straight away, though. Mary saw that to get qualified opticians to buy into her vision (of lowering prices and selling higher volumes) she first had to prove the concept. 'We had to get through that first year successfully so that we had some satisfactory figures to show other opticians so that they would join the group' she recalls.

During the first year she and Doug set up five entirely company owned stores. They had to prove that the model of dropping prices and selling larger volumes was commercially viable if they were going to get opticians to invest their own money in the business. Up until that point, Mary says opticians would typically see around 20 people a week but would make this sustainable by charging high prices. Specsavers wanted to slash the prices and treble the number of customers.

'We had to get through that first year successfully so that we had some satisfactory figures to show other opticians so that they would join the group.'

Crucially, they had to prove that opticians would be able to make a good living this way. Those first five company sites gave them the figures and profits on paper that proved that this was a good way of doing business. What's more, they knew that the first partners would be taking these figures to their banks to get their loans to invest in the joint venture partnership.

Although Mary didn't want to run her own chain again, it had to be done to kick start her new business. The first joint venture sites opened in 1985, although Mary says that convincing new partners of the merits of the venture was a challenge, at first. Most newly qualified opticians either went into employment in a large optical chain or set up their own small independent practices. However, they argued that by following the Specsavers model (dropping their prices and increasing their customer base) they would grow the market and increase repeat business from existing customers. They attempted to convince joint ventures that they would have a bright future with Specsavers, and a valuable business that they would one day be able to sell.

Their pitch was clearly compelling. Growth was slow but steady, and by the end of the first year of launching the partnership model, they had more than 20 partners on board with their own stores.

Leading by innovation

Mary says that their passion to give consumers a better deal in optics was what drove them to set up and grow the business, rather than financial gain, and she believes this has been a major factor in the company's success. Indeed, Specsavers has frequently ploughed profits back into the business to improve its products and services.

Ultimately, Mary and Doug have remained faithful to their founding vision, and a business formula that Mary describes as win-win. They have continued to lead by innovation and drive the company forwards by continually investing in state of the art eye equipment, product innovation, staff training and customer satisfaction research. The company diversified into hearing centres in 2002 and in 2008, a new website enabled customers to buy online. Specsavers is also now the largest provider of home-delivery contact lenses in Europe.

The company has received a lot of recognition for this innovation, collecting numerous awards including many for its famous 'Should have gone to Specsavers' advertising campaign. Specsavers has been voted as the most trusted optician brand by *Reader's Digest* eight times, while Mary was made a Dame in the Queen's Birthday Honours List in 2007, the same year that she was named the Most Outstanding Businesswoman at the National Business Awards.

Where are they now?

International expansion began with the Netherlands in 1997, and Specsavers now operates in 10 countries across the globe. More than 2,000 partners run more than 1,300 stores worldwide (the UK has 620 optical stores and 119 hearing stores, which accounted for £828.1m of sales in 2008/2009). The company employs over 26,000 staff around the world (including over 500 at its Guernsey base) and has more than 18 million customers on its database.

Even after 25 years, Specsavers is still very much a family business. Doug and Mary's three children are all involved in the company – their son John is joint managing director, daughter Julie is country manger in the Netherlands and their other daughter Cathy is an audit manager.

Of course, more competitors have sprung up over the years, but Specsavers was the trailblazer and retains a leading 35% share of the UK market. The company has continued to thrive in spite of the recession, which Mary believes comes down to its emphasis on offering customers value for money. 'Against the backdrop of what is turning out to be the worst global economic depression since the 1930s, with extremely difficult trading conditions, we have spent the best part of the past two years spearheading our launch and expansion into Australasia.'

'That we achieved this in the face of strong competition is testament to the professionalism and commitment of the entire Specsavers team, and particularly our joint venture partners who rose to the challenge by extending their opening hours, providing excellent service and offering consistent value for money' Mary says.

The company remains totally committed to the 'family values' ethos and treating others as you wish to be treated. This was formalised in 2008 when Specsavers signed up to a global ethical trading policy. The business also supports numerous charities. Since 2003 a quarter of a million glasses have been collected and recycled by Specsavers stores for Vision Aid Overseas for use in developing countries, and the company recently raised £130,000 for Diabetes UK.

Moonpig

Capitalising on cards

Founder: Nick Jenkins

Age of founder at start: 32

Background: Sugar trading

Year of foundation: 1999

Business type: Personalised greeting cards

Country of foundation: UK

Countries now trading in: Worldwide

Current turnover and profit: £20.9m and £6.7m

Nick Jenkins' business idea was simple. He would take the bog standard greetings card that has been around since Victorian times, and create a website where customers could personalise their own humorous cards. With even a miniscule share of the £1.7bn greetings card industry, he, and his customers, would be laughing. The problem was, just as Nick launched Moonpig.com in 2000, the dotcom bubble dramatically burst, leaving many an online venture dead in the water. Like many entrepreneurs at this time, Nick had a great idea, but struggled to get the funding he needed; Moonpig couldn't have launched in tougher conditions. Ten years on, and several rounds of funding later, the business is not only known for its cards, but also for being one of the few dotcoms from the turn of the century that has not only survived, but thrived.

Adding value

After graduating with a degree in Russian from Birmingham University, Nick Jenkins embarked on a career in sugar trading, moving to Moscow and working for Marc Rich, the Swiss-based commodity trading firm. Later he participated in the management buyout of the company. By 1998, after eight years in the industry, he decided to head back to the UK, prompted to some degree by finding a death threat from a former client nailed to his apartment door, but mainly motivated by the desire to start a business of his own.

To hone his business knowledge, Nick spent a year doing an MBA at Cranfield University and during the course, developed a number of start-up ideas. Nick's interest had been sparked by a new breed of companies, dubbed dotcoms, which seemed to be gaining ground and making headlines. He recognised the potential that online businesses had, and was sure that this would be the route to his business success.

While at Cranfield, Nick researched different business models carefully. He decided he wanted to take an existing product, and somehow transform and improve it, using the internet and existing technology. What he did not want to do was

Nick Jenkins wanted to improve an existing product, and take it onto the web

just sell an existing high street product at a lower margin, as so many dotcoms seemed to be doing. He reasoned that this model was too easy to copy, meaning that competitors could easily enter your market – the result being that the cheapest would win, making it an unattractive business venture. Nick also wanted to make sure whatever he sold would be easy to deliver: it must fit through a letterbox. He also wanted a business that would hold only minimal stock.

Nick wanted to take an existing product, and somehow transform and improve it, using the internet and existing technology.

Thinking his business proposition through in this way helped Nick rule out a number of possibilities, and made sure he was confident in the model he had chosen. With these very specific criteria in place, Nick came up with the idea of an online greeting cards business. He had often personalised humorous birthday cards for his friends using Tippex and a marker pen, and struck on the idea of combining the internet with digital printing technology to make it possible for customers to create their own personalised cards online. He thought customers would love to personalise the captions on existing, bestselling greeting cards with their friends' names, ages, in greetings or in jokes.

Nick worked out that he could create a profitable business where customers bought a single personalised card, with prices starting at £2.99 plus postage. The cards would be sent out on the same day, either directly to the recipient, or to the sender to pass on to someone else. Judging from the positive reaction he had had to his own rudimentary efforts he was confident that the idea would catch on. Operating as an online business, he would also be collecting payments upfront, leading him to think that cash flow would be good.

During his last weeks at Cranfield, Nick took the idea to Paperlink, a successful greeting card publishing company without an online presence, and offered them a small stake in the company if they would let the as-yet-unnamed company use their greeting card designs. Miraculously they agreed and this was enough to convince Nick that the idea he had was worth pursuing.

What's in a name?

With an idea in place, Nick's next step was to name his greetings card business. He knew word-of-mouth would be essential to promote the business so he needed a name that was really catchy. It couldn't be more than two syllables and needed to be phonetic, so it would be easy to remember, and easy to spell. He also decided not to use any symbols in the name – hyphens or numerals – as these could be passed on incorrectly in conversations.

His initial choice was Splat.com, but it had already been taken, along with every other two-syllable dotcom domain name he could think of. After several frustrating days of searching through the domain name registry, Nick entered the name Moonpig, which had been his nickname at school. It was available, and seemed to have all the right attributes of being phonetic, simple, and a bit cheeky which reflected the cards he would sell.

Nick knew word-of-mouth would be essential to promote the business so he needed a name that was really catchy. It couldn't be more than two syllables and needed to be phonetic, so it would be easy to remember, and easy to spell.

Creating a logo was the next step. Nick knew a strong visual sign would help to increase recognition among customers. 'The logo had to reinforce the memory of the name. When customers see the logo and hear the name they will never forget it' says Nick. For some companies, creating a logo can be an expensive exercise, but from the word go, Nick knew he had to keep a sharp eye on costs. At this stage, he hadn't even worked out how much he would need to launch the business and what, if any, investment he would be seeking. So he commissioned a cartoonist to design the Moonpig logo, for around £200 for three days' work. The logo turned out to be very memorable: a grinning pig in a space helmet, with a moon in the corner. Moonpig.com was born on 4 October 1999.

Nick knew it wasn't enough to have a strong brand: 'a key part of branding is to ensure that the product lives up to the brand.' So from day one he ensured they didn't compromise on quality: 'we have always picked the best card designs available and printed them on the best quality board. Customers are not interested in the technology they are interested in the reaction the card gets when the recipient opens it'.

Ready for take-off

Nick calculated he would need at least £200,000 to buy the necessary printer equipment and software – digital technology was still in development and an expensive proposition at the time. He would also need cash to pay for premises that were big enough to house the equipment – he had found a small, ground floor office space in Chelsea that would fit the bill, but did not come cheap. While property in this area was expensive, the office was only five minutes from Nick's flat and upon his return from Russia, he'd decided he did not want a long commute to work. He also needed to buy in the skills needed to turn his idea into reality. He needed to pay for a web development agency and to hire staff. His first employee was Jo Foley, a recent History of Art graduate.

Nick ploughed £160,000 of his own money (from his share of the Marc Rich sugar trading management buy-out) into the business and raised a further £125,000 from three friends who were keen to invest in Moonpig. He didn't actually ask these friends to invest – they heard Nick talking about his idea and wanted in. The three friends were all experienced investors, sufficiently wealthy for it not to be an issue if the business collapsed. This was perfect for Nick, who was keen to get the website off the ground, before securing venture capital, as having a product and customers would help to make the business a more attractive investment. Many a dotcom had secured huge amounts of funding in recent months and Moonpig aimed to repeat that success.

Immediately after registering the company in October 1999, Nick hired a website design agency to help him build and design the site, with the aim of going live by Christmas 1999. In the end making the site proved more difficult than Nick had expected as the agency did not meet his expectations, meaning the site was late, only ready to launch in April 2000. Nick held a launch party and invested in some PR to publicise the business and drum up initial sales. Even then, the website crashed at the launch party!

Fed up with the inconsistent service from the website agency, Nick decided to bring the whole IT function in-house and hired Jay Jetley, a software developer, to build a completely new site, which finally launched to the public in July 2000.

In orbit

At the time of the launch of the second site, the business had nine employees. As well as the graphic designer and programmer, Nick had hired two more people to fill similar roles, a general assistant, a marketing director, a bookkeeper and a customer service assistant. They conducted a small marketing campaign to generate some initial sales, which Nick admits was pretty hit and miss. He tried a number of affiliate marketing deals, some PR and invested in search engine optimisation, but none of these were as effective as the power of viral marketing. In fact, Moonpig's profile was most effectively raised through word-of-mouth – people received a card, were taken by it, went online and ordered one for someone else. While this 'customer gets customer' form of marketing was working, sales in the first year were slower than Nick had anticipated, 'steady rather than remarkable', he says. He remembers how he used to put the orders taken each day in a bag and cycle to the post office himself to send them.

Although it was working, word-of-mouth alone was not enough to grow the business as quickly as Nick had envisaged in his revised business plan. They weren't helped by the fact that broadband technology, which customers needed to access the site properly, was still quite slow and clunky. This meant Moonpig lost a lot of customers who didn't wait for the site to load, or were frustrated with the time it took to make a card.

In the business's first year of trading, it distributed around 40,000 cards, and made a loss of around £1m on sales of £90,000. The losses were mostly incurred on overheads, such as staff, printing equipment, software development and marketing.

Poor timing for launch

However, between starting the business and seeking venture capital funding, the climate for investment had turned distinctly sour – in fact, Nick's timing couldn't have been worse. In May 2000, internet fashion retailer Boo.com had declared itself bankrupt after burning through £120m of venture capital, and companies such as Lastminute.com, which had floated on the stock market and reached incredible valuations, were seeing their share prices collapse.

'The timing for launching the business and seeking funds was appalling as the bottom had fallen out of the market,' recalls Nick. 'But in hindsight, had I raised VC funding [at the start] we probably would have been pressured to spend too quickly on land-grabbing activities, and we would probably have gone out of business very quickly.'

By 2002, the economy was slowly starting to emerge from the shadows of the dotcom bust but things were still bleak. In a drastic bid to cut costs and reduce its overheads, Nick had no option but to carry out a round of redundancies.

'It wasn't such a painful experience as it could have been,' he recalls. 'Having assessed my options for some time as the recession continued, it meant we gave our staff plenty of warning and all those who left managed to secure jobs elsewhere. The advantage of starting and trying to grow a business during a downturn is that it couldn't get any worse. If we could make our business model work in those conditions, then we believed it could only get better when the economy picked up.'

'The advantage of starting and trying to grow a business during a downturn is that it couldn't get any worse. If we could make our business model work in those conditions, then we believed it could only get better when the economy picked up.'

Capacity also proved problematic in the early years. Unsurprisingly, Moonpig's business flourished at peak seasonal times of the year, such as Christmas and Easter – the business would typically sell up to 15,000 cards a day in the run-up to Christmas for example. But it was a different story at other times of the year, when the business would only sell between 1,500 and 2,000 cards a day. It meant Nick had to be flexible and creative when it came to office space. At Moonpig's busiest times, when its office was near capacity with people stuffing envelopes, many other employees worked from home to free up desk space.

Funding issues

Still on the hunt for investment, Nick realised he would need to go the extra mile to convince outside investors to part with their money in light of the economic conditions. He needed to rewrite the business plan, to show they wouldn't spend millions on land-grabbing marketing campaigns, and would be smart in their investments. Nick was confident the strength of the business lay in the product itself. He had always been convinced that the product would spread virally, but he did need capital to cover the running costs of the business while it grew to profitability, and the point where it was generating more cash than it was spending.

Nick had originally anticipated that the business would break-even in year

The Dangers of the Internet

Colin only logged on to check his email. 4 hours later, he had bought a C-reg Vauxhall Astra and married a 17-year-old Texan.

Inspired by cards he'd made for friends, Nick wanted customers to be able to personalise the cards

three, but in fact, it took five years and six further rounds of fundraising from private investors for Moonpig to reach profitability. After sending potential investors a personalised card most of them grasped the concept very quickly. Nick also injected more of his own cash at each round to encourage the other investors. 'Luckily I hadn't invested all of my cash in the first round of investment,' acknowledges Nick. 'Following on with my own money at each round made it easier to convince other investors to part with their cash, as it underlined my commitment to the business.'

> 'Following on with my own money at each round made it easier to convince other investors to part with their cash, as it underlined my commitment to the business.'

He admits that it was a struggle getting new investors on board and keeping existing ones. In total, the business raised £2.5m between 1999 and 2003 and Nick jokes that by this time, everything that was not bolted down to the office floor had gone. One of the major investors was Duncan Spence, a serial investor in the greetings card industry.

Completing several rounds of funding taught Nick some important lessons, not least how to structure a deal. From experience, he believes that it can be all too easy to give away too much company equity in the early days to secure funding. 'I learnt a lot in terms of how to structure a deal from a legal and shareholder point of view' he says.

Despite the ups and downs he experienced with funding, Nick maintains the first four years of the business were more exciting than daunting. By 2004, it seemed that all the hard work was finally paying off – sales were continuing to grow and the lines between loss and break-even were blurring. Sales had grown steadily from the beginning, based largely on word of mouth and referrals. As every product was unique and was branded with the Moonpig.com domain name, the more it sold the more customers it attracted. By 2005, the business was making a profit.

Over the moon

Moonpig's profitability coincided with a turning point in the business, when it branched out into different card designs in late 2004. As well as offering personalised cards, Moonpig started creating cards that looked like spoof magazine covers, such as *OK* and *Hello!*.

The idea for the cover spoofs was inspired by a card that Nick had received for his birthday, where a friend had done a mock cover in the style of *Country Life* magazine.

The addition of spoof covers took advantage of the growth in broadband internet connections and popularity of digital cameras. Customers could now upload their own photos to Moonpig's website, and use one of 200 templates to create their own card. Within a year of launch, these covers were accounting for 20% of the company's turnover, which had grown to around £1.2m, double that of the previous year.

As well as expanding its product base, Moonpig made the decision to expand overseas, starting with Australia. Nick says it was the logical step towards growth as the country is culturally very similar to UK card buyers. The distance made it impossible for Moonpig to import cards from the UK – it would have taken up to five days for a card to arrive and the postage costs would have been too expensive, so they set up production down under.

The introduction of spoof magazine covers proved a hit, and soon accounted for 20% of turnover

Where are they now?

Moonpig now accounts for over 90% of the online greetings card market and now sells more than 10 million cards a year which, if laid out end to end, would stretch from London to Moscow. More than 2.5 million people visited the site in 2008. Despite the onset of the credit crunch, spend per customer on Moonpig products has not changed. In February 2009, it sent out 99,000 cards in one day, a record number. Moonpig's profits had more than doubled from £2.54m to £6.7m during the financial year to April 2009. Nick believes the continued success of the business is down to the fact that it has developed a product that is different from those available on the high street.

In 2007 Nick promoted Iain Martin from the role of Commercial Director to Managing Director with responsibility for the day to day management of the business. At the same time Nick took on the role of Chairman to focus on long-term strategy. Jo Foley, the first ever employee, is now the Marketing Director.

By mid-2006 it was clear that the Chelsea office would not cope with the Christmas demand and the production side was moved to Guernsey. Recently the company opened a new 33,000 sq ft factory which is able to produce several hundred thousand cards per day.

While the company now has slightly more to spend on marketing than it did in the early days, and uses daytime television and street hoardings in their advertising, many of its customers are still acquired through viral marketing and word-of-mouth. 'The original premise when we set up the company was that if the product was good enough, our customers would sell it for us, and that's certainly been the case,' Nick says.

FOOD

Jane Asher Cakes

Rising to the challenge

Founder: Jane Asher

Age of founder at start: 44

Background: Actress and writer

Year of foundation: 1989

Business type: Cake making and sugarcraft

Country of foundation: UK (cakes), worldwide (sugarcraft online)

Countries now trading in: UK

Current turnover: £500,000

Jane Asher needs little introduction. A television and film actress, she has two BAFTA nominations and a Sony award to her name and has starred opposite the likes of Michael Caine and Laurence Olivier. But Jane's talents don't stop at acting – she has also built a formidable career creating fantastic party cakes and sugarcraft earning her the title of the 'guru of British baking'. Her timing was questionable though, as she decided to start a cake making business in 1989 when the UK was on the brink of recession. However, by maintaining her own high standards for 20 years, and keeping a tight rein on the purse strings, Jane Asher Cakes is now recognised as a market leader in its field.

Homemade talent

Jane's love of cake making stemmed from an early age, when she used to help her mother bake in their kitchen. Later, as a young mum herself, cake making became a hobby as she spent hours making novelty cakes in the shape of animals and fairytale characters for her three children. She also attended evening classes in general cookery offered by her local council. Her cakes were so creative and unusual that a friend suggested she try to get a book of her designs published.

Actress Jane Asher's party cake books were so popular she decided to make it into a business

Jane had been acting from an early age, and had established herself as a successful actress. She thought her profile might help her get published, but she was turned down flat by several publishers. She explains this by saying, in those days, 'it wasn't the done thing for actresses to write books'. It took many approaches to find a publisher, but eventually Pelham Books signed her up in 1982, and her first book, *Jane Asher's Party Cakes* was published.

The book was a surprise bestseller and other publications soon followed, as well as a cookery television series. Jane's cakes were becoming increasingly popular, and she started noticing the effect on the baking industry. 'Cakes in those days were mostly pretty ordinary, and it wasn't until I wrote my first book, that bakeries began to make them more unusual, more personal and funny' says Jane. 'It was when I began to see the cakes from my books being reproduced in bakeries in London and overseas that I decided to do it myself and start the business' she explains. She wanted to open a cake shop, which specialised in bespoke, 'couture' cakes, made to the specifications of every client, and using her innovative designs.

When Jane began discussing the idea with friends, she met with negativity – a lot of people tried to warn her off setting up a business during such tough economic conditions.

But when she began discussing the idea with friends, she met with negativity – she remembers a lot of people tried to warn her off setting up a business during such tough economic conditions. The mid-1980s were characterised by an increase in consumer spend and a property boom but by the end of the decade, inflation had reached double digits. Like many entrepreneurs however, she paid no attention and carried on with her plans regardless.

Setting up shop

Jane began by writing a simple business plan, with the help of a good friend – Tim Coates, the former managing director at bookseller Waterstone's – although, she remembers the plan was 'sheer invention, really', something she was not proud of but believed was realistic. She then found a potential premises for the cake shop, in an old art gallery in Chelsea, near to where she lived. In order to refit the shop and turn the basement into a kitchen, she would need to raise substantial funds. So, armed with her business plan, she walked up the road to her local bank and there and then persuaded the bank manager to lend her the money – something that she admits just wouldn't happen these days. The bank manager was able to make a personal decision on the risk of the loan and lend her about £80,000.

She believes that raising this finance was very much down to luck and the fact that she had a 'sparky and rather bold' local bank manager. She also acknowledges that her name and reputation helped considerably – the bank manager even mentioned that his wife had read her books.

The Chelsea shop has been in the same location for two decades

Armed with her business plan, Jane walked up the road to her local bank and there and then persuaded the bank manager to lend her the money.

A new market at a tough time

Jane planned to open Jane Asher Party Cakes in 1990 – at a time when it looked as though a recession was looming on the horizon. The recession was officially declared in January 1991, after starting in late 1990. Unfortunately Jane's business model meant that the cakes would be priced depending on the time taken to make the cakes, meaning they could vary from the affordable to the expensive. It was a tough time to launch a luxury goods business, as consumers were cutting back on such items. 'My business was classed as a luxury product, and, although people will always buy a cake for a special occasion, it is an area where they can cut down, and buy one a little cheaper than when times are good' acknowledges Jane. It seemed that all the odds – and the economic climate – were stacked against her, but Jane was determined to succeed and believed that her product was new, exciting and special.

'My business was classed as a luxury product, and, although people will always buy a cake for a special occasion, it is an area where they can cut down, and buy one a little cheaper than when times are good.'

To her advantage, Jane was entering what she describes as a 'pretty new market' and was planning to develop her cake making business in a direction that few, if any, of the potential competitors were taking. 'There were very few businesses of a similar type around, and none that would do everything we were capable of' she says. 'I used artists, for instance, to reproduce photographs, newspapers or paintings onto cakes.' In the early 90s, this creative decoration was new and exciting, and Jane hoped that her bespoke designs would generate enough interest to help the business take off, even in a harsh economic climate.

Beginning to bake

Jane kitted out the shop, and put in a new kitchen. She then needed to hire cooks and front-of-house serving staff before she could open. During the interview process, she employed some unusual interviewing techniques. At the time that she was looking for employees she was appearing in the comedy of manners, *School for Scandal*, at the National Theatre and interviewed prospective staff in her dressing room in full 18th-century costume. It was there that she hired David Trumper and Ruth Clark, who now manage the business for Jane. She was looking to employ staff who were not only trustworthy but who would develop as the business did – indeed, David started off in a junior role but soon rose up the ranks. Jane was very much one of the team from the beginning, and helped with the baking and decorating, although she had to juggle her 'other' career too: 'I never really stopped my "real" job of acting altogether, so I could never be there full time,' says Jane.

With staff in place, and the shop kitted out, they were just missing the vital ingredient: customers. Jane remembers spending the first few days staring at the telephone, wondering how on earth people would find the business or even hear about it. She believed it was a question of gritting your teeth and using any means possible to let the world know you're there. They relied on footfall from the street initially, but after a couple of months, Jane assembled a portfolio of pictures of her cakes and sent an energetic and charismatic friend around lots of hotels, restaurants, party organisers and caterers to show them what she could do. As Jane says, 'that really got the ball rolling.'

Learning from mistakes

Initially, Jane took no deposit when customers ordered cakes but she soon realised this was a big mistake. Every now and then a customer would cancel the order well after she had begun to make it (sometimes a broken engagement, for example, could mean an expensive wedding cake had been made for nothing) or they would just fail to turn up to collect their cake. 'We learnt to take a 50% deposit AND to sketch the cake customers wanted, together with a detailed description which they had to read through and agree to,' explains Jane. This also helped stop the occasional problem when a lack of communication meant the customer had had a very different idea of what their finished cake would be like than Jane and the other bakers had. Jane remembers an interesting moment when an American customer, who had asked for an exact copy of the Parthenon on top of her cake, exclaimed, on coming to collect it, 'Oh God! It's all broken!!' Once Jane explained that that was how the real Parthenon was, she was quite happy.

Pricing cakes was also a challenge. Jane admits she 'underdid prices like mad' at the start and did not take into account the hidden costs of what she was producing. Her products were labour-intensive and inevitably expensive, and while people were surprised by the prices she had to charge, Jane always tried to keep them as low as she possibly could.

Spreading the word

Undoubtedly Jane's name and reputation gave her a platform to spread the word about her business. She acknowledges that having a certain amount of fame can help get your business noticed, but she's adamant that that's not enough: 'a brand is only as good as its last product'. It's a double-edged sword: 'you do get coverage but you also have to ensure you follow it up with first-rate goods and quality. It will be remembered if one of our cakes isn't absolutely the best.'

Jane acknowledges that having a certain amount of fame can help get your business noticed, but that's not enough: 'a brand is only as good as its last product'.

As an established actress, Jane's fame meant that she could get away with spending very little on marketing. In the early days she used editorial, television shows and word of mouth to publicise her business and her portfolio that had grown to around 1,000 cake designs. 'I was able to achieve publicity pretty easily, which was an initial help in getting us going,' she says. 'This was partly because the product is so photogenic, but also because, as an actress, I had a known profile and was able to capitalise on that.'

Jane's cakes received some great reviews during the early and mid-1990s, appearing in magazines such as *House and Garden*, *Good Housekeeping*, *BBC Good Food*, Sainsbury's magazine, and countless others. This exposure, which specifically focused on her cakes, and not her acting, directly generated business for the cake shop.

Even if you don't have the added advantage of being a celebrity, she says it's important to promote your business whenever you get the chance and particularly in a downturn. She believes that keeping your company's name in front of consumers' minds is paramount in a recession, as you have to fight harder for your market share.

The need to diversify

By the end of the first year of trading, the business had reached a turnover of £150,000; profit, however, was much harder to come by. Jane had to pay back the large bank loan, and bespoke cake making, by nature, required very high labour costs. While the UK headed deeper and deeper into a recession, it became all too clear that her 'couture' cakes were not going to keep the business going and Jane realised she had to generate income from somewhere else. She advises budding entrepreneurs to 'be ready to diversify – it's something I did after bitter experience. You may need to step sideways depending on the market – my initial core business of expensive cakes wasn't going to work on its own'. So a year after starting, Jane pursued various avenues to try and keep her bespoke cake making business afloat.

Initially, Jane wanted to start selling bakeware and cake decorations, alongside her cakes, but knew this would require a large investment of stock. Soon after starting, Jane also realised the business needed more kitchen space in the basement. To solve this problem, she leased the property adjacent to the cake shop, and knocked through the basement to create a larger kitchen. Since she didn't have the money to invest in stock, she turned the shop space above the kitchen into a tea room, where people could sample her cakes with a cup of tea or coffee. Listed in guide books, the tearoom proved very popular with tourists and

From the outset, Jane wanted to diversify into sugarcraft, but had to wait until she had enough money to afford stock

celebrities alike. It brought in just about enough money to cover the additional rent, and pay for the extra kitchen space in the basement, but never made money in its own right. Jane says that she always viewed it as a means to an end – 'I always intended to change the upstairs use into selling baking and decorating supplies – far more suitable to the cake business'.

Jane also looked for other ways to expand the business. One option was to sell her range of cakes in supermarkets – which was only made possible by her celebrity status. Jane had originally considered Marks & Spencer, who were interested, but Jane turned them down, as they offered her a 'very, very tough deal'. Sainsbury's then jumped at the chance to work with her and in 1992, started to stock the Jane Asher brand of cakes. The supermarket also sponsored a twice-weekly cookery slot on GMTV that Jane would present. Jane admits that this partnership 'really saved the business'. After a few years of a fruitful partnership, however, she withdrew her cakes from the supermarkets, as she felt the product was becoming mass produced in a way she felt she couldn't put her name to.

Jane also launched a website in 1993, which helped generate more publicity for the business. It also meant that Jane Asher Cakes could start selling cakes by mail order, ordered on the website and delivered all over the UK. This also helped to underwrite the couture cakes that Jane admits were incredibly hard to make money on.

Even with various facets to the business, it took a few years to break even. Jane says that cake making 'is a very silly trade, we spend hours doing these things that are demolished in seconds'. She believes that the cake making business is definitely not something to go into purely for the money – even today, she admits, the business has only registered a very small profit.

Trading through recessions

In the early days, Jane's business was more of a passion than a money-spinning venture, but she learnt quickly what it would take to keep her business afloat. 'Starting and growing a business in recessions is tricky,' she says. 'One of the advantages is that if you can start in those conditions, then it can only get better. But cut costs wherever you can.'

She adds that before spending any money, it's important to ask yourself whether you really need to spend it, as too often businesses are not as pared down as they may think they are. Ensuring you are getting the best deals from your suppliers is also key, especially as costs of raw ingredients are constantly rising. She believes that it is all too easy for costs to creep into your budget so it is really worthwhile regularly checking through what you are spending.

She also believes it is important to never compromise on quality – even when times are hard. She is proud of the fact that her business today is still very close to the original concept and believes it is what continues to set her apart from the competition. 'There are ways of getting round things that would make our labour costs much cheaper but there are some things we've decided to keep as we believe they make a difference' she says. 'For example, we still use fresh eggs, butter and real brandy in our cakes – you'd be surprised how many well known bakeries use bought-in mixes or dried eggs.'

'Starting and growing a business in recessions is tricky. One of the advantages is that if you can start in those conditions, then it can only get better. But cut costs wherever you can.'

For budding entrepreneurs thinking of starting up in a tough economic climate, Jane strongly recommends planning ahead, and having contingency plans in place. She also believes it's vital to surround yourself with good, professional advice, something she regrets not doing enough of. Jane is now an advocate of business support organisations and networks, which can help with guidance and make you feel as if you are not alone.

For Jane, diversifying was the only way of keeping her business afloat, as she recognised her initial business idea just wasn't viable on its own. 'I compare it to couture dresses – they are seriously expensive, but hardly ever make the designers any money – it's the perfumes and off-the-rack ranges that underwrite the couture side' explains Jane. 'Just like us, it's the mail order, simpler cakes and the sugarcraft sales that enable us to keep up the very high standards of the handmade and decorated cakes that are our core business, and have been from the beginning.'

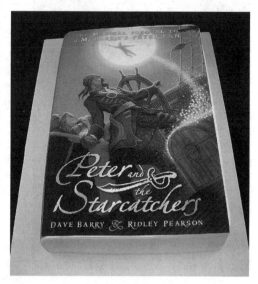

Jane began by painting photographs onto cakes, but now new technology means she can print onto icing

Where are they now?

In 1998 Jane moved ahead with her original plans, and closed the tea room, opening a sugarcraft and bakeware business (sugarcraft is the art of creating flowers and decorations out of sugar, and painting them with exquisite detail). She renamed the business Jane Asher Party Cakes & Sugarcraft, to reflect the change. 'Diversifying into sugarcraft sales presented new business opportunities' explains Jane. 'Unlike the cakes, which are limited to UK sales, sugarcraft could be sold all over the world, meaning we could continue to grow.'

After her experience with the quality of the 'Jane Asher' branded cakes sold in supermarkets, Jane was wary about lending her name to other products. However, in 2000 she partnered with Victoria Foods to produce a range of cake mixes. Initially, she had her reservations: 'the image of cake mixes was very poor in those days – probably rightly – and I felt that, far from my brand bringing the Victoria Foods mixes up, their products could drag down my brand' she recalls. It was only after

Jane's cakes continue to be popular, and although there may be tough ecomonic times, there will always be weddings!

Victoria Foods produced mixes from her own recipes that Jane was convinced that they were of a high enough quality to warrant the Jane Asher name. She is now extremely proud of them.

Jane also launched a range of gift food and bakeware for the homeware department at retailers Debenhams. Her association with Victoria Foods and Debenhams put her at number three on a list of Television Celebrity Brands, compiled by the *Radio Times* in 2003, with an estimated brand value of £41m.

With birthdays, weddings and anniversaries to celebrate, cake making is, and will remain, big business. Jane even made the wedding cake of at least one of the entrepreneurs in this book! The British cake market was worth close to £1.8bn in 2007, a figure that is forecast to grow by almost 5% by 2012. The recession of the late Noughties has lead to an increase in home-baking; and with a strong brand, Jane believes she is in a good position to take advantage of this market growth.

Charlton House Catering

The taste of success

Founder: **Robyn Jones**	
Age of founder at start: **30**	
Background: **Chef and catering manager**	
Year of foundation: **1991**	
Business type: **Contract caterer**	
Country of foundation: **UK**	
Countries now trading in: **UK**	
Current turnover and profit: **£81.3m and net profit of £2.1m (to end March 2009)**	

Robyn Jones wanted to shake up the world of corporate catering. Sick of the underwhelming food provided by large multinational catering companies, and faced with redundancy, Robyn set up Charlton House at the height of the recession in 1991. Today, the business, which provides staff catering services to blue chip organisations, is one of the UK's fastest growing independent contract caterers. The company has a turnover of £81.3m, with clients including the UK corporate headquarters of BUPA, Sony and Network Rail. Not bad for a company that started off with an old wallpaper pasting table as a desk and banana boxes as filing cabinets.

Redundancy breeds an entrepreneur

Robyn Jones's first taste of the catering industry was as a humble dishwasher. Seeing how a kitchen worked ignited a passion in her, and she decided to attend catering college in Derbyshire. On graduating, she became a cook at a private school in Suffolk and progressed to manager. Robyn gathered a lot of experience over the next eight years, working for a couple of dominant contract caterers, as well as a short stint on the Potato Marketing Board.

In 1990, Robyn joined construction firm Higgs and Hill, to help establish a contract catering division alongside the existing business. Yet in 1991, just a year into the job, she was made redundant from her £30,000-a-year position as the firm decided it could no longer invest in the new division. It couldn't have come at a worse time as the UK was in the throes of recession.

Redundancy was a big blow to Robyn's confidence as she'd only been in the job for a year. To make matters worse, Robyn and her husband Tim, an accountant, had recently moved house and taken on a large mortgage. She went for several interviews for other jobs but says her heart really wasn't in it. She really didn't want to work for another large catering firm, and deep down knew she wanted to go solo. Robyn had worked out that she would only need to earn between £10,000 and £15,000 to make ends meet. With this in mind, and with the backing of her husband, she decided to start her own staff catering company. She remembers the decision clearly: whilst gardening on a summer Sunday afternoon, she turned to Tim and said 'If I am ever going to set up on my own, now is the time to do it.'

'It may have seemed like lunacy at the time, given the economic climate and our lack of financial security, but we had a clear vision of how we could make it a success.'

Robyn Jones founded Charlton House in a quest for quality food

Robyn wasn't put off by the recession. She knew that many successful entrepreneurs had started during a downturn and believed it was a great time to get into a market and create a competitive advantage while other people might be put off by the increased risk. Robyn believes that that little 'edge of fear' when starting in a downturn can go a long way, and with no job to fall back on, there was everything to gain.

'There's nothing like a knock to focus one's attention' says Robyn. 'It may have seemed like lunacy at the time, given the economic climate and our lack of financial security, but Tim and I looked long and hard at it and had a clear vision of how we could make it a success. This was very important – there's no point building a flawed business so we had to get it right from the start.'

A focus on quality

At the time, the staff catering market was dominated by large multinationals such as Grand Metropolitan, Gardner Merchant and Compass. Robyn describes it as an 'extremely male-dominated and acquisitive sector' and says that staff catering in those days was all about volumes and bottom line, without much thought for the quality of the food.

Charlton House pride themselves on delivering local produce, and changing the face of corporate catering

Those were the days of the staff canteens, when many contract caterers used convenience foods such as packet mixes for soups, cakes and scones, and ready-made frozen foods. The focus was on making the most profit, so contractors would purchase from a central supplier in bulk rather than sourcing locally. Consequently, catering standards in the workplace were often very low.

Robyn wanted to completely go against the grain: putting the emphasis on fresh, home-cooked food, using quality produce and craft-trained chefs. This would set her business apart from the competition and carve a niche as a quality independent player, with an emphasis on freshly prepared food.

Robyn believed that such a focus was particularly important in an economic downturn, as companies start to scrutinise the finer details: what exactly are they paying for, and is it worth the price tag? Frozen ready meals certainly weren't.

'In a recession, everything is questioned and honed down; companies want value for money but more than that, they demand the very best quality for that outlay. In short, it becomes a buyer's market.' Robyn says 'we knew that we were in a position to give prospective clients exactly what they wanted – a highly tailored and personalised service. I was driven by the conviction that a fledgling Charlton House could be more responsive, creative, innovative, agile and keener to please than more established players'.

'In a recession, companies want value for money but more than that, they demand the very best quality for that outlay. It becomes a buyer's market.'

Cost-conscious

With a clear vision for the business in place, Robyn set out to raise some start-up finance. She didn't need much, as she could ask her first customer for a portion of the fee upfront, which was pretty standard procedure, in order to carry out the contract. She just needed enough to set up a small office, and support herself while she actually found that first, elusive customer.

Robyn applied for a Government Allowance of £50 per week for fledging businesses, but in order to secure this, she had to invest £1,500 in the business to show her commitment. Ever resourceful, she used her redundancy cheque of £2,500 to purchase a second-hand Peugeot 205 and a computer, leaving her with just enough money to fund the business.

With a large mortgage, two people living off one income, and a very limited amount of start-up cash, Robyn had no choice but to keep costs to a minimum. She cleared out the spare bedroom of her house in Henley-on-Thames to make room for an office; used an old wallpaper pasting table as a desk and banana boxes as filing cabinets. To save money, she designed and printed some headed stationery on her PC. She decided to create a PO Box number address because her house was called 'The Salt Lick' – not the most commercial sounding of addresses, particularly for a catering company! As caterers are contracted to manage catering services on site, and use the existing kitchen facilities, Robyn didn't need to invest in any equipment upfront, meaning her start-up costs were very little.

In search of the first customer

Robyn's entrepreneurial resolve was tested almost immediately. Her first, and most critical, task was to win her first clients. She set herself what she felt was a realistic goal of getting three. In her naivety, however, she thought that her greatest challenge would be gaining her first client. In fact, it was gaining her first appointment. It is somewhat of a vicious circle – as catering businesses work in their customers' onsite kitchens, without an initial customer, Robyn had nowhere to show prospective clients who Charlton House were, and what they could produce.

Armed with only a telephone, a telephone directory and endless enthusiasm (there was no money left over to print marketing literature) Robyn sat in her makeshift office and began cold calling. For six months she sat at her desk from 8.00am until 5.00pm each day making calls. To keep herself motivated and focused, she wouldn't have a cup of coffee until she had spoken to a potential client, or eat lunch until she had made an appointment. Inevitably, she ended up both thirsty and hungry more times than she can remember. Six months is a long time with no outcome, and Robyn admits she considered returning to work as a waitress and cook to earn some money – but never considered going back to work for a large corporation.

To keep herself motivated and focused, she wouldn't have a cup of coffee until she had spoken to a potential client, or eat lunch until she had made an appointment.

Robyn had expected it to be hard – catering is a difficult industry to crack, with just a few ingrained contractors – but she didn't think it would be this hard. Although Robyn was right that companies were reviewing their costs, they'd also be taking a gamble on this fledging business, and she admits that in a recession 'people aren't as prepared to take risks. Many companies decide that it is not worth the risk of changing contractors in a volatile financial marketplace and will work with existing contractors to find cost saving initiatives.'

Perseverance was key, and Robyn had to keep a positive selling attitude at all times, staunch in her belief that her business idea would work... eventually. When potential clients asked about existing customers, Robyn honestly admitted there weren't any as yet, but that they could be the first. In some instances her name helped because receptionists assumed that she was a PA putting her male boss through – a Mr Robin Jones. Robyn also used a few tricks of the trade, such as using the word 'we' when talking about the business, to give the impression it was bigger than it actually was.

During the six months of cold calling, both Robyn and her husband devoted every waking moment to the business, determined to get it off the ground. Her husband Tim was holding down a full-time job, supporting them both, but also worked on Charlton House's business plan with Robyn after work.

Break through

Her determination paid off in late 1991 when she thought she'd won her first contract with charity, Guide Dogs for the Blind. Her delight was short-lived, however, as although she had been verbally informed that she'd won the business, she found out at the final hour that her contact had decided to put the business out to tender (where other catering companies pitch for the work). Robyn was aghast – she'd spent months on a proposal that she was told had been accepted, and now she was back to square one.

In the end, she won the tender. She believes the manager put the risk of going with a new business to one side as he 'realised that he was going to get a better service from my first contract than from being one of 35 run by somebody else's area manager!'

To generate some cash flow, Guide Dogs for the Blind agreed to pay Robyn on the first of each month, enabling her to recruit her first member of staff, who would manage and run the contract, while Robyn drummed up more work. Her first employee, Alan Barnett, was a friend from the catering industry. Alan had served 22 years in the catering corps of the Royal Air Force and had recently retired to take up a position with a large multinational contract caterer. He was not entirely satisfied with the move and consequently joined Charlton House.

Robyn personally oversaw as much as she could of the contract, including purchasing and food safety, even serving food, to be close to the customers and staff. When it came to finding suppliers, Robyn approached people that she had worked with in the past and t who herefore trusted her. Consequently, she was able to ensure good credit terms and keep her cash flow healthy.

Nine months after she had started out, Robyn had a site to show prospective clients, and a happy customer. She moved from her spare room into small serviced offices (with a proper desk), and two other contracts soon followed: one for a charity for visually impaired people and another which came from a friend's recommendation.

Robyn was acting as sales representative, personnel manager and book-keeper all at once, and admits that juggling several roles wasn't easy. She admits she may have lost a few sales opportunities in the early days by not devoting enough time to follow leads. Her husband Tim, meanwhile, took care of the accounts in the evenings.

The hard work paid off – in September 1992, Charlton House ended its first financial year with 16 members of staff, a turnover of £340,000 and three contracts under its belt. More importantly, the business had surpassed its original business plan and went into profit in 1992, recording a net profit of £28,200.

The proof's in the pudding

The business's big break came in 1993, when Charlton House entered and won the Booker Prize for Excellence under two categories: Best Young Business and Best Caterer. Robyn still didn't have any marketing literature, but what she did have was a Booker Prize and a track record of running several successful contracts.

Then came one of the biggest milestones in the company's history, which Robyn sees as a 'turning point for the company'. Fittingly, it came about from Robyn's ability to spot opportunities. Sitting in her office one day, she noticed a big office block being built across the road and decided to try and win the catering contract there. The building turned out to be the UK corporate headquarters of Sony and Robyn secured a lucrative contract worth £400,000, in the face of much bigger competition. Robyn believes they won the contract because they were small, agile, and could offer Sony a more personal, attentive service. Charlton House grew rapidly as a result of this contract and by the end of that year, turnover stood at £1.2m and it employed 62 people.

The same year, Robyn hired the first of many senior staff, employing an operations manager. This appointment took a lot of pressure off Robyn and freed her to concentrate on building the business further. This involved attracting media coverage, which helped promote the business without spending much money, and

Charlton House staff restaurant at the international law firm, Lovells at Holborn Viaduct

was an area that Robyn thrived in – it wasn't until 1999 that she hired a PR consultant. Positive and regular media coverage helped the business to build a reputation in the industry – today 30% of all new business comes as an extension of existing business.

The media also picked up on the radical changes Robyn was bringing to food standards in the UK workplace. Charlton House was not only producing superior quality food, but started offering to refurbish clients' staff restaurants before starting a contract. Robyn recognised that her clients were starting to pay attention to staff facilities, so that the staff canteen was becoming a 'valuable HR resource to help attract, retain and reward employees.' A great way of diversifying, while keeping their core value of quality, they worked closely with commercial kitchen/restaurant design companies to ensure that the new facilities met the style of the food offer and the standards of the company.

Growing the business

Unsurprisingly, the business had outgrown its existing premises and it relocated to Henley in Oxfordshire, not far from Robyn's home. In 1995, with the business continually expanding, it made sense to invest in premises for the long term. Robyn and Tim purchased a converted barn in the heart of the countryside in Berkshire, where Charlton House is still based.

In 2000, Tim came on board full-time to handle both the financial and strategic side of the business. The company had built a reputation for the quality of its food and service and Robyn was investing heavily to retain such standards. Two years later, the business hired Michelin-starred chef, David Cavalier as its director of food. He had previously worked at restaurants including Peacock Alley in Dublin, London's L'Escargot, and Mossiman's. While the chef's decision to move into contract catering might have seemed a little odd to those in the industry, it proved a shrewd move. According to Robyn, David's appointment enabled the business to recruit and retain better chefs for longer than other caterers, as employees could sense they had a long-term future within the organisation. Robyn had also recognised that the business's customers were eating out more and she needed to bring what was happening on the high street more directly to the staff-feeding environment, in order to retain clients' interests and attract new business.

Keeping focused

Charlton House was built on a quest for quality. Although the company has grown, Robyn insists they maintain their high standards through 'a tight organisational structure which allows the ethos, values and mission to permeate throughout the company, from board level right through to our kitchen porters'.

Now, competition is tougher as standards within the sector have improved. Other companies are stepping up to the mark, and fresh, quality produce isn't so hard to find any more. The necessity, however, to provide quality **with** value for money remains the same as from day one. Robyn is steadfast that Charlton House 'never want to compromise quality in the interest of profit'.

'It's all about keeping quality standards high and not cutting corners in the interest of better profit margins.'

Having started at the height of a recession, Robyn believes cost control is everything in economically challenging times. She has learned valuable lessons that have stood her in good stead, such as placing great emphasis on cost control. The business operates to very tight profit margins, of just under 2%, far lower than the industry average. Robyn is proud of this, as it shows that Charlton House ploughs a large chunk of its income back into the business, investing in training and development, green initiatives and food innovation. It's also as a result of purchasing local high quality produce and supporting local food producers. While this means the company incurs higher costs, it sets the company apart from its competitors, many of whom purchase centrally and see the bottom line as the most important factor. Robyn explains, 'it's all about keeping quality standards high and not cutting corners in the interest of better profit margins.'

Where are they now?

In 2007, the business, which had grown organically thus far, completed its first acquisition, taking over corporate and venue catering specialist Chester Boyd.

And in October the same year, Charlton House launched a new division specialising in the public catering sector, called Charlton House Restaurants, targeting prospective clients such as art galleries, museums and other cultural and heritage sites, one such client being London Zoo.

Charlton House now has 150 clients and employs 2,000 people nationwide. It is still winning new business, and retaining current contracts with enormous success.

How They Started in Tough Times

In Robyn's eyes, over the years, Charlton House has helped to change the 'staff canteen' into a new concept of the staff restaurant, and it continues to set standards for others to follow.

With hindsight, she says carving a niche in a bad economic climate can pay off, particularly if you hang onto your core values and survive the early years. With clients demanding greater value for money and personal attention, she believes a small, entrepreneurial business can thrive by offering a tailored and more responsive service. She even wrote a letter to her ex-boss, thanking him for making her redundant, as she would not have set up the business otherwise.

Masala Masala

Business is the spice of life

Founder: Priya Lakhani

Age of founder(s) at start: 27

Background: Barrister

Year of foundation: 2008

Business type: Food production

Country of foundation: UK

Countries now trading in: UK, Middle East

When barrister Priya Lakhani quit her well-paid career to start her own range of Indian sauces just as the UK entered a recession, people thought she was mad. But Priya was sure she'd found a unique product that customers would want. She began by painstakingly researching her market, to ensure she pitched her product to perfection. Just one year after handing in her notice, the Masala Masala range of chilled Indian cooking sauces was being stocked by Waitrose, Ocado, Harvey Nichols and a range of other independent outlets.

Inspired by spice

In October 2007, newly married Priya Lakhani was working as a media barrister. Her job involved long hours working at various newspapers, but although she was shattered, Priya found herself unable to sleep at night. During the early hours of the morning, she spent her time coming up with new business ideas – complete with market research and product planning. One idea, a lingerie project, had even got as far as the prototype stage.

Because of her stressful job, Priya didn't have time to cook from scratch every evening so often bought the fresh pasta sauces found in the supermarket chillers. Given the popularity of Indian food, she just couldn't understand why an Indian equivalent didn't yet exist. The aisles were full of jars of pastes and packets of spices, but fresh, chilled Indian cooking sauces just weren't available. Priya was convinced there was an opportunity to produce a quality chilled Indian cooking sauce – and was keen to be the first mover in the market. She started working on the idea, spending weekends researching the industry, developing a brand and forming her business plan.

It wasn't until the idea for Masala Masala took hold that Priya seriously thought about giving up her legal career. 'Being a barrister was risk free' says Priya. 'I had a very secure income and compared to a lot of my peers, a very comfortable life for a 27-year-old. But after I came up with the idea for Masala Masala I just couldn't stop it. It was like an infection.'

> '*I had a very secure income and compared to a lot of my peers, a very comfortable life for a 27-year-old. But after I came up with the idea for Masala Masala I just couldn't stop it. It was like an infection.*'

Priya calculated that she had enough cash to get started on her own, but she knew she would feel more comfortable about the new venture if her parents were in full support. Despite her enthusiasm for the project, there was the small matter of convincing her parents that giving up a lucrative legal career to embark on a risky entrepreneurial journey was a wise decision. 'My parents loved the fact that I was a barrister. My mum was so proud she would tell supermarket cashiers what I did for a living. Also, my dad was a business owner and he knew how hard it was. He'd been through the ups and downs and didn't want me to go through the same thing.' Although her parents hadn't been supportive of her other entrepreneurial ideas, when she told them about Masala Masala, they simply couldn't understand why she hadn't started work on it sooner. In fact, Priya's mother eventually become her creative director and owns half the company.

Priya Lakhani gave up a career as a barrister to start a range of sauces

Doing her homework

Once Priya had her parent's blessing, she ploughed all her spare time into researching her idea. It took her nine months to perfect the plan, and pluck up the courage to leave her job, but as she explains, 'that time was so valuable. I spent a lot of time in the British Library – a great resource which I would recommend to anyone starting a business near London'.

Priya began researching the pasta sauce market which was the closest type of product to the one she intended to launch. She noticed that while the long-life products had seen a recent decline in sales, chilled product sales had increased by 18% between 2007 and 2008. Fresh products were in style, and Indian food was still as popular as ever. Priya was confident there would be consumer demand for an authentic Indian product. 'The British foodie likes authenticity and more people are starting to realise that Tikka Masala is not Indian, it was created somewhere between Bradford and Birmingham.'

However, the fact that a similar product didn't exist made it a harder sell. Being a first mover in any market has its benefits as well as its disadvantages. Priya knew she'd have to educate her customers before they would buy her product, as few people would think to look for an Indian cooking sauce by the fresh meat in the supermarket chillers. Priya needed to market the product well, and target the right customers on a tight budget.

She decided to pitch the product at the premium end of the market. Her research had suggested that fresh products with fresh ingredients would mainly be bought by more affluent consumers. The added expense of creating a fresh product – the costs of chilled distribution and a shorter shelf life – also meant that the product had to be priced accordingly, retailing at roughly £3 per pot. 'A company can generate higher margins with lower sales volumes in a few premium retailers, or lower margins with higher volumes with discounters' explains Priya. 'Some companies achieve both, but we felt we needed to launch with smaller premium retailers so we could ensure we could deliver to them.'

While Priya accepts that launching a premium product in the middle of one of the biggest economic crises in modern history does not fit in with everyone's plan, she's adamant that there was still a market for quality food even in tough times. 'A lot of supermarkets focus on economy and value lines. But you also have to remember there are a lot of homeowners who haven't lost their jobs and, as a result of lower interest rates on their mortgage payments, have more disposable income than ever before. Not everyone needs to be shouting about the economy of their product.' Even during a recession, people have to eat – and as consumers are eating out less, a premium supermarket product can do better in tough times as people choose that instead of eating at a restaurant.

'A lot of supermarkets focus on economy and value lines. But you also have to remember there are a lot of homeowners who haven't lost their jobs and, as a result of lower interest rates on their mortgage payments, have more disposable income than ever before. Not everyone needs to be shouting about the economy of their product.'

Together with her husband Rahul Bakrania, she worked out that the venture would need £25,000 to develop the sauce, and for the manufacturing of the pots and labels. They had enough savings to cover this, so didn't need to seek a loan from the bank.

Full steam ahead

In August 2008, after nine months of thorough research, Priya took the plunge by quitting her legal career and and officially started her business. Priya and Rahul agreed that they would either sign up a big customer within the first few months or shelve the project until the industry was ready for it. 'I was really keen to launch the product but I didn't want to struggle with it for years. Either customers were ready for it or they weren't, but we knew we weren't going to continue pouring money into it. If we spent enough on product design, we thought we could just shelve it until the time was right to try again.' She says she was convinced that they would get into a supermarket though, because she had ensured that her product would fit their customer base exactly.

The first step to launch was to come up with the recipes. Priya asked her mother to produce seven sauces, which were taste-tasted among the family, and quickly whittled down to five choices. Next came a few weeks of product testing. Friends and acquaintances were asked to try the sauces, and give their opinions before Priya let the general public have their say, getting people to taste and smell the products outside London tube stations.

To decide on a name for her cooking sauces, Priya stood outside Bond Street and Liverpool Street stations and asked members of the public their opinions. Masala Masala proved most popular. Next, Priya developed the brand. She wanted it to look traditional and authentic, but also contemporary – and it needed to stand out on the shelves. With no connections in the world of design, Priya googled 'brand designers' and chose what she felt was the most suitable. She got in touch and gave them a strict brief. After just one round of design, and a few tweaks, she finalised her brand's design in just three weeks.

Armed with her recipes and branding, Priya began to look for a manufacturer to create the sauces in bulk, and found that this proved more of a challenge than she initially thought. The response Priya received was mixed. While some found her plans overambitious, others simply ignored her completely. 'I was laughed out of the door by some manufacturers, suppliers and people who'd been in the industry for 20 years. They just couldn't understand why I wanted to give up a legal career to do it. They didn't believe I would be in the supermarkets within months and just thought I was wasting their time.' However, there were a lot of people eager to help. 'I found manufacturers who only did dry products who not only recommended other factories, but actually gave me the names and contact details of relevant people.'

With plenty of recommendations, Priya found a manufacturer she was happy with and lined up a deal to produce the sauce. But she soon discovered getting your product 'supermarket ready' is a costly affair. One thing that makes it notoriously hard for food producers to get into the supermarkets is that buyers are not interested in seeing a mock-up. They want the real deal complete with packaging and branding, and pot and label manufacturers are not in the business of supplying a few hundred units. Priya says suppliers were driving a hard bargain back in late 2008. 'Suppliers knew the recession was coming when we launched, but I still had people tell me it was going to cost me double what they charge others because we were new and so small.' To meet the minimum order, Priya had to order 5,000 pots and about 3,000 labels for each sauce, and kept these stacked up in her parent's garage. 'Before you know it, just to get a good prototype done properly, you're spending £15,000.' With no track record, supplier credit was not even an option. Invoices had to be paid before products were even delivered which meant that she had to monitor cash flow tightly.

'Before you know it, just to get a good prototype done properly, you're spending £15,000.'

Making headway

While working on manufacturing the product, Priya had been calling supermarkets and stores asking to speak to 'chilled sauce buyers'. The problem was, this category didn't exist - there was a buyer for ready meals or a buyer for long-life ethnic sauces, but her product fell between the two. In September 2008, Priya officially launched her new Masala Masala sauces at The Specialty and Fine Food Fair in London, hoping to drum up some interest in her product. This worked, as a buyer from Harvey Nichols attended the show and loved the product immediately. With the breakthrough she needed, things quickly progressed, and the contract was signed in September 2008, a mere eight weeks after Masala Masala launched.

Despite securing the Harvey Nichols deal, Priya says trade shows have not proved consistently worthwhile as a way to grow the business. 'A couple of them were a waste of money and I wouldn't do them again. They can cost £5,000 each and it's so expensive to market a chilled product at them that even if you sell out of your stock, you only just break even.'

Starting out in a home office, Priya soon realised that the company was taking over her married life so she decided to take on outside office space to establish a clearer work / life balance. Masala Masala moved into a small central London office space which Priya was able to negotiate at a low rate because it had been empty for so long. The office was in the basement, and had no natural light, and only one air-conditioning unit which serviced the whole building – except for her office! She also purchased two fridges and two freezers so she could store sample products in her parents' garage alongside the excess pots and labels. Masala Masala then hired its first member of staff, as a marketing intern.

Keen to not rest on her laurels, Priya then targeted the biggest upmarket supermarket, Waitrose, as she felt it was the perfect place for her product. To save on courier costs, she dropped samples off to the Waitrose and Ocado head office personally. This led to a conversation with their buyer on the phone and she got her first order from them in March 2009 without ever meeting the Waitrose buyer. At the

Priya wanted to ensure the brand was traditional and authentic, but also contemporary

time, another major supermarket was also keen to stock the range, and Priya admits that deciding between the two was the single biggest decision she has had to make during the life of the business. 'It certainly was one to keep you awake at night. In the end we chose an exclusive deal with Waitrose. The truth is, it's a premium supermarket and it suited our product perfectly.'

The original deal Waitrose offered was for three months' supermarket exclusivity in exchange for a launch in just 100 of their stores. But just before the products were due on the shelves the Waitrose buyer called Priya and informed her they had decided to take the product national straight away.

Hard bargain

After Masala Masala had secured its supermarket deal, Priya used some additional savings and a bank overdraft to keep cash flow healthy – the ingredients, pots, labels and manufacturers all had to be paid for before she received payments from the retailers. With orders coming in from well-known customers, it proved relatively easy to persuade her bank to give her business an overdraft, despite the much-reported tough bank lending conditions of the time.

Priya would often find herself sorting out VAT returns at 2am with her husband, and often sent invoices out late. But the strong relationship she had built up with her buyers meant that Priya's retailer customers were chasing *her* to invoice them! This was a big help with keeping cash flow positive.

Marketing strategies

In addition to the trade shows she attended, Priya knew she needed to educate consumers about her new product. Priya chose Masala Masala's marketing activities very carefully as it is an area it's easy to spend lots of money on and results are not at all certain. 'With a food brand you just can't be naïve. You can't expect to be as well-known as Heinz within the year because big TV marketing campaigns cost millions.' The best return on investment came from in-store promotions and campaigns online at Ocado.com or in Waitrose's magazine. These included features suggesting Masala Masala for evening meals alongside more detailed recipes on how to cook with the sauce. Once she'd established good relationships with the buyers, they gave her plenty of advice on how best to promote the products in-store. 'Our relationship with Waitrose and Ocado is very special. They've spent a lot of time on the phone with me and I recognise that's unusual. I wasn't experienced in this market so I asked for a lot of help. The success we've had with promotion or marketing strategies has been largely down to them.'

'With a food brand you just can't be naive. You can't expect to be as well-known as Heinz within the year because big TV marketing campaigns cost millions.'

During 2009, Priya also won numerous entrepreneurial awards, including the *Daily Mail* Young Entrepreneur of the Year, and was included on the list of *Growing Business* Magazine's Young Guns. This has given the company very valuable PR, and helped promote the brand further.

Giving something back

An important part of Priya's plan for Masala Masala had always been to use the company in part for charitable purposes. She built a plan for the Masala Masala Project, which feeds somebody in India a hot meal for every pot of sauce sold, into the business model from the outset. 'It's all very well saying you'll give a percentage of profits to charity but I knew if I didn't do it right from the start I'd regret it. It also gave me that extra get up and go in the mornings and I enjoyed telling people about it.' Every month sales are totted up, and the appropriate amount of cash is given to the company's NGO partner in India. Priya has never, and still won't, work with any supplier or retailer that isn't completely behind the Masala Masala Project as well as the commercial side of the business.

Where are they now?

Masala Masala reached profitability almost a year to the day after launching. Priya's careful financial planning has meant outside investment has not been required, which has perhaps shielded the business somewhat from the credit crunch. The business now operates with a small team from its North London office, and consists of a small team of four, including a part-time bookkeeper.

Currently, international distribution in regions such as the Middle East account for less than 5% of turnover but a few prospective deals could see a much wider reach for the product in the future. Priya's main focus now is to increase sales through the existing domestic distributors. 'Right now we want to keep our existing clients happy. If you try to grow too fast it can damage you. We're small and there's only one of me, and I can't manage it all.' Priya intends to increase marketing spend as and when the company's overall budget grows and luckily she knows where to go for advice on where to spend the cash. 'I always go to the supermarket buyers and ask them for help. I think one of the tricks of Masala Masala is that we're not afraid to ask questions. I'll approach people and say "look, I'm a former lawyer and have no idea what I'm doing. Can you help?".'

New products are also in development and the Masala Masala brand is gaining a strong and loyal fan base. Priya's ambition is for her brand to ultimately become a household name. One of things Priya has found most surprising about starting the business is the amount of calls she now gets from the suppliers who had originally ignored her or laughed at her requests for information when she was first starting. She insists she's not bitter but still forwards them the emails she sent to them a year earlier – emails that were previously ignored by the very suppliers vying for a piece of Masala Masala today.

PR AND MARKETING

Kitcatt Nohr Alexander Shaw

Marketing agility

Founder: Paul Kitcatt, Marc Nohr, Vonnie Alexander, Jeremy Shaw

Age of founders at start: 45, 34, 34, 52

Background: Advertising and direct marketing

Year of foundation: 2002

Business type: Direct and digital marketing agency

Country of foundation: UK

Countries now trading in: UK

Current turnover and profit: £10m and £6m (gross profit)

You might not recognise the name Kitcatt Nohr Alexander Shaw, but you'll probably be familiar with their work. The direct and digital marketing agency is responsible for creating advertising campaigns for the likes of Waitrose, John Lewis and the World Wildlife Fund. It has won Agency of the Year twice in the last three years and in 2009, it made *The Sunday Times* list of the best small companies to work for. With a turnover approaching £10m, the agency has thrived since its launch in the rocky economic climate of 2002. In the last year, it has managed to defy much of the cost-cutting that has befallen other agencies in the sector.

Advertising slump

The early Noughties was not an ideal time to set up an ad agency. In 2001, the advertising industry saw revenues severely plummet, as the dotcom bubble spectacularly burst, and the world's economy felt the effects of 9/11. For many companies, advertising spend is closely related to corporate profitability and the general state of the economy. So, with business confidence decreasing, many firms were drastically cutting their marketing and advertising budgets.

Such a climate, however, did not seem to faze Marc Nohr, Paul Kitcatt, Jeremy Shaw and Vonnie Alexander. Having all held senior positions at various agencies, and fed up of making profit for someone else, they decided it was time to try running a business for themselves.

All four founders were about to start new jobs when their paths crossed in 2001. Marc had left his job as managing director of a direct marketing agency in

Founders Marc Nohr, Vonnie Alexander, Jeremy Shaw, and Paul Kitcatt wanted to work for themselves

the summer of 2001, to decide on his next career move. Paul and Vonnie had both left their agency – Paul to start a business and Vonnie travel the world. It was Jeremy (with many years' experience of managing, leading and growing marketing agencies) who introduced Marc to Paul and Vonnie, and suggested they start an agency by combining forces.

To the founders it certainly seemed it was a case of right place, right time, and they sought to take advantage of the state of the market. Marc recalls, 'it was a tough climate for some of the larger agency players and many direct marketing agencies were seen as lumbering giants and had taken a bit of a beating. It seemed a good time for a new challenger in the marketplace as we believed we had a different offering.'

Differentiation is key

The founders were determined to stand out from the competition, not by focusing on specific types of media, as other agencies did, instead, it wanted to concentrate on 'behavioural change' – using marketing to alter the way consumers approached brands.

'We saw ourselves as an agency that was "classic modern"– a "Paul Smith of direct marketing",' explains Marc. 'Other agencies seemed happy to be doing whatever the fashion was at the time – brand response [marketing that aims to get people to buy from the brand], CRM [customer relationship marketing, which revolves around loyalty programmes] and integrated services [offering a range of disciplines, such as direct marketing and promotional marketing].'

Like many small companies, they had the advantage of offering a flexible service, and were therefore easier to work with. Marc recalls, 'our services weren't necessarily cheaper than established agencies, but being smaller than many of the other players, we had lower costs to bear.'

'We saw ourselves as an agency that was "classic modern"– a "Paul Smith of direct marketing".'

The agency also began at a time when they could take full advantage of the rise in new technology. While traditional marketing campaigns were dominated by established channels such as newspapers, television and radio, new advertising tools such as online marketing were becoming increasingly popular. Both clients and the industry were looking for a different approach to traditional marketing communications, and many agencies found themselves having to learn a new set of skills in a very short space of time. Kitcatt Nohr Alexander Shaw were perfectly placed to be at the forefront of this, as its aim was not to focus on specific types of media, meaning it could adapt to new media quickly.

Marc believes they were also set apart from the competition by their sheer determination. 'We turned down good job offers to start the agency and we could have lost our homes. My wife had also just had our second baby – that was motivation enough for me' adds Marc. This meant they were 'leaner, meaner and more focused' than their competitors.

Setting up shop

Given the way the advertising industry worked, the founders had two options: to set up as a specialised division of an existing agency, or to set up on their own and enjoy a period of independence as the agency grew. If an independent business was to succeed, the usual route would be to sell to a bigger competitor, as their organic growth would be limited by lack of investment. However, an investment group called Mentor Marketing Services sought to change this pattern and introduce a third option. With their backing, entrepreneurs would be able to grow their agencies without losing control of the business, or having to sell. Mentor specialised in providing capital to marketing services companies, and was backed by four veterans of the marketing industry.

For the fledgling agency starting out on their own, backing from Mentor looked like the most attractive option. This would offer the founders more freedom and the ability to be more entrepreneurial, and they would also benefit from the advice of Mentor. This option also meant they wouldn't have to sell the company off if they didn't want to.

Apart from rent, the biggest expense the agency had was the cost of people. This was where they would have to invest most money, and the founders knew they needed significant sums under their belt to stand any chance of survival. The four founders raised £100,000 between them by using private funds and remortgaging their houses, and in December 2001, they secured around £200,000 from Mentor. The process was relatively easy – Mentor believed in the agency's proposition and after some delicate negotiation, was more than willing to invest. The deal meant that Mentor owned a 50% stake, built on a ratchet principle – if the business grew and met certain performance targets over an agreed period of time, Mentor's shareholding would subsequently reduce.

In that same month, the agency took shape. They named the agency Kitcatt Nohr Alexander Shaw (each of the founders' surnames), although longer than most agency names it was important for the founders to keep their identities at the forefront of the business so that prospective clients would recognise the level of expertise at the agency. They set up their roles with Paul as creative partner, Marc as managing partner, Vonnie as client partner and Jeremy as partner/chairman. In the early days, the founders had been using Paul's kitchen table as an office, but soon after receiving Mentor's investment, they rented office space in Hoxton, east London.

Getting their first client was relatively easy. Burnett, the direct marketing company that Marc and Jeremy had met at, had gone into administration in January 2002, and Kitcatt Nohr Alexander Shaw put in a bid for three of their accounts and associated staff. The recent investment from Mentor gave them a platform from which they could negotiate the deals and also bolstered their reputation. 'We won two of them through a combination of hunger and hard work,' says Marc. One of these was children's charity the NSPCC (which still retains their services today).

But it wasn't all good news. One of the other two accounts that the agency thought it had secured fell through at the last minute. The founders had taken on a number of other people in preparation for the extra work, and so had to inform them that the roles were no longer available. Despite this knockback, the founders propelled the business forward with the two accounts.

Getting things moving

Kitcatt Nohr Alexander Shaw knew that a key part of winning business would be coming up with great ideas and presentations to pitch to prospective clients. However, this necessary creative process could take weeks and even months, with no guarantee of success at the end. It could also be an incredible financial drain on resources: you're pumping money into something that you don't know will yield results. Furthermore, as a rule of industry, agencies have to be invited to pitch, after which a shortlist is then drawn up – Kitcatt Nohr Alexander Shaw had to wait nine long months before they secured their first invitation.

During this time they worked on the NSPCC account, and focused on making further industry contacts to try and get on pitch lists. They made concerted efforts to gain coverage in the trade press and the founders phoned their contacts on a regular basis to drum up business. The marketing industry runs on reputation, and all founders knew the importance of investing time and money in this way. They made sure they networked with journalists and new business intermediaries, to build the fledgling company's name.

Eventually, their networking paid off and they were invited to pitch for the Rail Passenger Council. They won the pitch, and began work for the RPC in October 2002. It was the one break the agency needed. Within a few months, it had won several accounts, including work for the National Blood Service, Amnesty International and a brief to re-launch radio station Jazz FM. In fact, Kitcatt Nohr Alexander Shaw didn't lose a pitch for the next 18 months. 'We were on a roll after getting our first pitch and we quickly attracted brands that liked our direct marketing proposition' says Marc.

Marc acknowledges that Kitcatt Nohr Alexander Shaw was able to use the economic climate to their advantage: 'the recession provided us with opportunities to go to our clients and offer them a solution that would work in such a climate. It also made us hungrier and more aggressive with regards to winning business.'

Much of the founders' determination to succeed was also borne out of necessity. The investment from Mentor would only have lasted till the end of the business's first year, and with their homes on the line, failure was simply not an option. Well aware they had launched in a recession, the founders ensured they knew the cost and value of everything the agency did, giving it the best chance of meeting Mentor's targets.

'The recession provided us with opportunities to go to our clients and offer them a solution that would work in such a climate. It also made us hungrier and more aggressive with regards to winning business.'

Ahead of the game

Before 2002 was out, the agency needed space for 10 staff, and Kitcatt Nohr Alexander Shaw began renting an office in London Bridge. The agency broke even in its first year and recorded a profit in its second. Clients were already referring to it as 'an integrated agency' reflecting the breadth and depth of its skills. This was an indication of how rapidly the marketing services industry was changing, as more and more clients were looking for an agency that didn't confine its work to print media and television. The Kitcatt Nohr Alexander Shaw plan was working.

By 2004, digital marketing began to feature prominently in pitches, alongside more traditional methods of marketing. The number of people online was growing, spurred by the rapid uptake of broadband technology. Clients were gaining confidence in including online channels as an integral part of their marketing mix, using techniques such as search, email and viral marketing – but most marketing agencies had yet to cotton on to this trend. It was an opportunity that Kitcatt Nohr Alexander Shaw spotted ahead of the pack. 'In marketing services, you need to be fleet of foot and ensure you respond to the needs of the market' explains Marc.

'In marketing services, you need to be fleet of foot and ensure you respond to the needs of the market.'

Four years into the business, the agency made a substantial investment in digital – being a start-up, Marc says, gave it more flexibility to scale and diversify quickly. In 2005, Kitcatt Nohr Alexander Shaw took a 5% stake in digital agency Underwired, a specialist in websites and online advertising. While the business's core services had not changed, what had altered was its focus – digital integration has been its single biggest investment.

The two founding partners of Underwired were actually close friends of the Kitcatt Nohr Alexander Shaw founders. They were starting up and were looking for some

Kitcatt Nohr's direct marketing campaign for Waitrose at Easter

desk space and as Marc explains, starting a joint venture with them on digital seemed to be the first step towards helping them get off the ground. The two agencies worked closely across new accounts won by Kitcatt Nohr Alexander Shaw, including Virgin Holidays, Friends Reunited and VSO. 'We did much of the creative thinking within our department – but relied on Underwired's expertise to help shape and realise our ideas,' explains Marc.

Gaining independence

By this time, the agency's income had grown from zero to £3m and the founders sought to buy out their original investor, Mentor. While the agency's performance had been good, it wasn't good enough to meet the terms of the original ratchet agreement, where Mentor's shareholdings would gradually decrease to nothing. So instead, they had to buy Mentor's shares back.

This was a brave move, and showed the high level of confidence the founders still had – they had to take out personal loans to buy out the investors. Mentor, meanwhile, walked away with a three-fold return on its investment in four years. The founders now owned more than 90% of the company.

In 2006, the agency's hard work paid off when it was crowned Direct Marketing Agency of the Year by an industry trade magazine, following a string of new

The agency secured some high-profile clients, such as upmarket car makers Lexus

accounts won that year, including Waitrose. A number of clients were also won without a pitch, as the agency was able to use word of mouth, PR and its contacts to impress clients such as LA Fitness, Sightsavers and Channel4 Learning. The agency impressively achieved a 100% client retention rate. Its creative output also received much attention, garnering more than 20 awards that year. One client even went so far as to say that 'Kitcatt Nohr Alexander Shaw is the benchmark to which all our roster agencies should aim.'

Going from strength to strength

Over the next two years, Kitcatt Nohr Alexander Shaw expanded rapidly. It invested in two related agencies: a media planning shop and a data and analytical consultancy.

It also sold its stake in Underwired and created an in-house digital offering. Marc explains, 'clearly, as digital became more central to what we were doing, a joint venture made less sense than having digital at the heart of our agency.' The partners felt the time was right to develop its own service at the heart of the agency, rather than running digital across two companies.

In 2008, just as the credit crunch was starting to bite, the agency excelled on the new business front, bagging 10 new clients including the global digital marketing account for Glenfiddich Single Malt Scotch Whisky, and work for PepsiCo, Britannia Building Society, Lancôme, and upmarket car makers Lexus. Despite this glut of new business, Marc admits that the current recession has resulted in an incredibly tough time for marketing services companies, Kitcatt Nohr Alexander Shaw included.

'The recession has affected everyone,' admits Marc. 'By the fourth quarter of 2008, there was a lot of uncertainty among clients – many of them were unsure what the following year would bring so they cut costs or suspended decisions on their budgets.'

To ride out the recent recession, the management took a pay cut for six months and staff were offered the opportunity to reduce their hours and work on a flexible basis in return for reduced pay. The agency, however, made sure it did not compromise on areas it believes are key to its growth and which help it to stand out from the competition, such as staff training and investing in the best senior talent.

Where are they now?

As one of the few remaining independent agencies in the sector, it's not surprising that Kitcatt Nohr Alexander Shaw has received its fair share of attention and more from prospective buyers. At present, Marc says there is no plan to sell – but the partners would not rule out anything if the time and strategic opportunity were right. For the moment, though, they are still enjoying growing the agency on a day-to-day basis. 'We have to work continually to attract and retain clients and the most talented staff – from that everything else flows' says Marc. 'We'll achieve this with an emphasis on quality rather than quantity.'

We Are Social

Social butterflies

Founders: Robin Grant and Nathan McDonald

Age of founders at start: 34

Background: Digital marketing, and film and video

Year of foundation: 2008

Business type: Social media marketing

Country of foundation: UK

Countries now trading in: UK

You couldn't escape the phenomenon of social media if you tried. The use of blogs, video logs, podcasting and wikis have transformed the way people use the internet. Social network sites such as Facebook and Twitter have transformed the way we interact with each other. This hasn't gone unnoticed by consumer businesses – it's the perfect tool to increase brand recognition, and at record speed. This is exactly what inspired Robin Grant and Nathan McDonald. With more than 10 years of digital marketing experience between them, the pair took advantage of the growth of social media to found an agency in 2008 which is dedicated to helping brands exploit the medium.

Social media growth

Robin and Nathan met at digital marketing agency Tribal DDB in 2002, where they worked as producers and production managers, before moving into account handling and strategy roles. Nathan had previously worked in film, video and publishing, having started a filmmaking magazine in Sydney, Australia. Since graduating in 1996, Robin's background had been in digital creative agencies and he had been a pioneer of social media, writing a blog way back in 1997, long before the term 'blog' was even coined. As social media emerged, Robin remembers his interest was in the effect it could have on society, rather than commerce.

After leaving Tribal DDB in 2003, Nathan spent the next four years at agency MRM Worldwide, now one of the UK's top five digital marketing agencies, while Robin worked at two other leading agencies until 2008. During this time, they were able to see the impact social media was having on their clients – as companies dabbled online, and saw promising results, they gained confidence and interest. Robin and Nathan, who had stayed friends, both saw the possibilities in starting an agency solely dedicated to the social marketing medium. Robin explains, 'we were increasingly recommending social media strategies to our clients, but the businesses we were working in were not ideally set up for the type of campaigns we wanted to run.' They were convinced that they would need to start their own agency dedicated to social media in order to harness its power; and despite a gloomy-looking economy, prospects for the digital marketing industry were actually on their side.

The onset of the credit crunch in 2008 had forced companies to cut costs, and to achieve this, many of them slashed their marketing spend. This meant a sharp decrease in untargeted, traditional advertising formats such as television and print. Online advertising, meanwhile, was benefiting from the dismal economic conditions.

As companies cut their budgets, digital marketing proved an attractive proposition. 'Social media is an area where clients can test and learn, where they can dip in and out – it doesn't entail building a big, expensive website,' says Nathan. It is particularly appealing in a time of recession as it offers flexibility, and is easily measured, so companies could quickly see the results of their campaign.

Robin Grant and Nathan McDonald focused on social media, and set their agency apart from the competition

'Social media is an area where clients can test and learn, where they can dip in and out – it doesn't entail building a big, expensive website.'

Figures released from the Internet Advertising Bureau (IAB) in 2008 showed that internet advertising continued to buck wider advertising industry trends, with spend rising 17% to £3.3bn in 2008. The reasons for this were twofold: advertisers wanted to tangibly track the results of their investments, and budgets were increasingly shifting from traditional media to more cost-effective online channels.

The way people were communicating was also shifting away from broadcast media and towards online communities within social media. Teenagers, for example, were spending less and less time watching television; instead opting to spend time on Facebook or surfing YouTube.

Consumers were also increasingly seeking out opinions online about products and services before making purchase decisions. Robin and Nathan were quick to recognise that opinions shared online were now more trusted than a brand's own website, and a lot more trusted than advertising. 'There's a proven link between online conversation and sales – people are talking about brands at all hours of every day, in countless forms of social media' explains Nathan.

A unique offering

While the market for social media was not brand new, it was developing at a rapid pace. This sudden growth meant there were very few specialist players already established – around three or four, according to the founders. Various other marketing agencies were talking about expanding their offering to cover social media, but this would be tagged onto the marketing mediums they already offered. Robin and Nathan knew that focusing wholly on social media would offer them the best positioning in the market, and set themselves apart from established agencies. Robin explains, 'we felt there was enough of an opportunity for a specialist player that could structure itself in the most appropriate and effective way, rather than trying to work within a traditional agency model.' This was an advantage of starting the agency structure from scratch; they could really do things their way.

Launching in a recession did not, says Robin, put the agency at a disadvantage. Operating in such a fast-growing sector of the market meant that the majority of their competition came in the form of big agencies. As Robin explains, they were one step ahead *because* of the recession. 'While we were small and nimble, the bigger agencies had hiring freezes and were undergoing restructures and downsizing' he says.

> 'While we were small and nimble, the bigger agencies had hiring freezes and were undergoing restructures and downsizing.'

They felt they had a high chance of succeeding if they were able to keep overheads low, and offer an effective service at reasonable cost. This, says Nathan, is a great thing to offer in a recession; as clients lose confidence and patience with larger, slower, more expensive service providers, they will turn to smaller, more flexible agencies.

Their social marketing agency would, for example, help clients track down key blogs and start conversations with the bloggers, introducing them to client's products and services or running more complex conversational campaigns. The founders set out to help brands 'listen to these conversations and provide metrics to quantify them', turning online conversations into data which could be analysed and used effectively. It would use social tools such as

Twitter to pinpoint users already conversing about a product, and, over a period of time, start natural conversations with those people, on behalf of the brand.

Hitting the ground running

Once they had discussed the idea in early 2008, it was only a few months before Robin and Nathan decided to take the plunge in May 2008 and promptly resigned from their jobs.

Instead of finding investment, setting up formally and then looking for the first client, through coincidence, the founders did things a little differently: they secured a client contract, before they had even set up properly. With little more than their name, We Are Social, decided (the 'Ronseal' (do what it says on the tin) approach), the agency won its first client.

Robin had worked alongside key people at internet telephony provider Skype in one of his previous roles. They had heard that Robin was starting a social marketing agency and contacted him directly in June 2008, as they were actively looking for an agency with expertise in social marketing. While their 12 years of experience stood them in good stead, Robin and Nathan say they were also fortunate enough to start up at a time when Skype was preparing to launch a major new version of its flagship product. It was a case of being in the right place at the right time; and only after they had won the business did they register the company. Skype weren't put off by the fledgling business, even though Skype had not previously worked with them or even met Nathan; instead they were attracted by its focused proposition.

It was a case of being in the right place at the right time; and only after they had won the business did they register the company.

As it was their first brief, the founders were able to devote substantial resources and time to the relationship. We Are Social devised a social media strategy to engage bloggers and developed video and conversational content around the launch. The launch was a great success; and once this had happened, We Are Social put in some long-term strategy programmes. This included a 'listening and responding' programme, where the agency tracked blogs and forums and responded to posts immediately. For example, when the front page of *The New York Times* reported that the Chinese Government was intercepting Skype messages, the agency tracked several thousand online responses on the subject, to monitor people's responses and give Skype the opportunity to tell their side of the story, and protect their online reputation.

Back to basics

Once their first campaign was up and running, the founders turned their attention back to the set up of the business. Having discussed the amount of finance that they needed back in May, they still hadn't decided exactly how they would finance the business as all their attention had gone on the Skype campaign. Robin and Nathan discussed investment opportunities with some of their industry contacts, who the founders saw as potential partners. They were all interested in getting involved: some were willing to provide office space in return for a small portion of equity and others were prepared to invest up to half a million pounds in return for a bigger share in the business.

In the end, however, both Nathan and Robin decided they wanted to retain entire ownership of their business, and so, We Are Social had very humble beginnings. Nathan and Robin reasoned they could get going with the very basics: business cards and a couple of cheap laptops. So, instead of the half a million they were offered in investment, the agency was started with around £2,000. To save on start-up costs, they deferred paying themselves for the first three months and lived on money they had saved. 'The only real investment we made was forgoing salary for that period,' explains Robin. 'We were not that fussed about sacrificing our salary. We knew we had enough to pay rent and to eat and from the early days, we could see that our idea was working. We didn't need to hire any freelancers to start with.'

They worked from home at the start of the business and met each other several times a week in internet cafes. They were also able to work in Skype's offices regularly, and built a very good relationship with them. Skype were delighted with the launch of Robin and Nathan's campaign, and continued using the agency. We Are Social still manages Skype's network of global and local blogs, user forums, its Facebook page, LinkedIn groups and Twitter presence.

Client contact

After the initial success of the Skype campaign, Robin and Nathan had hired an account director in mid-August 2008, to drum up new business. Sandrine Plasseraud had previously worked for an agency that worked with Ford, and had heard that Ford was looking for an agency to help it develop a social media strategy. Through her contacts, Nathan and Robin arranged a meeting and found themselves up against two other more established agencies. After a tough process, We Are Social eventually won the work, and Nathan recalls 'winning wasn't that easy – we were just good!'

From September, the agency helped Ford launch their Fiesta model, using a pan-European conversational campaign to encourage activity among bloggers. They also created and ran a campaign blog. Once they had won the Ford campaign, the actual work was pretty straightforward to carry out for two experienced social marketers.

Gaining the first few clients may have been a case of being in the right place, at the right time, with the right contacts, but Nathan and Robin knew that generating further new business would be a challenge. While they had a few clients under their belts, these campaigns were ongoing, and none were ready to be used as testimonials to impress potential clients. It was going to be hard to win business without any case studies or examples of work to back up their vision.

Non-stop networking

They set about networking at every opportunity, making full use of their existing contacts to arrange business meetings. Even if one potential lead was not interested, they often knew someone who was. But time and time again Nathan and Robin invested time and money working on pitches to gain new business, only to find that they had not won the work and would not progress beyond the pitch stage. It was 'frustrating, scary and worrying' for the founders, but they never thought twice about what they were doing. If anything, they say it just made them more determined to make the agency work.

Nathan explains, 'it became clear that we needed to develop a different approach to new business'. In some cases, this meant finding partners, such as other agencies, who they could work with to develop a brief, 'ensuring we weren't putting all of our eggs into one basket'. They learnt to be clearer about who they were approaching and why, and became better at recognising when a particular pitch was not going to come to fruition.

Their persistent networking paid off – it eventually led to a meeting with a PR company where they pitched and won part of Remington's business, with a brief to generate online conversation about products in the company's hair and male grooming range.

In October 2008, We Are Social won a brief to help actor and writer Stephen Fry expand his social media presence on Twitter and other sites. The work came about through a friend of Nathan's who worked as a digital producer for Stephen Fry across his audio books, podcasts and websites, and who had heard of the work they were doing at the agency.

Nathan and Robin began by making Stephen Fry's new website more 'social'. This included enabling the site to display social feeds, and advising his management on how best to run the forums and communities around it. As part of this, We Are Social helped Stephen to set up on Twitter, as a way for him to stay in touch with his fans on his travels. He's now one of the most well-known celebrity Tweeters, and is followed by more than 700,000 people.

Cost-effective marketing

One of the ways We Are Social kept its overheads low from the start was in its marketing. As you'd expect from a business that specialises in social marketing, We Are Social used the tools of its trade to advertise its services, with daily blogs on its site, and an active presence on Facebook, Twitter and LinkedIn. 'We practise what we preach, and a large part of how we talk to our potential clients is through our blog and by being active users of Twitter' explains Nathan.

'We practise what we preach, and a large part of how we talk to our potential clients is through our blog and by being active users of Twitter.'

Robin adds that in the fast-moving world of social marketing, reputation is key and has enabled We Are Social to attract and retain its client base. Its reputation has been established not only by the work it has undertaken, but also by the way it talks about its activities through its blog and other social media channels.

During the first few months of the agency, they also decided to use an external PR agency. While it is an expense many businesses forego while starting up, the founders believe this has been vital to the growth of the business's profile in the trade press. 'PR was a great way to reach clients,' says Robin. 'Social media is important and influential in the industry but it's still early days and a lot of clients aren't very social media savvy and still enjoy reading trade magazines.' Robin had worked with the founder of the PR company at a previous agency and had been very impressed, so it was an obvious choice. 'It is a significant cost but we don't feel that it is that expensive.'

On the up

Once the company had a few clients under its belt, Nathan and Robin were able to build a portfolio of relevant and credible case studies which made winning business a lot easier. In early 2009 they won two more clients, Directgov and the *Telegraph* newspaper, and in the summer of 2009, won business with Dunlop, Coca Cola, Nokia and Eurostar.

As business grew, Nathan and Robin hired more account managers and account directors to cope with the extra work. They hired a mix of senior, mid-level and junior staff, to ensure they had both the expertise and the manpower needed to run each campaign. Taking on new staff has also presented new challenges – Nathan says that being responsible for people's salaries and livelihoods has increased the founders' levels of commitment to the business.

Where are they now?

We Are Social established itself as the market for social media was on the rise, and the fast-paced nature of the industry continues to present new challenges on a regular basis. For example, Robin believes that if a big network agency decided to take social media seriously and throw a lot of money at it, then We Are Social would face serious competition. But as yet, he says, these agencies have either not seen the potential or had the money – which is another benefit of the recession.

He adds that while these agencies may have more time and resources than We Are Social, their offering is still likely to be limited. There is the danger, however, that some clients will always want to use a one-stop-shop agency over a specialist one, as they would prefer not to manage too many agency relationships. This is a risk the business is willing to take, as they feel the benefits outweigh the dangers.

Eurostar's webpage, where We are Social blog and update news regularly

The future prospects for social media look healthy, which is good news for an agency such as We Are Social. According to Nathan, turnover has exceeded initial forecasts and the agency is in profit, with money ploughed back into the business for future growth.

In the space of a year and a half, the London-based business has changed rapidly, in terms of both size and culture. With a client list including Microsoft, *The Economist*, Barclaycard, and Orange, and around 20 employees, the agency is going from strength to strength. There are no geographical boundaries with the internet or with social media, and We Are Social's growth plans are likely to include international expansion, which will present more challenges for the business. It is clearly a well-placed business doing well in a fast-growing sector, and seems destined for more success.

Marmalade PR

A fruitful opportunity

Founders: Lucy Hackett, Alexandra Nelke, David Pugh, Kate Shanahan

Age of founders at start: 33, 33, 29 and 35

Background: Public relations

Year of foundation: 2008

Business type: Public relations agency

Country of foundation: UK

Countries now trading in: UK

PR isn't all glamorous launch parties and networking events. It's a highly competitive industry where, in order to succeed, you have to be the very best. When the 2008 recession hit the UK the competition stepped up a notch, with both large and small agencies pitching for the same business. It was in this climate that Lucy Hackett, Alexandra Nelke, David Pugh and Kate Shanahan launched their PR company, Marmalade. Despite negativity from friends and family, they believed there was room for another agency, one that would offer clients value for money in a time of recession, along with a high quality of service. It's a gamble that appears to have paid off – Marmalade recently celebrated its first birthday and counts Olympic gold medallist Rebecca Adlington as one of its clients.

New directions

At the age of 33, Lucy Hackett is a veteran of the PR industry, having worked in the sector for the last 15 years. In 2001, she joined one of London's leading consumer PR agencies, rising to the role of managing director (MD) and overseeing fashion, sports and retail accounts for clients that included Speedo, Argos, Timberland and Cadbury. As MD, she helped to recruit other senior members of staff, including Alexandra Nelke (who specialised in fashion PR), David Pugh and Kate Shanahan, who had both previously worked across major FMCG (fast-moving consumer goods) accounts.

By 2008, Lucy was becoming increasingly frustrated with running a business for other people. There had been some decisions and directions taken at the agency that she had disagreed with, but as an employee, she felt powerless to make a difference. Having worked in both big and small agencies and encountered the same frustrations, Lucy felt disillusioned and was on the lookout for a fresh challenge.

The economic climate had also prompted her to have a long, hard look at the PR industry and her future employment prospects. By mid-2008, the full impact of the global financial crisis was sinking in. She felt that the worsening economic conditions had changed people's opinion about PR. With clients slashing their marketing and PR budgets, the industry had become much more competitive, forcing agencies to prove to clients how they could offer value for money. Lucy was convinced there was room for an agency that could go back to basics, offering PR without the tie-in of monthly retainers, and with guaranteed service from the most experienced of staff at all times, rather than junior members. 'The days of paying huge sums of money for campaigns and not worrying about results were long gone,' she says. 'Too many big agencies were going out to win business but weren't putting much effort into servicing the relationship.'

The recession had also sparked fears over job security. Their former agency had suffered a dip in new business compared to the previous year, winning only a handful of pitches. Lucy felt that the reliance on the staff as individuals was huge and she worried that the agency had become complacent about some of its bigger clients. If the agency were to lose one or two of these clients, their jobs might be on the line.

The founding members of Marmalade, Lucy Hackett,
David Pugh and Alexandra Nelke (courtesy of PA Photocall)

'The days of paying huge sums of money for campaigns and not worrying about results were long gone. Too many big agencies were going out to win business but weren't putting much effort into servicing the relationship.'

Right place, right time

It just so happened that Alexandra, David and Kate were also all thinking of exploring new opportunities at that time, including freelance consulting. By the end of May 2008, each of them had handed in their notice, confiding in each other about their future plans to go it alone. This prompted Lucy to take a long, hard look at her situation – having recently split up with her husband she was keener than ever to have a change in both lifestyle and work. It was only after they had handed in their respective notices that they began discussing a new agency. Lucy explains, 'when we did start talking, it quickly became apparent that we had one shared dream – to set up an agency with an offering that would work in the current market. It would offer highly experienced staff, a transparent service with low overheads, flexibility with regards to payment terms and value for money.'

'It quickly became apparent that we had one shared dream – to set up an agency with an offering that would work in the current market. It would offer highly experienced staff, a transparent service, and value for money.'

All four were on a three-month notice period but Lucy was put on 'gardening leave', where she had to carry out her notice period at home and was not allowed to commence any other work until the leave expired. This enabled Lucy and Kate to work on the business plan over the summer and tap into contacts to assess what business opportunities were available. This also meant that all four of them could continue to earn money up until the day the new agency would begin operation.

The minute their notice periods finished at the end of August 2008, the plan was that the agency would open its doors for business. They appointed roles focused on their strengths: Alexandra handled the marketing/creative side, Kate was Company Secretary and handled all the legalities, David focused primarily on new business, and Lucy put the administrative systems in place. The name Marmalade was chosen by chance. A horse race happened to be on television one summer's day when the four partners were together and a horse called Duke of Marmalade, who was enjoying a winning streak at the time, won. He went on to win six consecutive races over the summer. It seemed a lucky omen and the name stuck.

Standing out from the crowd

Having more than 40 years, experience between them, none of the founders had any illusions about the challenges that lay ahead of them. The public relations industry is a crowded one, with huge PR giants, and small, niche agencies. It was important for Marmalade PR to set itself apart from the competition. They decided to do this in two distinct ways.

Marmalade aimed to solve what they saw as an ongoing problem in the PR industry. Well aware that there would always be agencies offering (or at least claiming to offer) similar levels of expertise as Marmalade, they wanted to change what Lucy describes as 'the unfortunate reputation PR has for empty promises.' All too often in PR, the most senior staff are present for pitches and important meetings, while the campaign is actually run by a very junior, inexperienced team, sometimes even by 'graduates who had been in the job for less than six months'. Marmalade were determined to be different.

The partners would all work on new business, using their pool of contacts from the industry. Once the business had been secured, the agency would allocate a team accordingly – always involving one of the founders, sometimes supported by a freelance consultant. For bigger business or more short term, intensive periods, two or even three founders would be involved on a day to day basis. Therefore, at least one of the founding partners would work with each client. They would attend all client meetings, be the first people that both clients and journalists spoke to, and personally ensure each campaign ran smoothly.

Marmalade aimed to solve what they saw as an ongoing problem in the PR industry.

The agency also aimed to differentiate itself in terms of how fees were paid. Most PR agencies set an amount for a fixed period, regardless of the level of work carried out. Marmalade wanted its monthly fee to match the work done. They aimed to be very transparent with their fees. They would set monthly budgets according to how busy they expected to be. They would then be sure to keep the client in the loop, and charge them accordingly: some months, there may be additional, unforeseen opportunities to charge for, while in other months the agency wouldn't have achieved as much as they expected, so would lower their fees. They would not just take the client's money regardless. Lucy admits this was a 'risky proposition'. she says, 'With a long-term set payment, you can plan ahead and you know what money is coming in when. From the start, however, we weren't keen on tying clients down to long-term, non-flexible contracts.'

Marmalade was also positioning itself as an expert in sports and fashion PR primarily, with additional expertise and experience in lifestyle. This in itself did not make the agency stand out, although the combination of both sport and fashion was a more unusual one. Other agencies tend to specialise in one specific area or work across numerous industries.

Negative feedback

It wasn't just challenges within the industry that Marmalade was seeking to overcome. The founders also had to deal with the reactions of their friends and family. Many of them questioned the decision to launch a business during a recession, particularly as all four of them were leaving secure, well-paid jobs behind. But as Alexandra recalls, on countless occasions they were also told that some of the most successful businesses were set up in a recession, which put paid to any negative remarks.

The management team at their previous company was also less than happy to see four of their employees set up a rival agency. But the partners at Marmalade were more than aware of this and were determined to leave on the best possible terms. They had no desire to take away any of the agency's business or staff, and so posed no actual threat to their previous agency.

Cash is king

The four founders raised £20,000 in total from their savings to help kick start the business. They debated whether to look for additional outside investment but ultimately decided against it. Although this would have enabled them to start and grow more quickly, they wanted to retain control over the business. Having less money at the start would also encourage them to work harder and keep an eye on costs. 'As we had no investment, we also had no money to lose, so it would have just been a case of having to admit defeat and going back to working for someone else' says David. 'That alone proved a huge driver for each of us. If we had had the cushion or security blanket of a lump cash sum at the start, we would probably have spent it on office space, support staff and salaries. We wouldn't have managed to achieve what we have done. It was a scary and risky decision to do it for ourselves but ultimately a good one.'

'If we had had the cushion or security blanket of a lump cash sum at the start, we would probably have spent it on office space, support staff and salaries. It was a scary and risky decision to do it for ourselves but ultimately a good one.'

The initial funding was aimed at covering basic salaries in the first few months. They wanted to keep start-up costs as low as possible, as they did not want to begin incurring costs until they had a steady stream of regular income. So, from the start, they called in favours. Kate's husband, a barrister, helped with the legal side of setting up the business, including registering the name. Their website was built for free by Alexandra's sister, a web designer based in San Francisco. They also made it a priority to ensure they had access to an expert in financial advice – this came in the form of a friend of the partners who they had worked with in the past, who helped guide them through areas they had little expertise in, such as cash flow issues and forecasting.

Tapping into contacts

As plans for the agency took shape, Lucy was approached by an industry contact she had met the previous year. Rob Woodhouse, the founder of Elite Sport Properties (ESP), a leading Australian-based sports management company, was looking to set up an office in the UK in preparation for the London 2012 Olympics. Lucy explained the set up of their new agency and the two decided that, should they both go into business at the same time, they would work together.

Rob had already secured British Olympic gold medal swimmer Rebecca Adlington, OBE, as one

One of Marmalade's first clients was Rebecca Adlington, appearing here on the cover of Observer Sport Monthly

of his clients, following her win in the Beijing Olympics in August 2008. He was looking for an agency to help in the run up to Rebecca's campaign for the London Olympics. ESP soon became Marmalade's first official client when it opened its doors for business in September 2008. Marmalade handled a range of media campaigns for Rebecca, from features and news stories to media training, TV appearances and photo shoots. Rebecca, now a household name, has featured in *The Observer Sports Monthly*, *The Sunday Times Magazine*, *YOU* and *Grazia*.

Despite having secured their first client, and a high-profile one at that, none of the founders were prepared to rest on their laurels. The experience of the last few months at their old company, where new business opportunities had been much harder to win than in previous years had taught them that nothing could be taken for granted in a tough economic climate.

Drumming up business

With client budgets shrinking as the recession hit, and both large and small agencies vying for the same business, Marmalade opted for a flexible approach. They would offer to carry out project work to prove their credentials to clients who were slightly nervous about working with a start-up. Instead of hiring staff, they used freelancers where necessary to save on the burden of committing to annual salaries.

Marmalade knew good relationships within the industry were paramount. It built a relationship with the industry trade magazine, *PR Week*, to ensure new business wins were announced. As a PR agency, Marmalade was no stranger to networking and knew it was one of the best ways of spreading the word about the business for free. They made full use of social business networks such as LinkedIn, with each founder building a profile at the earliest opportunity, and attending as many key industry events as possible, including London Fashion Week and the Splash Awards, the swimming industry's annual awards.

> *As a PR agency, Marmalade was no stranger to networking and knew it was one of the best ways of spreading word about the business for free.*

Marmalade also made sure they regularly updated their website with the latest news, along with case studies of their work. They launched an e-newsletter and sent it out to their growing database of contacts; this proved to be one of the most cost-effective ways of marketing.

In the first few months of the business, the founders worked tirelessly to win new business, attending many meetings and preparing presentations for pitches. On more occasions than the partners care to remember, many of these meetings proved to be a waste of their time and resources, as ultimately, it would transpire that potential clients did not have the money necessary for the campaigns. David also recalls working closely on a pitch for nine months with a prospective client, only to see the work go elsewhere. Worst of all, though, the founders spent a few months producing work for a client who never paid them a single penny. The client was a new business too, and as they didn't have any money, Marmalade couldn't get paid. Lucy says they decided to cut their losses on this one: it would have taken too much time and effort to fight, when they could be focusing on winning new, paying business.

Cutting back

Like many start-ups, generating cash flow proved to be a huge problem from the start. Lucy, Alexandra, David and Kate had no choice but to make sacrifices. With no investors' money to fall back on, the founders often did not know if they'd be able to pay themselves on a month to month basis, let alone find the additional money to pay for marketing materials, client hospitality and travel – areas that are taken for granted in PR. They had enjoyed expense accounts at their previous company, but at Marmalade the reality was quite different.

'Cash flow is a huge issue,' says David. 'Payment terms were very inflexible, sometimes set as much as 60 days from invoicing, together with the first payment being a month in arrears. This meant we could be waiting for up to 90 days before being paid.'

In order to help their cash flow when doing work for smaller businesses, Marmalade tried to ensure it got half of the money paid upfront, but in the early days, it was a question of ringing round their clients to ask what money could be paid when.

The agency also covered fashion, representing boutique jewellers Leblas, seen here featured in the Financial Times

None of them drew salaries for the first three months and Lucy and Alexandra, both single at the time, even decided to move in together to halve their monthly rent. With no actual office space, they all worked on laptops from each other's houses; in Kate's case, often having to work around her small children if they were not at school. Their only big expense was a new computer, a printer and a scanner, which were housed at Lucy and Alex's flat.

Despite the expense the founders also joined a members' only club, The Hospital, in London's Covent Garden, which caters to those from the media industries. This enabled them to conduct client meetings in professional surroundings as well as access the technology required, without the cost of offices. Membership was cheaper for those under 30 so it fell to David, then 29 at the time, to join, saving Marmalade some money in the process.

Parting ways

Three months in, however, the business was dealt an unexpected blow, when Kate and her family decided to move to Dubai, where her husband had been offered a job. Whilst they hoped to continue working together, the reality proved difficult, so Kate resigned as a company director and re-distributed her shares in the business. The agency was confident it could continue as it had originally set out and, if anything, in the short term it helped to cut back on costs.

It also enabled the founders to hire their first full-time employee to assist on an administrative basis. Up to then, the agency had been using a mix of work experience interns recommended by contacts and were paying only travel and expenses to keep costs to a minimum. The new staff member enabled them to spend more time servicing their clients and focusing on new business leads.

Six months after launch, Marmalade decided to move into its first offices. Lucy says this was a difficult decision, not least because it substantially increased their overheads but she believes the advantages have far outweighed the risks as the move has provided the agency with a much needed base, somewhere to meet clients and store products.

Marmalade now rent space at the Press Association (PA) in central London. They were offered the space through an old colleague, and it turned out to be ideal due to its flexibility. They can choose to make the space smaller or larger depending on its requirements and projects, and it can use facilities such as meetings rooms. Most importantly the PA was happy to negotiate a rent that would increase on a three-month basis but the agency would never be held to a period of more than three months, allowing it added flexibility. 'It was the moment we first felt like we were a fully-fledged working business, Lucy says.

In September 2009 Marmalade celebrated its first birthday. In the first year, the founders learnt some hard lessons fast, and are now much more diligent regarding new business – initial meetings are done over the phone and budgets are agreed, firmed up and paid in varying amounts before, during and after the work.

Where are they now?

Marmalade now has a total of 11 clients, including SWIM, founded by former Olympic swimmer Karen Pickering MBE; Elite Sports Properties; Mission Sports Management; rapidly growing home furnishing company Dwell; and boutique jewellery brand Leblas. They are also focusing on building the profiles of the Olympic athletes on their books, from cyclists and swimmers to gymnasts and modern pentathletes – all with the 2012 London Olympics in mind.

SERVICES

Impact International

Making a personal impression

Founders: David Williams, Robin Witham and Paul Broom

Age of founders at start: 22

Background: Lifeguard, experiential learning and personal development courses, teacher

Year of foundation: 1980

Business type: People development

Country of foundation: UK

Countries now trading in: 18

Current turnover: £13.7m

When three 22-year-old lads wanted to start a training and development business in the depths of the 1980s recession, it seemed all odds were against them. The economy was looking gloomy, companies were slashing training budgets; and none of the founders had any money. What they did have was an idea: to offer different and innovative personal development techniques that took people out of the classroom and into the outdoors. By building the business slowly but surely, and providing a new way of learning, Impact International has been able to make a real difference to day-to-day company life for three decades.

People are low priority

In the early 1980s, 'people development' was the last thing on a business's agenda. The UK had entered a recession before the rest of the world, and cost-cutting was number one on every To Do list. Unemployment was on the rise, and many companies were just trying to stay afloat. Training was often one of the first, and easiest, budget cuts to be made.

But while you might cut costs in the short term, this solution comes at great sacrifice. Good people are invaluable in a recession: companies that invest in training have a skilled and productive workforce that, at the end of the day, will help them survive, an asset over companies with less skill to offer. This is something uni friends David Williams, Robin Witham and Paul Broom recognised, at a time when others were turning their backs on training programmes.

Founder David Williams

Against the grain

Although only 22, the founders had some solid experience behind them, and had seen the positive effects of outdoor, imaginative learning techniques. David had previously worked as a lifeguard, trained as a teacher and held various posts in training at Lakeland Training Group and Outward Bound (an educational charity that uses outdoor experiences and challenges to help and develop young people). At Lakeland Training

Group he held the position of director of training at the age of just 21. Here he met Robin and Paul, and the three grew to be friends.

David, Robin and Paul wanted to shake up traditional training programmes. They wanted to create a training programme that would enable people to learn through their own experiences, real situations, consequences and achievements, instead of conventional classroom-based activities. They called this 'experiential learning'. 'We had a dream of delivering experiential learning that was inspirational, motivating and truly memorable' says David.

Impact International would also be the first privately owned company offering such training. While there were similar existing businesses, such as Outward Bound and YMCA, they were not-for-profit companies. The founders also aimed to target executives and primarily target the commercial sector. The founders knew that what they wanted to offer would be unique – no other training company was offering this breadth of learning methods.

'We had a dream of delivering experiential learning that was inspirational, motivating and truly memorable.'

The fact that the country was in a recession didn't bother the founders one bit. With a commendable amount of guts, the three founders decided to run their own courses, driven by the belief that their methods and activities could make a real difference to people's personal development.

Entrepreneurs in training

In March 1980, the three founders gave up their jobs at Lakeland, to concentrate full-time on starting the business. The idea was simple, and relatively easy to set up: they would deliver training sessions in hotels, village halls, mountain huts and self-catering units that also had an outdoor activity facility, such as climbing or canoeing. This would mean they did not need any premises to begin with. The business would be based in the Lake District, where the founders had been working, due to the amount of outdoor activities available in the area.

They decided not to go looking for investment, and none of the founders had any savings to use as start-up capital, but as David says, 'when the chips are down, you fight harder'. So the founders' only option was to start on a shoestring. Impact International started from David's kitchen table in a rented house in Cumbria. The company name, Impact International, was inspired by a closely-guarded secret from the founders' student days. To save on the cost of equipment, they bought materials to make their

Members of an Impact training programme in 1982

own and stored it all in David's coal shed. They made canoes, waterproof clothing, helmets and belts themselves, and intended to use down payments from delegates to buy boots, other climbing equipment and life jackets in addition to borrowing kit. They bought a run-down minibus (begged from David's dad's firm) to transport them and their equipment to the course locations. David remembers he paid for this in £10 notes so he could really visualise how much it cost. They painted it in their chosen corporate colour of blue by hand (although the paint ran out halfway through).

Impact International planned to run five-day courses and tailor the skills taught to the needs of the client and participants. As they would find out, this could range from helping young offenders to avoid re-offending, to helping corporate leaders manage their people more effectively. They would ask for a 20% deposit from the companies, and the remainder was billed on delivery. They were able to pay for the accommodation and use of facilities once the course was finished, meaning they could keep cash flow reasonably positive.

Enthusiasm pays off

From David's kitchen table, they began the hunt for potential customers. The founders got a book from the library which had details of all the registered companies in the area. They sent out mailshots to these contacts, all individually typed on David's grandmother's typewriter, which rather annoyingly cut out the letter 'o' if the key was pressed too hard. Attracting potential customers in this way was no easy task, but the founders made a point of documenting who they had contacted and followed leads meticulously.

As David recalls, selling is always a challenge when times are hard – you have to be even more enthusiastic. The founders were helped by their solid background in training, as well as the unique programmes they were offering: their mix of personal development training and outdoor activities was well received. David explains, 'people were very excited about our work as it was such a brand new proposition'. He adds, 'We also had excellent reputations for this kind of work. If you have the right ideas and you and your people are passionate about your products and services, then you can be successful whatever the economic climate is like. If you ever lose your entrepreneurial spirit then you'll struggle.'

Unexpectedly, David recalls one of the biggest challenges the founders faced was that many potential clients were put off by their age. At 22, more than a few organisations thought they were too young to be selling and delivering executive development. Ever the entrepreneur, David quickly came up with a solution so as not to lose any business leads – he employed facilitators who were older than the founders to act as first point of contact.

'If you have the right ideas and you and your people are passionate about your products and services, then you can be successful whatever the economic climate is like. If you ever lose your entrepreneurial spirit then you'll struggle.'

Impact's first logo

The early days

Eventually their persistence paid off. The business's first few clients were as diverse as it gets, and not all from the commercial sector as Impact International had first imagined. They also persuaded a couple of clients they already had relationships with (from David's previous employment), to try one of their training programmes. They ranged from young offenders with care orders on intermediate treatment programmes (aimed at breaking criminal tendencies) to deputies from the coal board taking their first tentative steps into leadership, and civil servants from the Post Office, learning how to become entrepreneurial leaders.

Even with the first few clients on board, keeping costs to a minimum was still a priority – particularly in a time of recession. The company pumped any money generated back into the business, and they relied heavily on cash flow. The founders even slept in sleeping bags outside the hotels where they were hosting training sessions to save money! None of the founders drew a salary in the first year of business – David's wife was a hairdresser's assistant at the time: they both lived off her wages and ate tomatoes on toast.

Business started slowly, and at first, Impact International had enough clients to run about one programme a month. To fill in any quiet times, the founders ran day activities for boy scouts, holiday makers and school groups, including canoeing, climbing, walking, caving, orienteering and sailing. By the end of the first year Impact was running a course every week. Word of mouth is key in the training and development industry, and with successful courses behind them, Impact were able to prove their credentials and attract a steady flow of business.

Not all business was won easily, however. David remembers one instance when Impact lost a big business opportunity because the client, a multinational oil company, thought their courses were too cheap. They learnt from this mistake, and revised their prices. David says he has never knowingly underpriced anything since. He believes that if you believe in the value of what you're offering then you should never let yourself be talked down in price – but you must have faith that you can deliver value at the price you are asking.

Eighteen months into business, the original partnership ended and Robin left Impact. At this stage, David and Paul hired their first official employee, a full-time facilitator, who is still with the company today.

Spotting opportunities

After two years of gradual growth, Impact had built a reputation for successfully changing the working behaviour of apprentices and supervisors from two of their earliest clients, the Post Office and British Coal. It wasn't until the coal strike of 1984–1985 that the National Coal Board's investment in training started to dwindle.

Cragwood was Impact's first property, on the banks of Lake Windermere

Until then, it had invested heavily in leadership development for its deputies and Impact would run training programmes for up to 20 miners at a time.

The training sessions were going well, but Impact was getting some recurring feedback from its delegates. 'Delegates returned to the workplace from their Impact experience full of passion, ideas and energy, but this was not always encouraged back in the organisation, which was incredibly frustrating for them' David explains. Taking this feedback on board, Impact made a strategic decision: they decided to start tackling the upper echelons of organisations, teaching them to recognise and foster talent and create the right environment for ambition, innovation and creativity.

This came to fruition in 1983, as the UK economy was slowly emerging from a recession. Impact developed a new programme specifically for managers of the recently privatised British Telecom, called High Impact Training. The concept was completely new: taking senior executives from the civil service into the outdoors to improve their management and leadership skills, to train them up to lead one of Britain's first newly privatised businesses – BT. The programme gained massive media attention from the BBC, Granada and Channel 4. This was invaluable PR, and led to the business delivering 37 week-long courses in their third year. Following the coverage, the company also won contracts with Marks & Spencer, Apple Computers and a number of government departments.

Property planning

By 1985, Impact was well established enough to think about expanding the business. Up until this point, Impact had been using other hotels and accommodation to host their training programmes, and were able to fill them to capacity. The next step would be to run the programmes from their own accommodation. They wanted to remain in the Lake District, and asked a local estate agent to find them a lakeside property which could accommodate 20 people, with outbuildings and an office.

In one day, the agent found the perfect venue: Cragwood, a private house on the edge of Lake Windermere. That afternoon, David and his team arrived at the house in their outdoor gear and knocked on the door. They offered the owner a £60,000 deposit (all of the money Impact had saved from the company profits thus far) if he promised to take the property off the market. He agreed, but when Impact met the bank later that week, it refused to lend them the rest of the money needed to buy the property, as the company had no experience of the hotel industry.

The business had got itself stuck between a rock and a hard place: the deposit they had paid was non-refundable. Fortunately, the company's accountant put in a good word for them and they managed to secure a loan of £280,000 to secure the property and convert it for Impact's use. David found out later that the accountant had also put in £10,000 anonymously. Some of Impact's clients had such faith in the business that they even paid future deposits upfront to help pay for the rest of the conversions.

David and his team arrived at the house in their outdoor gear and knocked on the door. They offered the owner a £60,000 deposit (all of the money Impact had saved from the company profits thus far) if he promised to take the property off the market.

The Impact team and their friends and family pitched in to get the hotel ready for the grand opening. They worked on the property at nights and weekends, and transformed the four-bedroom house into a 12-bedroom hotel within eight weeks. It was here that David and Paul, with a team of six facilitators, established Impact's first residential base, saving massive costs for the company in the process, as they now did not have to pay for the use of hotels. Of the eight members of the Impact team who moved to Cragwood House in 1985, five are still with the organisation.

Expanding the business

In 1989 Impact made its first forays into international markets. This hadn't been part of their immediate plans, but an opportunity landed in their laps that was too good to miss. A Swiss company offered to sponsor Impact to look at the Japanese training market, by funding a month-long scouting mission. Following a successful trip, a joint venture was established between the Swiss and UK companies. At a time when the business world was enamoured with Japanese management techniques, it seemed strange to advocate western methods in the country. But Impact strongly believed its methods would work just as well in Japan, and so took its style of management training there, despite the popular view of the superiority of Japanese management philosophy.

To set up Impact's training programme in Japan, they sent over a team to start and run the programme. The team then recruited local staff who were sent to the UK headquarters for training. The local team then gradually took over more and more responsibility from the UK team, until they were self-sufficient.

Developing a second office was not without difficulties – Impact struggled for seven years to make a profit in Japan but their belief finally paid off. It was able to buy out the Swiss company, and Japan is now the business's second biggest office.

Impact's programmes include team building and leadership development

The lessons learned here provided a framework for Impact's approach to entry into new markets, combining a global approach with cultural sensitivities. Over the past 15 years, it opened offices in Thailand, Australia, New Zealand, China, Singapore and Hong Kong.

Where are they now?

Impact has expanded within Europe, as well as globally. Between 1997 and 2002 they opened two other sites in the UK and established offices in Italy, Poland, France, Sweden, Turkey and Ireland. In 2001, at the height of the fallout from the dotcom boom, Impact opened an office in New York in response to client demand and a growing recognition of the value of training people during harsh economic times.

Impact has also branched out into other areas besides training. Its sister companies include Eclipse, an events management company founded in 1989 (which complements its training activities), Zinco, a graphic design company (which designs and produces all its marketing material) and Cragwood Construction, a team of builders and gardeners, which help maintain its sites.

For a company with its roots in people development, it is fitting that in 2009 it was named as one of *The Sunday Times* best small companies to work for. Impact now employs 250 people full-time with a further 100 retained associates worldwide. The business operates from 18 offices around the world and delivers training in 37 countries each year.

With a turnover approaching £14m, David believes that the business has stayed true to its original purpose. Even today, keeping costs down is an area that is continually revisited. Company employees travel economy, share hotel rooms and stay in budget accommodation such as Premier Inn or Travel Lodge wherever they can.

David advises any aspiring entrepreneur to 'follow your intuition, but also do your research carefully'. He warns: 'never make a decision you can't reverse. Think of it like climbing a rock face – never step up to a ledge that you can't get down from'.

Foxtons

Building a vast business estate

Founder: Jon Hunt

Age of founder at start: 28

Background: Army gunner, then estate agent

Year of foundation: 1981

Business type: Estate agent

Country of foundation: UK

Countries now trading in: 24 offices in the UK

When Jon Hunt opened his own estate agency during an economic slump in 1981 he was determined to make a success of his business. This meant working longer and selling harder than any other agency; a practice which has often described as 'going to war' for its customers. With this inherent determination, Foxtons has survived the rise and fall of the London property market over the last three decades, and emerged victorious. From the outset, Jon ensured his agency was different from traditional agencies, and without doubt, it was the founder's sheer tenacity that brought Foxtons through more than one property crash. But Foxtons isn't without its controversies – it has weathered undercover reports into its practices, and faced scrutiny in the media. Nevertheless, there can be no doubt that the business Jon Hunt founded is nothing but a success. Jon made his exit with impeccable timing, when he sold the business at the peak of the property market for a cool £390m in May 2007.

An enterprising mind

Jon was involved with property from an early age. Educated at Millfield, an independent school in Somerset, he spent some time in the army as a gunner before getting a job as a negotiator for an estate agent covering the Guildford and Woking areas when he was 19. The job gave Jon valuable insight into the property industry: he learnt the ropes, and also discovered many things that he felt were wrong within the industry. These included working practices that he felt were old-fashioned, inconvenient opening hours and little evidence of hard selling. Jon describes the estate agency market at the time as a 'staid industry dominated by old brands'.

At the age of 19, he borrowed a £100 deposit to buy a one-bedroom flat in Woking, Surrey, which was priced at around £4,500. Two years later, he sold the flat for just under £8,000, already displaying some of the shrewdness that would stand him in good stead in later years. It was only a matter of time before Jon spotted an opportunity to do something he knew well, and to do it better.

In 1981, aged 28, together with business partner and school friend Anthony Pelligrinelli, he set up a two-person estate agency in London's Notting Hill. Anthony stumped up the £30,000 cash required to run the business for the first year. They hired a secretary, set up an office in an old pasta bar and installed a phone line. Notting Hill wasn't one of the cheapest of London's areas, but it proved a shrewd decision. Jon decided on the name of his estate agency easily: Foxtons was the name of a village close to his Suffolk home.

The long hours pay off

'The business wasn't at all innovative when I opened in 1981,' admits Jon. However, it rapidly became apparent to him that if you weren't different, you wouldn't have any advantage over the established brands. There were around 20 other estate agents around Notting Hill, all operating in a traditional fashion – five and a half days a week, closing at 6pm on weekdays. Jon decided to address one of the problematic issues he had with the estate agent trade, and differentiate himself in the process. So, instead of opening for 40 hours a week, and closing on the dot at 6pm each day, Foxtons worked a 76-hour week, including Saturdays and Sundays, closing at 9pm. For the next eight years, Jon worked gruelling 12-hour days, but he was right on the money – Jon explains that their success was down to the fact that these hours fitted with the demands of living and working in London. These extended opening times are a strategy that has survived for the long-term, and still proves successful today: 40%

Founder Jon Hunt felt he could make a splash in the world of estate agents, and he was right

of their viewings are carried out in the evening and at weekends, proving there is huge demand for these alternative opening hours.

It rapidly became apparent to him that if you weren't different, you wouldn't have any advantage over the established brands. For the next eight years, Jon worked gruelling 12-hour days.

This dogged dedication and innovative approach helped Jon to maintain his focus, even through a recession. 'When Foxtons opened in 1981 I had no idea there was a recession going on' he says. 'I didn't read the newspapers let alone the business pages. We worked 13 days in a row then had one day off. Everyone in the company was focused entirely on selling our clients' properties.'

'If you have the urge to do your own thing, then prevailing interest rates, stock market highs and lows, unemployment figures and housing statistics make not a jot of difference to whether your tiny insignificant company will succeed or not' says Jon. 'In this business it is purely down to hard work and commitment to your clients and of course a large spoonful of luck.'

> '**If you have the urge to do your own thing, then prevailing interest rates, stock market highs and lows, unemployment figures and housing statistics make not a jot of difference to whether your tiny insignificant company will succeed or not.**'

Location, location, location

Armed with a distinct point of difference, Jon's choice of location for his first office was a shrewd move. According to Jon, Notting Hill and North Kensington were anything but trendy areas, meaning there was potential for development. By 1981, Notting Hill was moving upwards – albeit slowly – and was becoming a desirable area in terms of property, having become more and more gentrified in the late 1970s.

With no marketing budget, the location of the Notting Hill office proved the best marketing asset Foxtons had. It was on the bustling high street, right opposite the tube station. As Jon explains, people would literally walk in off the street and ask Jon to buy or sell property on their behalf. From the start, Foxtons had hundreds of walk-ins every week. When he spoke to friends who had agencies in relatively poor locations, it showed him without doubt that the location of your shop or office is a critical factor in its success – why swim upstream? It taught him to pay a little more rent, but to always get the best location you can possibly afford.

Sell, sell, sell

At the end of the first year, Foxtons sold a large land deal to Wimpey Homes, which generated a £20,000 fee. This gave the business enough cash to survive the following year, and meant Jon could try a rather radical marketing technique. Determined to do things differently and make his mark, in 1982, Jon introduced a 0% commission fee. This undercut competitors, who charged around 2.5%–3% commission on

Foxtons' first office was situated opposite the tube in Notting Hill

sales prices. This was unheard of in the industry and encouraged more customers to use Foxtons, boosting the business's reputation .

Foxtons did a steady trade throughout the early 1980s, and Jon slogged long and hard to make his business a success. As the economy recovered from the recession, Foxtons was ready to benefit from the substantial property boom of the mid-1980s.

After a year of charging 0% commission, Jon changed tack completely, and began charging sellers a fee similar to, or higher than the rates his competitors were offering. After making a name for himself by charging no commission, he justified this U-turn by promising house sellers that he would achieve a better price for their properties – up to 10% higher, in fact. Such an aggressive strategy worked and Foxtons met their promise. 'We were not cheaper, in fact we were more expensive and we never ever negotiated on our fees' Jon recalls.

Foxtons logos through the years, from 1981, through the 1990s to the early 2000s

'We set out our stall and 99.9% of our customers were happy to pay our fees to sell their properties efficiently'. This was also the start of Foxton's often-quoted mantra, 'our clients expect us to go to war for them'. To sell properties, Foxtons agents, encouraged by Jon, were expected to work longer, sell harder, to do whatever it took to get the business, and then sell the property.

Growing gradually

Jon's shrewd business move of returning to a commission charge generated a substantial amount of income, and meant that the business could expand. Jon opened the second office in Fulham Broadway in 1985 and a third in South Kensington in 1987.

Jon says employing the right people was crucial to growth. From the early days it was obvious to him that good, strong minded people would make a good business. During the first 17 years of the business, Jon was entirely responsible for interviewing prospective employees, either over the telephone or face-to-face. He was looking for exceptional characters, many of whom are now the key directors, managers and top negotiators in the company.

Employing the right people was crucial to growth. From the early days it was obvious to Jon that good people would make a good business.

As the number of employees grew, sales meetings were held. Originally these were monthly 7am breakfast meetings, until a young Australian negotiator pointed out that Jon was the only person awake! Jon then changed the time of the meeting to 7pm on a Friday – when all business for the week would have closed.

Innovative marketing techniques also paid off. In 1986, Foxtons launched its first in-house newspaper and magazine, and was the first estate agent in London to do so. This free publication was circulated in the neighbourhoods around the Foxtons offices. The result of this, Jon says, were leads that equated to overnight success. It's a clever marketing technique which has been carried through to today – the business now publishes local property magazine *Area*, which is distributed on a monthly basis to around one million homes.

Changing the business model

As well as Jon's determination and strong work ethic, Foxtons' expansion can also be attributed to a post-recession boom in the UK property market. By the mid to late 1980s, property prices had surged, particularly in London and the south-east. The Government was encouraging home ownership, which made it easier for consumers to get access to mortgages. Between 1983 and 1989, figures show that the average UK house price more than doubled, going from around £31,600 to £68,800, an increase of 117%.

All this was to change in August 1988, however, when Nigel Lawson, the Chancellor of the Exchequer at the time, announced that double mortgage tax relief would end later that year. This had enabled unmarried couples to claim tax relief on mortgage interest. Following this announcement, young couples rushed to get a foothold on the property ladder before the tax relief ended, resulting in a huge, but short-term boost to the property market. As a result, property inflation went through the roof and sellers revelled in the money they made.

Yet as soon as the cut-off point for mortgage tax relief was reached, the public's interest in viewing and buying properties virtually plummeted overnight. Estate agents around the country struggled to sell even their competitively priced properties, precipitating the property crash that occurred in 1989. London and the south-east were the first to be hit by the crash. For Foxtons, which had focused mainly on residential sales to date, the property crash dealt the business a devastating blow and one that it was completely unprepared for. 'During the August 1988–January 1994 recession, Foxtons had no significant lettings department and as a consequence, it barely hung on – we were close to going bust every day,' recalls Jon.

Foxtons quickly learnt from this devastating period, and took the decision to diversify. Jon decided that lettings would become an equally important side to the business – so much so that if and when the next recession came, lettings would be able to pay for the business's operating costs. In 1995, Foxtons produced a dedicated lettings magazine for Londoners to boost this side of the business. And true to his word, lettings have boosted the business in the most recent recession to hit the UK – while house sales slumped, the lettings market boomed.

New directions

In 1991, Foxtons worked on creating a recognisable brand. Until the company was a reasonable size, Jon didn't spend any time thinking about the Foxtons brand and brand values. It was only when he started talking to an advertising team that he began to understand the value of a strong brand, and the importance of appealing to your market. 'You have to adapt your brand to the market conditions – in the roaring 1980s, we had a very modern looking Foxtons "F" and as the 1990s property depression hit, we changed this to a more traditional, dustier "F",' says Jon. 'You certainly don't want to look racy when your customers are having a tough time'.

In 1992, with the property market proceeding slowly on the road to recovery, Jon opened an office in Chiswick, followed by Battersea in 1994, in Putney the following year and offices in Park Lane and Islington in 1997.

In 1998, Jon appointed two other directors, to whom he was able to delegate management duties. Peter Rollings now looked after the front end sales staff and Lesley Martin took over recruitment and HR. This left Jon free to focus on growing the business. He concentrated on opening new offices, and staff numbers grew to 1,600 people.

In the late 1990s, the business also invested heavily in its website as a means of advertising and marketing the business, which Jon says has 'paid dividends' over time. They were one of the first agencies to really embrace the power of the internet in aiding property searches, and again Jon made sure they were quick off the mark, launching their website in 1999. Over the following years, Foxtons also used new technology to its advantage, using tools such as RSS ('really simple syndication' or 'rich site summary', a tool that alerts users to new content on a website), podcast and vodcast feeds, Google Earth, and text and email alerts to advertise new properties.

By 2001, the housing market was relatively healthy, and prices were forecast to rise. This was the year that Foxtons launched their first fleet of Minis. At that time in the estate agent world it was quite usual for estate agents to have company cars, to drive themselves and customers to and from appointments. Foxtons turned this necessary transportation cost on its head, and used the cars as an advertising tool, so that they became mini-billboards for the business. Branded cars had always been

The first specially designed Mini Cooper

on Jon's agenda, but it wasn't until the Mini came along, that he jumped at the chance to use the iconic shape and character of this car alongside Foxtons branding. Jon found a young designer, Roberto D'Andria, and commissioned him to design Minis for Foxtons, buying him every book about Minis he could find. According to Jon, the launch of

800 Minis onto the streets of London was an overnight success. The first design was called the 'Italian Job' and was inspired by Mini Coopers' racing history. The company has released a new design every year since.

Foxtons turned this necessary transportation cost on its head, and used the cars as an advertising tool, so that they became mini-billboards for the business.

Expansion abroad

In 2001 Jon decided to expand Foxtons overseas, by making a $20m (£12m) investment in YourHomeDirect.com, (later renamed Foxtons Inc), a discount commission estate agency started by Glenn Cohen a year earlier. It hoped to encourage business by placing a 2% commission on consumers buying and selling homes, compared to the standard 6% of traditional brokerages (commissions in the USA are typically much higher than those in Britain).

In 2004, Foxtons fully acquired YourHomeDirect.com, which by then had grown to 400 employees and operated in 10 locations. The acquisition reportedly came after Jon fell out with Glenn, who left the business having sold his remaining shares to Jon.

Undercutting competitors may have been a tactic that worked in the UK, but it wasn't a model that could be replicated everywhere, and especially not, it seemed, in the USA. Despite spending millions on marketing campaigns, the business made massive losses and their commission strategy was later modified to 4%, but still struggled.

Stormy times

In 2006, Foxtons featured alongside two other agents in an undercover BBC documentary that showed alleged underhand sales practices, including faking signatures on documents and showed staff bragging about having misled clients. At the time, Jon denied the allegations but said, 'there were several things we had done... that were wrong.' Foxtons felt that the programme was edited unfairly with inaccurate weighting to the allegations against them compared to the other agents featured in the way that the imagery and shots were cut.

It wasn't the first time, though, that the estate agent had courted controversy. In 2003, it had been accused of destroying rival 'For Sale' signs outside properties. And at one point, the company was also forced to make a public apology when one of its 'For Sale' signs wound up in the front of Alastair Campbell's house, who was the press secretary to then-prime minister Tony Blair at the time. Not only was this house not listed with Foxtons, it wasn't even for sale. This didn't seem to dent Foxtons relationship with the PM though – in 2004, it advised the Blairs on the purchase of their £3.65m property in Connaught Square, and then became their letting agent.

Surprisingly, the negative publicity that followed the BBC documentary did little to dent the business's prospects. In response, Foxtons implemented a programme which enabled employees to receive an intensive week's training which covers legal compliance and 10 hours of training after being at the company for three months. The company also signed up to the industry's voluntary ombudsman code. Foxtons was still able to take full advantage of the property boom in the UK at the time and continued to expand across the capital and the leafy suburbs of Surrey.

Over the years, the media have spent many column inches discussing various Foxtons controversies. Tales of their ruthless sales meetings are widely reported, but Jon explains the real structure and purpose of the weekly meetings, and says it is without doubt one of the most successful things that Foxtons does. A digital presentation shows the individual business that each sales person has executed that week. He dismisses reports printed in the media that the sales person with the lowest amount of money generated gets fired: 'To say the lowest income producer gets fired each week is absurd. Some of my negotiators banked more than £1m a year, in fact one individual banked £2m a year, having spent most weeks never doing a deal. However, most sales people love recognition and if you call out a good set of numbers, everyone is impressed.' Jon explains that the meeting also acts as an accounting tool: 'By 8pm on a Friday evening you know exactly how much money you have made or lost during the previous seven days –monthly management accounts are redundant.'

Where are they now?

In November 2006, the estate agency hired Credit Suisse to prepare for a stock market listing, with a reported potential valuation of between £300m and £400m. The aim was to raise funds to finance its US venture and the expansion of Alexander Hall (their mortgage broker) in the UK, but the US business continued to underperform.

By contrast, Foxtons in the UK was thriving. By 2007, it had grown to 20 offices in London and Surrey and recorded revenues of more than £100m. With such impressive figures, it was not surprising that the estate agency was on the radar of several buyers. Such was the interest from buyers that Credit Suisse decided to conduct an auction. Jon eventually sold the business in May 2007 to BC Partners for £390m and is reported to have pocketed around £300m for his stake in the business as at the time of sale he owned more than 97%.

It turned out Jon sold just at the right time. Five months later, in October 2007, the US enterprise, Foxtons Inc filed for bankruptcy and made 350 out of 380 employees redundant. An economic downturn and property slump in 2007 had seen US house sales fall to near a five-year low. Jon believes that hard work and luck go a long way when working in the property market and the fact that he sold the business just before the credit crunch devastated the property market would certainly support his belief that luck can play a big part in success.

There's no denying that 2008 and 2009 have been a difficult climate for all those involved in the property market, and Foxtons has been no exception to the rule. In January 2009, it emerged that Foxtons had breached lending agreements with its banks. BC Partners has even publicly questioned its decision to buy Foxtons, just prior to the onset of the credit crunch. Foxtons now has 24 offices in London and Surrey.

Jon has spent the last year looking to return to the residential market where he made his name and fortune, this time with a foray into the serviced apartment industry. The property slump in the last year has done little to dampen his enthusiasm and he believes it has created the perfect time to find the right deals. Still a shrewd operator, Jon looks at the recent recession as an opportunity. 'At the moment, it is a property man's dream, where you have cash in the pocket and a distressed market,' proving he still has the determination which helped him to make Foxtons such a success.

dunnhumby

Delivering on data

Founders: Edwina Dunn and Clive Humby

Age of founders at start: 30 and 33

Background: Geography graduate and mathematician

Year of foundation: 1989

Business type: Data consultancy and marketing services

Country of foundation: UK

Countries now trading in: 20

Current turnover and profit: £220m and £42m

More than 13 million households in the UK use Tesco's Clubcard, the loyalty scheme operated by the supermarket retailer. Hardly any, however, have heard of dunnhumby. The data consultancy and marketing company has been described as the 'brains' behind the scheme, having helped Tesco to launch it nationwide in 1995. dunnhumby was founded by husband and wife team Edwina Dunn and Clive Humby in 1989, at a time when the UK was plummeting into a recession. Armed with a firm belief in their pioneering idea, and not much else, the husband and wife team needed to convince clients of the value of customer data, as well as build data technology from scratch. Today dunnhumby operates worldwide and turns over £220m, generating profits of more than £40m.

Data insight

Every day we are inundated with sales and marketing messages – via the telephone, by post or by email. And they're becoming increasingly relevant to us: things we're interested in, recent purchases or products we want. This is made possible through increasingly sophisticated customer data and software. Many companies know not just your name, age and address, but the type of food and drink you like, the number and ages of your children and where and when you like to travel on holiday.

Back in 1989, this kind of data did not exist. At the time, Clive Humby and Edwina Dunn worked for market analysis company CACI, which used census data to predict consumer lifestyle patterns. They had met at the company several years before and later married. Clive, a mathematician by training, had joined 11 years previously as a systems analyst, rising to chief executive; while Edwina had joined after graduating with a degree in geography and was now vice-president, after nine years of service.

While working at CACI, they came up with a vision to use data in a different way. This involved retaining and analysing customer data based on behaviour, which would enable companies to deliver marketing that was more relevant to their customers. They wanted to set up a consultancy to advise companies on how better to manage their customer data to this effect.

They approached their employer with the idea, but were met with a cold reception: CACI was not willing to invest its profits in this new concept. Clive was adamant this idea should be pursued, and his disappointment in the company's lack of vision led him to resign from the business in order to pursue the vision on his own. As Edwina was married to him, she recalls, 'I was literally fired 10 minutes later as they felt I would be competing with the business.' She received a substantial payout – enough to dissuade her from claiming unfair dismissal.

Their timing was less than perfect: they left senior roles in an established company just as the rosy economy was changing for the worse. But for Clive and Edwina, staying put wasn't an option. 'We could have got jobs elsewhere but we were very passionate about our idea' explains Edwina, and she admits that the idea to go it

Husband and wife team Clive Humby and Edwina Dunn are the brains behind Tesco Clubcard

alone came from frustration more than anything else. As they left their jobs, they hadn't even drafted so much as a business plan.

Rocky road

Edwina and Clive had recently taken advantage of the UK's 1980s property boom and had taken out a huge mortgage on a property in Chiswick, west London. With no prospect of salaries for the immediate future, they started their business in a spare room with only a few thousand pounds. With the mortgage to pay, they had no option but to plough everything they had into making their marketing consultancy company a success. Edwina recalls the effort it took, 'You work very hard when you start something from scratch – it becomes so real'.

They chose to combine their surnames – Dunn and Humby – to create their company name. They thought this through carefully. With around 10 years' experience of customer data between them, they felt it important to make the most of their reputations in the industry, and they thought it would help to attract clients to their fledgling business. According to Edwina, there were also too many companies using 'marketing' in their name and it was important that they stood out from the crowd.

'You work very hard when you start something from scratch – it becomes so real.'

To get their first client, they used their existing contacts list, approaching a few with a simple explanation of what they could offer, and how it could impact on their clients' business. Within two months, they found their first client, food wholesaler Booker Cash and Carry, which operated in the business-to-business sector. Edwina and Clive thought this field was sufficiently different from the one they'd been involved in at CACI. Celebrations for the win were short-lived, however, as CACI sued them – unbeknownst to dunnhumby, CACI had also been pitching for the Booker business. CACI accused Edwina and Clive of using specialist knowledge gleaned from CACI to secure the deal. The case ended up in court – not only did Edwina and Clive face huge bills, but as CACI had taken out an injunction against their business, they couldn't trade either. The frustrating thing was that dunnhumby had not stepped out of line – Edwina recalls that the case 'confused the judge enough for him to grant the injunction.' There was nothing they could do but ride it out.

Raising funds

With no prospect of income for the near future, and the UK sliding deeper into recession, they wrote a business plan to attract funding. What dunnhumby was proposing to do – use behaviour to determine customer actions – was completely new. Having a unique selling point is a must for any new business, but offering a completely new service also has its downsides: as Edwina explains, there was nothing to compare their business to so it was a challenge setting both budgets and expectations. They worked on this to ensure it was as accurate as possible, and Edwina believes that if you write a strong business plan, have thought the business and the numbers through carefully, and can show how you will make a profit, seeking finance is actually relatively straightforward. 'We wrote a good business plan – we'd been well trained at CACI, which was an entrepreneurial business.'

Having a unique selling point is a must for any new business, but offering a completely new service also has its downsides.

They presented their business plan to some of their industry contacts, including Geoffrey Squire, CEO of Oracle UK at the time and an angel investor. He had been a colleague at CACI and was so impressed by what the two were looking to achieve that he invested £250,000 in 1990. Edwina acknowledges that his investment was much more easy to secure, as he 'knew us on a personal level and was aware of our track record. He was confident that we would achieve what we had set out to do.'

The pair had also approached the banks and other private investors, and while all of them were willing to invest in the business, this was on the condition that they would own a majority stake in dunnhumby after the business had been running for three years. After some consideration, Edwina and Clive decided not to accept any other investment as they weren't prepared to sacrifice their ownership of the business. It seemed silly to them that in three years time, after working hard to get the business off the ground, they wouldn't even own the majority of it.

Change of focus

The court case with CACI dragged on for three months but Edwina and Clive eventually won and fought off the injunction. Despite not being able to trade during that time, Edwina recalls that the win made them feel more liberated and ultimately gave them more focus and determination to succeed.

The original idea was to offer consultancy and training services so that companies could analyse their data effectively. As they launched the business in earnest in 1990, however, both founders recognised that data technology would provide a competitive edge. 'We recognised from the start how important this would be to the growth of the business', recalls Edwina. Many retailers were throwing customer data away as they simply did not know how to store it or what to do with it. Data technology had always been part of the business's intention, but on a much smaller scale – it now became the main focus. They decided to invest heavily in building a data toolset from scratch.

With this data toolset, dunnhumby would collect the data that clients had on their customers, store this information and create profiles. Customers, for example, would be profiled according to what they bought and according to what they didn't buy. This meant that clients could then reach the best customers for their products, through activities such as direct mail. Clive saw this process of 'data mining' as both an art and a science.

Technology trials

This change in focus presented challenges of its own: again, what dunnhumby proposed to do was completely unique. Despite having a list of industry contacts to approach, both Edwina and Clive knew they would have do something extra to raise the profile of the business and explain the importance of the technology they were creating. This in turn would generate more consultancy work, which would help finance the creation of the data tool.

So they decided to carry out a survey called 'Computers in Marketing', looking at the role of computers in marketing and analysing data. They approached 1,000 companies and received 110 responses. The survey gained them extensive coverage in the trade press, enabling them to build their business profile and achieve positive PR. On the back of this, and by exploiting their existing contact list, they won clients such as car manufacturer BMW and the software company Lotus. The income from these clients meant dunnhumby was able to hire a systems designer recommended by their investor, Geoff, to help build the toolset.

The creation of the data tool took longer than Edwina and Clive bargained for, but they knew that this investment would pay dividends later. By 1992, the toolset was built and the business had bought its first data processing computer.

Word of mouth, a growing industry reputation and PR continued to attract a steady flow of clients. Turnover for the first year was around £150,000 and by year two, the business had made a nominal profit. The dunnhumby team was also growing, as Edwina and Clive recruited more data managers.

The big break: the Tesco Clubcard

The business was growing steadily, until 1994, when dunnhumby caught the eye of Tesco. An executive from the marketing department of supermarket Tesco had heard Clive speak at an industry conference, and was clearly impressed. He presented the two founders with a challenge. Tesco was trialling a loyalty scheme, the Clubcard, in nine of its stores and was interested in finding out if dunnhumby could help to measure and improve its performance. Edwina and Clive were told not to build their hopes up, however – this would be a one-off exercise as Tesco rarely used external companies.

By this time, dunnhumby had grown to around 40 people operating from a small office in Chiswick, near Edwina and Clive's house. Everyone pitched in to help prepare the analysis for Tesco, which was presented a month later to the same marketing executive – Grant Harrison. dunnhumby was analysing Tesco customer data based on what people did and did not buy in-store. Rather than sending promotional offers to all customers, data analysis enabled them to look at customers on an individual basis, identify their characteristics and buying patterns, and then target promotions and communications accordingly. The idea was to encourage repeat sales and tempt customers into buying new products that appealed to their existing preferences. In Edwina's words, the representative was 'blown away' by their work and invited dunnhumby to present it to the Tesco board, including Sir Ian MacLaurin, the supermarket's chairman. Their presentation was a rousing success.

The opportunity to work with Tesco proved the break dunnhumby needed

'The board directors told us that we knew more about their customers than they did' recalls Edwina. 'The analysis we prepared showed them how much the Clubcard could improve Tesco's results – the costs of the scheme were relatively high but so too was the extra spend generated from customers.'

> 'The board directors told us that we knew more about their customers than they did.'

National scheme

Tesco was so impressed with dunnhumby's analysis of what the scheme could achieve that it decided to roll out the Clubcard to all its stores nationwide. Tesco tasked its in-house IT leadership with the challenge of delivering the Clubcard roll-out. When IT said they couldn't guarantee they could implement it, and that it would probably take them 5 years to do so (dunnhumby had quoted 10–12 weeks), at a cost of £50m, it was the big break that dunnhumby needed. By this time, its data toolset was so sophisticated that it could implement Tesco's requirements for under £1m.

'We convinced Tesco we could do it; we knew that we only needed *some* of the customer data, *some* of the time, rather than *all* of the data, *all* of the time (the traditional IT approach)' explains Edwina. dunnhumby not only had to collect the data, it had to store it, analyse it and then target the rewards to millions of customers at home. None of this had ever been done on this scale before, so it wasn't a matter of doing it faster than someone else, it was about being the first ever to achieve it.

Winning the Tesco contract meant dunnhumby needed to double its staff numbers virtually overnight – by 1995, the business employed around 80 people. Over the next few years, the success of the Clubcard scheme helped propel Tesco to number one in the supermarket retail wars. The information it received on consumer buying behaviour has helped to influence many of its key decisions, including the launch of its Finest range, its financial services products, its entry into non-food areas such as clothing, and the launch of Tesco.com, its online shopping service.

> None of this had ever been done on this scale before, so it wasn't a matter of doing it faster than someone else, it was about being the first ever to achieve it.

Dotcom fallout

dunnhumby had built its reputation on the strength of its work for Tesco Clubcard. By 2000, the heady days of the dotcom boom were in full swing, and technology businesses were starting up all over the UK, Europe and the USA. It wasn't uncommon for a business to receive massive venture capital investment, grow at a staggering rate, and float on the stock market for incredible valuations.

In this climate, dunnhumby was approached several times by City institutions with a view to floating the company, with some valuations reaching £1bn. Although tempted, both Edwina and Clive could not quite believe such valuations were possible and they declined to float the business. Instead, they accepted an offer from Tesco to buy a 53% stake in the business.

The fallout from the markets following the dotcom bust led to the 2001 recession and although dunnhumby had been growing steadily over the years and making a profit every year, the business was badly affected. It was, says Edwina, the worst chapter in the business's history, as many companies switched their budgets from customer insight to more 'sexy' online channels which were in vogue at the time. dunnhumby's expertise was in offline data – meaning it was not collected on the internet – and although they could analyse online data, it was not an area that dunnhumby was leading. Edwina explains that 'every other data company around us was building websites and this completely took our legs out from under us.' As a consequence, the business struggled over the next two years and chose not to stray from their area of expertise. 'We were very nervous at the time but we did grow a little and made a small profit. We decided to invest in our established clients like Tesco and carry on with our work in "bricks and mortar" as it was called then', says Edwina. Despite the exponential rise in online data dunnhumby continued to work hard and deliver excellent data for their clients.

Targeting the USA

By 1995 dunnhumby's work with Tesco had helped to put the business firmly on the radar. The phenomenal ongoing success of the Clubcard scheme meant that it was only a matter of time before other retailers approached dunnhumby to help replicate its success with Tesco. In 2003, with the worst of the recession over, dunnhumby began a 50:50 joint venture with Kroger, the largest grocer in the USA, calling the venture dunnhumby USA. It was tasked with transforming the grocer's customer initiatives using its Frequent Shopper Card, and to improve price, assortment and promotions.

It is a model they have successfully repeated elsewhere. In October 2006, they created dunnhumby France with Groupe Casino, the French grocery retailer, helping to build on their loyalty card and customer first programme. Business in the USA has grown considerably too, with clients such as The Home Depot, Coca-Cola and General Mills

dunnhumby's offices in Ealing, London. The company now employs over 1,200 staff in 20 countries

coming on board. dunnhumby also distributes customer 'profiles' to companies such as Procter & Gamble, Mars and Heinz. They now operate in 20 different markets globally.

Where are they now?

In 2006, Tesco increased its stake in the business from 53% to 84% for an undisclosed sum (reportedly £15m), leaving Edwina and Clive with a small stake in the business. At the time, both were still very much involved in the business and wanted to retain some ownership and control over the company.

Today, dunnhumby employs around 1,200 people in Europe, Asia and America and turnover is around £220m. dunnhumby worked with Tesco to roll out its Clubcard scheme across the globe, and is currently working on revamping and relaunching the Clubcard.

Edwina acknowledges that the most recent recession has proved challenging for the business but the fact that much of its work is with food retailers has given it some cushion of security. 'People still need to buy food, even in a recession, so that market is still relatively stable' she says. 'Operating on a global basis is challenging, however, as the business is definitely harder in some places than others.'

dunnhumby opened companies' eyes to the value of customer behaviour – they had the data, but they didn't have the tools to manage this data effectively. The data

How They Started in Tough Times

consultancy industry is highly competitive but Edwina believes that other players are relatively small compared to her business. And despite now being largely owned by Tesco, the business is still independently run. Clive is chairman of the business, and as chief executive, Edwina has guided the business into overseas markets and overseen new client wins. The founders now have a new vision: to be a billion-dollar company by 2010.

Red or Dead

Standing out from the crowd

Founders: Wayne and Gerardine Hemingway

Age of founders at start: 19

Background: Student and clothes designer

Year of foundation: 1982

Business type: Clothing and footwear retailer

Country of foundation: UK

Countries now trading in: UK

ashion labels come and go but Red or Dead has held its own in the public's imagination for nearly three decades. Founded by husband and wife team Wayne and Gerardine Hemingway in 1982, Red or Dead became a brand that inspired the masses and proved that fashion and politics could be mixed. Embarking on such a new concept during the 1980s recession could have been a big risk. But in Wayne's eyes, it provided an opportunity to introduce products and stand out against the competition – Red or Dead were the brains behind selling Dr Martens work-wear shoes as a fashion item, a fashion still popular today. All of this was a world away from the business's humble foundations in London's Camden market.

From idea to reality

Wayne says that the idea for Red or Dead was stumbled upon by chance. In 1982, he was doing a degree in geography and town planning at University College London (UCL) and was living in London with Gerardine, who had left school at 15 with no qualifications.

'It was a Thursday and we had run out of money, with rent due on our flat on the Monday' recalls Wayne. 'I'd spent the last of our rent money on a saxophone so we needed to get some extra cash – both for the rent and to raise funds for a band I was in at the time. We had heard of a clothes market in Camden that was just getting going and you had to get there at the crack of dawn. So we emptied our wardrobes into several laundry bags that we bought for 50p each at our local pound store.'

They weren't entirely inexperienced in the world of fashion. Wayne had a collection of 'far too many' second hand clothes and Geraldine had a wardrobe full of outfits she had made herself, some of which she didn't wear anymore.

'We had heard of a clothes market in Camden that was just getting going and you had to get there at the crack of dawn. So we emptied our wardrobes into several laundry bags that we bought for 50p each at our local pound store.'

They quickly realised that a stall at Camden could be the making of something bigger and better when they raked in roughly £100 on their first day, easily making the £6 they needed to cover their rent and recording a profit from day one. With such success it was an easy decision to go back again the week after, and then again the week after that. Gerardine and Wayne had noticed the public's appetite for vintage clothing and footwear and so decided to focus on selling this – describing it as 'style-conscious fashion inspired by jumble sales and second-hand clothes'.

Setting up shop

To maintain their one stall in Camden, Wayne and Gerardine needed a constant source of new supplies. They roped in friends who had a similar eye for this type of fashion to help. This team of fashionistas would trawl jumble sales, car boots and charity shops such as Oxfam for stock. The money they made was continually reinvested in the stock. 'We were buying clothes for 10p and selling them for £10, easy' recalls Wayne. 'We all went to big recycling rag yards and shoddy mills around the UK. This is where clothes recyclers saved the cool items before they were gotten rid of or shipped overseas.'

'We were buying clothes for 10p and selling them for £10, easy.'

In a few weeks Wayne and Gerardine had to open two more stalls in Camden market to meet customer demand. These were manned by the same friends who had helped source the products. Wayne believes it was their unique clothing that made all the difference. 'If you have a good idea that excites people, you have a chance. If you are starting a corner shop and there are dozens in the area already, you won't get anywhere.'

The biggest challenge in the first few months of business was sourcing enough clothes to match the burgeoning number of stalls. To keep up with demand, Wayne and Gerardine started importing – as well as trawling charity shops, they sourced second-hand clothes from abroad, in particular from Belgium and Germany, gathering contacts from their own research and by observing fashion trends. By the end of the year, they were running 16 market stalls and selling a mix of Gerardine's own creations and second-hand clothing and footwear brought in from all over the world. Takings over a weekend were anything from £5,000 up to £10,000.

Expanding empire

Wayne and Gerardine hadn't written a business plan, they were just taking each weekend at a time. In its first year of trading, the company grew organically and profits were ploughed back into the business, a pattern that was to continue as the business expanded. Wayne is proud of the fact that the business never borrowed money or had an overdraft. By the end of the second year of trading, in 1983, Wayne estimates turnover reached £250,000.

Following the continued success of their stalls in Camden, they began trading in a second location in London's trendy Kensington Market, renting a 180sq foot space for £12 a week. At the time, this location was the second most important shopping street in London for fashion after the King's Road.

Armed with a sewing machine and some fabric from the market in Blackburn (where Wayne and Gerardine were brought up), Gerardine made her first collection: eight items inspired by Russian peasant clothing. They coined the name, Red or Dead, as the name of the collection, a reference to Wayne's Red Indian background and the fact that the first collection that Gerardine did was Russian-inspired.

The collection caught the eye of buyers from New York department store Macy's, who happened to be visiting Kensington Market to get an idea of English street fashion. Macy's put in a large order within a week of the business having set up in Kensington Market. To this day, Wayne and Gerardine are still unsure as to how exactly this happened, but put it down to being in the right place at the right time. It was an exciting time for Wayne and Geraldine but one that they were not quite prepared for. 'Gerardine was egged on by all the other stallholders in Kensington Market to take the order' recalls Wayne. 'But up to this point, she had made all the clothes herself – she could only do three pieces a day so we needed some extra help.'

To meet demand, Red or Dead opened a small production unit in Blackburn, and Wayne roped the family in to help out. Wayne's mother left her job working in a pub, and Gerardine's sisters joined after quitting their jobs as secretaries. By this time, they had 16 staff in total, some based in Blackburn and some in London working on the stalls.

Youth culture

It took them five months to fulfill the Macy's order. Wayne says the biggest challenge was quality control and delivering on time, but with all hands on deck, they hit their deadline. Buoyed with the success of this order, Red or Dead began to make a name for itself selling affordable designer clothes and putting a new spin on existing products.

The idea was to develop innovative fashion items and make their products as affordable as possible. Red or Dead had found a niche in vintage clothes, and as Wayne explains, it was about being creative with the materials available; the early version of the eco-warrior. 'Our aim was always to be affordable and individual – we didn't necessarily think about being the cheapest' explains Wayne. 'We came into a new market with a philosophy that was about creating an accessible designer label. We were part of the youth culture and could serve it well; we knew the kind of clothes that would appeal.'

'Our aim was always to be affordable and individual – we didn't necessarily think about being the cheapest'.

One of these innovative products was Dr Martens boots, which were traditionally worn by postmen and construction workers. Red or Dead began to sell these work-wear shoes as a fashion item on its stalls, aimed at both men and women. The inspiration for this came from Wayne's decision to find 'all sorts of things I knew from growing up that would always be cool in a certain way.' This included jumble sales and kitsch items – an art form that Wayne is particularly passionate about.

In 1984, footwear became one of the company's main focuses. At first they sold 1950s and 1960s shoes, and then sourced items from the Far East. As Wayne explains, Red or Dead became a defining force for youth culture, in which they had a specific and powerful customer base. 'Deck shoes, Chinese slippers – we brought a lot of stuff back from the 1950s and managed to make it work' recalls Wayne.

With a healthy cash flow that was reinvested in the business, Red or Dead expanded rapidly, opening retail stores in Camden and Manchester in 1985, and two more in London in 1987 in Soho and Neal Street. The London stores attracted regular queues due to the success of the Red or Dead 'Watch' shoe (Dr Martens with a watch attached to them) worn by teen band Bros and celebrities such as Kylie Minogue.

Wayne puts this success down to the originality of their products, and the partnerships the founders had built with suppliers. 'We always remained on very friendly terms with manufacturers – if not close friends then we've certainly maintained good relationships' he says. 'We've never shafted anyone and never been shafted ourselves. Your business is only as good as the people who make the products for you. You have to get on with your manufacturers, a big network of people who can benefit from you if you do well. I've always said that the best thing to have is human value. If you want to get an idea off the ground, you need passion and you need to sacrifice time.'

'Your business is only as good as the people who make the products for you. You have to get on with your manufacturers.'

Opportunity in a recession

Wayne believes that in an economic downturn people are looking for new products and services and he sought to take advantage of this wherever possible. 'Whenever there's a change in the financial market, people's habits change and you have to look for a new angle to tempt money out of wallets.'

According to Wayne, the company didn't come up against any disadvantages by starting in a recession – it kept its overheads to a minimum, and as it started out with very little, Wayne says it had nothing to lose. He admits that raising finance in such times is a very hard proposition but he also maintains that you need less money as rents become more affordable and more space becomes available, leaving the way open to negotiate.

'Whenever there's a change in the financial market, people's habits change and you have to look for a new angle to tempt money out of wallets.'

'The companies that aren't very good start to fade away at a pace that keeps up with people's spending power – they might have less to spend but that is because there are less places for them to spend money on' Wayne says. 'In a recession people stop spending money on rubbish, they start being a bit more discriminating in what they spend.'

Making waves

Publicity came easily to Red or Dead but not through conventional marketing means. Wayne is proud of the fact that he never paid for an advert to promote the business throughout the entire time he was at the helm. 'I have never and will never be influenced by advertising – I try and go the opposite way when it comes to advertising' he says. 'As a brand, we were always seen as quite political in terms of where culture was going – we made sure we were relevant to the culture and political thinking of the time. We used fashion to address issues of the time and it got us talked about in the news pages. We knew how to generate media interest without spending any money.'

The business wanted to be the first designer company that sold to everyday people. In the mid-1980s Wayne and Gerardine were presented with a few ways to make this happen. 'Franchising came about because of two things', says Wayne. He explains how once stockists found that the Red or Dead products sold well in their stores they requested more stock. Through this, Red or Dead clothes started to be sold in high street retailers such as Top Shop and Miss Selfridge. The second way the Red or Dead brand spread was through its staff members, 'who fancied returning to their home town and opening a Red or Dead shop' explains Wayne. 'It was all done very organically, like one big family.'

The public clearly liked the Red or Dead concept; but it was a different story in the rest of the industry. In 1988 Red or Dead were banned from participating in London Fashion Week, because of their presence in high street stores. Wayne recalls that the organisers of London Fashion Week said 'designer fashion was all about elitism' and he received a letter saying Red or Dead's prices were too low. But this went against all that Wayne had hoped to achieve: accessible fashion. The fashion company was spurred on by the evidence: people wanted to buy the brand's products, even if the fashion industry didn't approve.

Red or Dead's popularity forced the fashion world to accept the label as part of the industry and the following year, in 1989, Red or Dead débuted at London Fashion week with a collection entitled Space Baby. It was the start of something big.

Fast expansion

By 1992, stores had opened in Leeds and work began on the concept of Dr Martens clothing. Just a year later, Red or Dead signed a deal to become the first designer shoe company to advise Marks & Spencer.

International expansion followed in the early and late 1990s, with further franchise stores opening in Tokyo, Prague, Tel Aviv, Copenhagen and Ontario. The UK economy had once again gone into recession but the harsh economic climate did not appear to affect Red or Dead's fortunes – Wayne believes that 'when a brand is hot, it is recession-proof'.

Hiring the right people was key to business expansion. Wayne and Gerardine sought a mix of people: some had business qualifications, some had done design courses, and some had no qualifications at all. What linked all of the staff was an ability to predict what the general public would want next in terms of fashion – the company employed people with instinct.

As Red or Dead grew, its philosophy remained the same but the business naturally became more formalised and in Wayne's eyes, less fun, losing some of the original spirit that had embodied the brand from its roots. 'The business was always very anarchic but as we grew and we became more organised, it lost some of this' he says. 'We had to complete business plans as we were dealing with large sums of money and several shops. Too much structure can dull creativity – that was our driving force but both Gerardine and I were spending an increasing amount of time dealing with other issues. It was a hard balance to strike.'

Future opportunities

It was partly this feeling and the significant financial reward that prompted the Hemingways to sell the business, although Gerardine was initially reluctant to do so and needed some persuasion from Wayne. 'Money was one of the big attractions of a sale' explains Wayne. 'We'd started with nothing and I had really fallen out with the idea of waking up in the morning for the business – I was bored with it and it was becoming a bit of a monster. I felt there was something more I could do. There was a sense of unfulfilment.' Both Wayne and Gerardine knew people were interested in buying the business and their accountant spread the word about their intention to sell.

In 1995, Red or Dead was sold to the Facia Group, which owned several other fashion brands including Sock Shop. A year later, however, Facia Group collapsed, prompting Wayne to buy back the business and safeguard around 100 jobs. On the same day he bought the business back, he sold it again in a multi-million cash deal, this time to Pentland Group, which still owns the brand today alongside brands like Speedo and Kickers UK.

Where are they now?

Red or Dead, owned by Pentland, is still prominent in the world of fashion, with lines in footwear, clothing, sunglasses, bags and watches. Pentland employs more than 12,000 people worldwide and in 2007, its global sales exceeded $1.8bn. Its target audience is still very much non-conformists, willing to push barriers and challenge the norm.

In 1999, Wayne set up Hemingway Design, which specialises in affordable and social design. Projects have included the Staiths South Bank, an 800 property mass market housing project on Tyneside for George Wimpey Homes, and a new settlement of 3,000 homes in Lothian.

Today, Wayne is passionate about helping start-ups to succeed in an economic climate that is not too dissimilar from when he first started out. Ten years on and Wayne remains undaunted in the face of another economic downturn. 'Recessions are a time for opportunity and creative thinking' he says. Last year, he offered free retail space to new businesses for two months via a temporary pop-up shop outside London's City Hall. Dubbed the KioskKiosk, it was aimed at small creative businesses that were being priced out of the high street as a result of high rents.

Wayne still has a keen interest in Red or Dead, and has derived an immense amount of personal satisfaction from having run and successfully sold the business. 'In a way, it was our baby. It's still going strong now and is a respected brand and a much-loved name.'

Go Sustainable

Green ideas flourish

Founder: Franz Hutcheson

Age of founder at start: 47

Background: Armed Forces, building surveyor

Year of foundation: 2006

Business type: Supplier of sustainable and renewable energy

Country of foundation: UK

Countries now trading in: UK

Current turnover: £320,000

G reener energy sources have become a hot topic in recent years – we're all increasingly aware of climate change, as well as the impact the escalating price of energy is having on our bank balances. In 2006, Franz Hutcheson set out to tackle both of these issues head on, when he launched Go Sustainable. His aim was to save the consumer money, while educating them about the value of using sustainable heating technologies. Hindered by changes in government policy, Franz had to struggle to keep his fledgling business afloat. But when the tides turned, and the recession loomed, he found himself in a position to really make an impact.

Energy conservation

After six years in the Armed Forces, Franz Hutcheson trained as a building and chartered surveyor in the 1980s, working on building projects including schools, hotels and housing accommodation. He worked as a surveyor for the next two decades, until, in 2006, he had his 'eureka' moment. While doing some further training, he learnt that the environmental impact of building works was putting pressure on architects, engineers and building operators to reduce the use of air conditioning and heating in favour of more passive (less noisy and therefore more energy efficient) cooling and warming systems. At that time, many of these heating systems had been mainly used on new-build projects as it was easier to install them from the beginning.

Having worked in the building industry for many years, Franz realised that this new technology was groundbreaking stuff: these systems would play a big part in the future of building works and energy consumption.

However, new technology using energy from the ground to heat buildings was becoming available to use on existing structures. This was known as 'heat transfer' technology. The Royal Festival Hall on London's South Bank is a prominent example of a building which uses this innovative technology. The building became an early example of sustainability, drawing its heating energy from the water in the River Thames.

Having worked in the building industry for many years, Franz realised that this was groundbreaking stuff: these systems would play a big part in the future of building works and energy consumption. Fascinated to find out more, he researched the subject thoroughly, and was soon convinced there was the potential for a new business specialising in fitting the new greener and more energy efficient heating and cooling equipment in homes.

Entrepreneur Oli Barrett, Go Sustainable founder Franz Hutcheson,
and Sara Rizk at the 2009 Startups Awards

In August 2006, he decided to use his savings of £20,000 to start his business, naming it The Sustainable Energy Company. He believed this name would give his company the impression that it was bigger than it was, meaning that people might take more notice of him than if they knew he was a small start-up – it also described his services to a tee.

Franz intended to offer different renewable 'micro-generation' technologies, which produce heat and/or electricity on a small scale from a low carbon source. Low carbon sources produce less carbon dioxide than traditional fossil fuels, meaning they are better for the environment. Franz intended to offer solar thermal hot water systems, ground and air source heat pumps, wood fired boilers using logs, and wind turbines (designed for domestic use). These inventions could all be used in the home, not just on a larger scale, and had already been proven to produce carbon savings. The Sustainable Energy Company would sell and install these systems, and Franz would use his contacts in the building industry to source the necessary supplies.

Back to basics

But before Franz could think about getting the business properly off the ground, he needed formal training about renewable energy sources. Between September and December 2006, he ploughed his savings into training courses, travelling all over the UK to take courses in electrical engineering, refrigeration, how to be eco-friendly and gas handling. He also spent £5,000 of his savings on a van that he used to travel from course to course. 'I'm one of those people who like to know what is happening in my industry – everything from the bottom up,' says Franz. 'The more training I did, the more I realised that using renewable energy was a niche that had mainstream potential'.

'I'm one of those people who like to know what is happening in my industry. The more training I did, the more I realised that using renewable energy was a niche that had mainstream potential.'

In between the courses, Franz worked from home, at his kitchen table, with nothing more than a laptop and a broadband connection. His next focus was his business plan. He aimed to raise money from the banks – he knew his savings would only go so far, and if he was serious about making a go of the business, he would need some

Solar Collector tubes

additional funds. Knowing nothing about business plans, however, he decided to use the services of a specialist business planning company, based in London.

He browsed the internet for companies and within an hour had found one that seemed to fit the bill. Franz explains how 'this might have seemed risky but I got a good feel for them and they knew what they were talking about.' The company helped to both write the plan and to attract funding from the banks. Although this was risky, not to mention costly (he paid around £3,800 in total), he believed it was worth it in the end as it saved him time and did a better job than he would ever have been able to do. 'You can do the business plan yourself but the challenge is writing it in a language that will appeal to investors' believes Franz. It took him just four weeks to secure a loan for £15,000 from a high street bank, which he achieved in November 2006.

'You can do the business plan yourself but the challenge is writing it in a language that will appeal to investors.'

Publicising the business

With the finance he needed in place, Franz turned his attention to marketing. With the help of a close friend, Phil Moore, who owned his own marketing agency, Franz came up with some ideas to attract customers. This involved designing and printing leaflets, which were produced at a discounted price through one of Phil's contacts.

The marketing strategy was simple. Franz would hand-deliver leaflets to towns in the north-east of England, where he was based, before targeting other regions around the UK. 'I was aiming at readers of newspapers such as *The Guardian*, those consumers who were slightly upmarket and who cared about the environment,' says Franz.

They also decided to put Franz's van to good use as a marketing tool. Phil designed a logo for The Sustainable Energy Company, and this and a phone number were painted onto the van. This meant that while Franz zipped across the country for his various courses, he was generating free publicity for the business.

Learning curve

As well as publicising his company and drumming up interest in his products, Franz says a big part of his business was very much about education. From his experience, when it came to renewable energy, most people had only heard of solar panels and even then, their knowledge of how these worked and the benefits they offered was limited. To get his knowledge across, he planned to do some presentations on the benefits of renewable energy sources. At the talks, Franz planned to start from scratch and explain why heating at ground or air source would be both beneficial and offer cost savings.

'In these rural areas, it was a matter of visiting church hall after church hall, speaking to the secretary in charge and booking a time to do the talk.' He felt the people in more rural areas would be more receptive to the idea of using renewable energy as not all of them would have heating supplied by conventional means such as gas, instead, using electric storage heaters or coal fires. To promote the talks, he leafleted the area, stuck posters on lamp posts and took out ads in local papers. He also attended local agricultural shows, rural development seminars and even farmers markets. His presence at these events not only increased his profile, but helped him make contact with architects, engineers, other suppliers.

His first few talks did not quite go to plan, however. He originally put a PowerPoint presentation together but quickly realised that this was one thing that was guaranteed to alienate customers. He then concentrated on making the presentations as interactive as possible, encouraging people to ask questions. 'People were not interested in looking at images and words on a screen,' explains Franz. 'I had to inject vibrancy in my presentations by focusing on the education angle and the benefits, such as being able to save people money on their energy costs.' He was wary about putting too commercial a message across in case it put potential customers off, and so he focused on the environmental and financial benefits.

Franz therefore tailored his talks to focus on the benefits of alternative energy supplies. Even if people were not interested in buying his services, he wanted them to understand how they could save on their energy bills. The early signs were positive as around 50 people on average would come to his presentations, which he held roughly once a week in different towns during late 2006 and early 2007.

Green shoots

Franz remembers how tough the first few months of trading were – he spent most of his time either training or talking about the business, rather than generating any sales leads. With business non-existent at the start, Franz found himself spending more and more money on training courses during the day (which could cost as much as £1,000 for a three-day course once you add in accommodation costs) and speaking to village halls at night. He'd got the start-up funds, he had the knowledge, people seemed interested – but he now desperately needed actual sales.

His hard work paid off when he landed his first contract in March 2007, six months after starting the business, and came as a result of one of his talks. The work involved installing a ground force heat pump for a retired couple living near Durham in north-west England. Their son was just starting out in the building trade, and Franz was able to build up a good rapport with his first customer by passing on some industry trips from his experience in the trade. 'In the building trade, it's vital that potential customers have confidence in you and believe that you can do a good job,' he says. 'You can't tell them it's your first job, but having done all the requisite training. I could say I had done it before. It's important to establish a good relationship from the start and to set expectations.'

'In the building trade, it's important to establish a good relationship with customers from the start and to set expectations.'

As a one-man band, Franz worked on his own, using just his van and a toolbox. He ensured he got a deposit up front (usually a third of the total cost of the work) which he would then use to purchase materials from industry contacts. So impressed were the couple with his work that they asked him to do the under floor heating as well, even though this had originally been contracted out to another firm. While Franz admits that this put him out of his comfort zone, he believed it was essential that he have a go at doing it, in order to build credibility for the business and extend

New type of ground source heat pump collectors in the form of panels

his skills. He badly underestimated the time taken to complete the job, however, originally believing it could be done in five days when in fact it took three weeks.

It was a learning curve for Franz, as he juggled long hours during the day while refining his business plan at night, drawing up new designs for leaflets that he planned to use for added publicity.

Mounting losses

Despite his marketing push, business leads were thin on the ground. Worse was to come, when Government policy changes relating to renewable energy threatened to deal a severe blow to his fledgling business. In March 2007, the Government suspended applications for grants to the Low Carbon Buildings Programme, pending a review. The scheme had been introduced the previous year and provided grants for homeowners towards the costs of installing micro-generation technologies.

Two months later, at the end of May, the Government completed its review and introduced changes to the Programme, effectively reducing individual grants for homeowners wanting to produce their own renewable energy. Future applicants would be limited to a grant of £2,500 for domestic projects where previously, grants of up to £15,000 were available for solar energy and £5,000 for micro-turbine schemes.

> This change in policy was huge blow to Franz's business. He had to wait at least three months before being able to sign off any potential contracts, during some of the crucial summer months – the building industry's busiest time.

Up to then, demand for the scheme had been immense, with monthly allocations of funding being fully subscribed within minutes. The changes meant that many people who wanted to apply decided not to, as many projects would now be too expensive –they would now need to contribute £4,000–£5,000 of their own money. The typical cost of buying and installing a solar panel system, for example was around £7,000.

This change in policy was huge blow to Franz's business. He had to wait at least three months before being able to sign off any potential contracts, during some of the crucial summer months – the building industry's busiest time. People who had expressed interest in his services now wanted to wait for the Government decision, to see to what extent the funding would be affected and whether they would then be able to afford to have the work carried out. This nearly caused him to abandon the business.

To keep himself motivated, Franz decided to attend more courses to continue building his skills and knowledge – it was the only thing that kept him going. He also completed jobs in the traditional building trade, taking on all sorts of projects to make ends meet.

By the middle of 2007, once the grant applications process was renewed, trade started to pick up again and Franz secured a couple more contracts. But the damage had already been done. The change in Government funding meant that business was practically non-existent in the first year, with barely a trickle of leads amounting to a total of five jobs. Consequently, Franz sustained a loss of £42,000 in his first year of trading, with most of his cash flow

Typical pipe work for ground source heat pump

spent on training, marketing, and travelling – he was so determined to make the business grow that he was prepared to travel anywhere in the UK.

Turning point

After a tough first year, yet another factor out of Franz's control proved to be a turning point for the business. In January 2008, oil prices hit $100 a barrel – the dollar had fallen, and there were concerns over a winter fuel supply crunch. Petrol and diesel prices had climbed to record highs, with diesel edging to £5 a gallon for the first time ever. This leap in fuel prices made consumers keener than ever before to cut their energy costs, in favour of more sustainable, cost-efficient sources.

The rise in oil prices coincided with more general economic instability, and the start of 2008 heralded an uncertain time for the UK economy. By the end of March, many economic experts were predicting that the UK could be heading for a recession, prompted by a deepening global financial crisis. Mortgage rates were increasing in the UK and this was having a knock-on effect on consumer spending – people had less disposable income and were becoming increasingly wary. Experts predicted that this indicated an economic slowdown that could last some time. At the same time, fuel prices continued to go through the roof.

While this made depressing reading from some, for Franz rising fuel prices were actually good for business as it made consumers think twice about their mounting energy costs. It seemed this was the catalyst that Franz needed to convince consumers of the benefits of switching to sustainable energy systems. Suddenly his phone was ringing off the hook, and he struggled to keep pace with the number of enquiries, completing as many contracts in the first six months of 2008 as he had done throughout the whole of 2007. All of his work thus far was in the domestic market, with some jobs worth as much as £20,000. This uptake in business coincided with a name change – Franz settled on Go Sustainable as he believed it was a more dynamic name that customers would find easier to remember.

> While this made depressing reading from some, for Franz rising fuel prices were actually good for business as it made consumers think twice about their mounting energy costs.

Ambitious growth

In November 2008, Franz hired his first employee, a heating engineer whom he had known from his past jobs in the building trade. He also moved into his first office, renting space in Phil's agency's office based in Gateshead. It was at this point that Franz decided to try a new advertising approach. Thus far, the leaflets had helped to draw in domestic business with some success, but for the company to start making the desired impact, he would need to make a bigger splash and aim for the public sector.

In 2009, Go Sustainable invested in print advertising, taking out a quarter page in the Bursar's Handbook, a bi-annual buyer's directory for the educational marketplace, which lists suppliers of every product and service that may be required in running a school, including building maintenance services. This set Franz back £2,000 but as well as the ad, a list of potential customers (and their contact details) who were interested in sustainable energy was included in the price. He also decided to target the NHS, through an e-zine of suppliers that it publishes on the internet. He paid £1,800 for a digital insert, and while Franz admits that this has generated very little direct response, he believes a presence in the e-zine tends to give prospective clients confidence in the company.

Where are they now?

The business has now expanded to five members of staff, including Phil, who joined the business as sales and marketing director in early 2009. In November 2009, Franz won the Silver Fox Award at the annual Startups Awards, an award given in recognition of business achievements for start-up businesses started and owned by those aged over 50.

The average price of a job carried out by Go Sustainable is between £7,000 and £8,000 and Franz makes a 40% gross profit on the back of this. In a time of recession, it can often pay to team up with a bigger supplier, and Franz has ensured that he has secured some partnerships with the manufacturers of the equipment he wanted to fit, including Mitsubishi and Ice Energy, which provide ground source heat pumps.

Not content with cornering the domestic market and tapping into commercial opportunities in his own area, Franz is now setting his sights on franchising the business throughout the UK. In a world where climate change and environmental issues are getting more and more air time, the future of Go Sustainable looks bright green.

www.crimsonpublishing.co.uk